WAR IN AFGHANISTAN

By the same author

SOVIET LAND POWER

War in Afghanistan

Mark Urban

Defence Correspondent, *The Independent*

St. Martin's Press
New York

First published in the United States of America in 1988

Printed in Great Britain

ISBN 0-312-01205-5

Library of Congress Cataloging-in-Publication Data
Urban, Mark, 1961-
  War in Afghanistan.
  Bibliography: p.
  Includes index.
  1. Afghanistan—History—Soviet Occupation,
1979- .   I. Title.
DS371.2.U72 1987   958'.1044   87-14375
ISBN 0-312-01205-5

8 9-B1102

For my brother Stuart

Contents

List of Maps

List of Abbreviations

AGSA	Afghan government intelligence service, May 1978–September 1979
APC	armoured personnel carrier
BMD	*boyevaya maschina desantnika*, (airborne combat vehicle)
BMP	*boyevaya maschina pekhoty*, (infantry fighting vehicle)
BTR	*brontetransporter*, (armoured troop carrier such as BTR-60)
CIA	Central Intelligence Agency (of USA)
DIA	Defence Intelligence Agency (of US military)
DRA	Democratic Republic of Afghanistan
dushman	meaning 'enemy', Soviet soldiers' word for guerrilla
DYOA	Democratic Youth Organisation of Afghanistan
DWOA	Democratic Women's Organisation of Afghanistan
GRU	Glavnoye Razvedyvatelnoye Upravleniye, Main Intelligence Directorate (of Soviet General Staff)
IAAM	Islamic Alliance of Afghan Mujahadeen, resistance party, same as IUAL
IP	Islamic Party, resistance group, with Hekmatyar and Khalis factions
ISA	Islamic Society of Afghanistan, resistance group
IM	Islamic Movement, resistance group
IRM	Islamic Revolution Movement, resistance group
IUAL	Islamic Unity for Afghan Liberation, resistance group
jihad	Holy War
jerga	council or meeting
KAM	Afghan government intelligence service, September–December 1979
KGB	Komitet Gosudarstvenoy Bezopasnosti, Committee for State Security of Soviet Union
KHAD	acronym for State Information Service, Afghan government intelligence service, January 1980–January 1986 (replaced Ministry of State Security)
LCSFA	Limited Contingent of Soviet Forces in Afghanistan
MRL	multiple rocket launcher
mujahadeen	fighters of God, anti-government guerrillas

MVD	Ministerstvo Vnutrenost Del, USSR Ministry of Internal Affairs
Nasr	Victory, resistance group
NFF	National Fatherland Front
NIFA	National Islamic Front of Afghanistan, resistance group
NLF	National Liberation Front (of Afghanistan), resistance group
PDPA	People's Democratic Party of Afghanistan
PLO	Palestine Liberation Organisation
Sarandoy	Kabul Ministry of the Interior Armed Forces
Shura	acronym for Council of the Union, Hazara guerrilla party
TVD	Teatr Voyennikh Destviy, Soviet Theatre of Military Operations
VDV	Vozduyushno Desantniki Voisk, Air Assault Forces (Soviet)
VTA	Voyenno Transportnaya Aviatsaya, Military Transport Aviation (Soviet)
VVS	Vozduyushno Voorezhenie Sil, Air Forces (Soviet)

Preface

This book is a description of the military struggle for Afghanistan. It concerns the objectives, operations, tactics and effectiveness of the forces involved in that struggle. The aim is to describe the war as objectively and in as much detail as possible.

Truth is an elastic commodity in Afghanistan. Both sides resort to exaggeration and plain dishonesty to publicise their cause. Cut away the rhetoric and a surprising amount of common ground emerges in guerrilla and government accounts of many incidents. For example *mujahadeen* reports that they had crushed enemy forces at Zhawar in April 1986 were in themselves an admission that the Afghan army had, as reported by Kabul, succeeded in fighting its way through to the fortress.

This book has been written from a very wide variety of sources. It is one of the few books about Afghanistan that exploits Kabul and Moscow sources. An enormous amount of detail has been disclosed by 'the other side', but unfortunately most writers in the West digest the guerrilla view too uncritically to make any use of it.

The book also makes use of many eyewitness accounts – some published, others related to me. Often these provide vital corroboration of the claim of one side or the other. It is not a work of personal experience; many of those have already appeared. Instead it is a summary drawn from many thousands of documents and accounts.

The chapters of the book are intended to provide an account of events with a certain amount of analysis. The key military actions are described and background is provided. Examinations of trends, development of forces and so on are built into the chapters, so that Chapter Four, 1981, contains a great deal more than just the main battles of that year. I have tried to confine my opinions to the Prologue and the concluding Analysis. Statements and opinions in the chapters are attributed, as far as possible, in the notes at the end of each chapter.

I have had access to some unpublished sources, such as US military maps of the country. The use of these – so much better than those which are publicly available – allowed a lot more sense to be made of battle accounts. As far as possible, the sketch maps in this book include relevant detail from these maps.

In some ways it would have been more sensible to have waited some years for the war to finish before embarking on this project. But by starting now the book has not been crushed by the weight of hindsight. Because the outcome is still in the balance I have been obliged to treat all of the research fairly – the gains and losses of both sides have to be reported. The argument cannot be stilted in favour of a particular outcome.

The narrative ends in July 1986 – although some details of events beyond then have been included. Obviously interesting events have happened since July 1986, but the demands of producing a book mean that a line must be drawn.

I would like to thank the many people who have given interviews for the book – their names are in the notes. I would also like to thank the staff at the International Institute for Strategic Studies, the BBC External Services, the Afghan Support Committee, the Friends of Afghanistan and Vincent Dowd for reading the manuscript.

Mark Urban
London

Prologue: Before 1978

Afghanistan is one of the world's most unruly states. Successive leaders have tried to confront local independence and failed. It is an independence born of geographical remoteness and of loyalties incompatible with the centralised state. In rural Afghanistan power lies in the hands of leaders at the village level: tribal chiefs, religious elders, and headmen. At this level there is a tradition of taking decisions by *jerga*, a meeting of village worthies. Even within the village *jerga*, disagreements often prevent decisions being reached. The result is an incredible history of disunity and feuding. Kabul has failed many times to wrest power from the villages and tribes. On occasions the army or *gendarmerie* have been sent into the hills to put down a local rising, but rural Afghanistan usually had the last say. To make matters even more complicated the objectives of 'the countryside' cannot easily be classified. There are a great many different peoples and tribes, each with its own aspirations and antagonisms. In terms of political cohesion it has long been an atomised nation.

There is no such thing as an Afghan national type. Instead, the people belong to a variety of different ethnic and religious groups. The Pushtuns have traditionally been the dominant group in most areas of national life. Before the revolution about 6.5 to 7 million Pushtuns lived in Afghanistan, concentrated in the south and west. They dominated political life and the army. History has given them their own quite separate identity. Pushtun national life is cut in two by an arbitrary 19th-century border, the Durand line. Across this border live the Pushtun people of Pakistan's North-West Frontier Province. The idea of unifying these communities into a single Pushtun nation, Pushtunistan, has, over the years, caused enormous friction between Pakistan and Afghanistan. Despite the rhetoric and sabre-rattling it would be true to say that, in the last few decades at least, the Pushtuns have never come close to getting their own state. Instead the people on either side of the Durand line have taken life more philosophically, and carried on as if the border simply was not there. The mountainous terrain and traditions of kinship and corruption in the border provinces have meant that state attempts to restrict their movements and trading have never been particularly successful. Among the Pushtuns there

1

are rivalries and bitter feuds. There are different Pushtun tribal groups. The principal ones are the Durranis in the west and the Ghilzai in the east. The Pushtun martial spirit and the resort to blood feuds have led to many conflicts between Pushtun villages, and between them and other Afghan peoples. Their attitude is summed up by the saying: 'Do you have an enemy?' 'Yes, I have a cousin'.

After the Pushtuns, the most important ethnic group in Afghanistan are the Turkic minorities who speak a dialect of Farsi called Dari. Among these people are 3.5 million Tajiks, a million Uzbecks, 125 000 Turkmens, and a few thousand Kirghiz. These Dari-speaking groups are concentrated in northern Afghanistan, close to the Soviet border. Many of them live in farming communities on the plain of the Oxus, or Amu, River. Initially very few of them settled south of the barrier presented by the Hindu Kush mountains. With time Dari speakers became important as city-dwelling traders and administrators. Just as the Pushtuns have close ties with their kinfolk across the Durand line, so the Tajiks, Uzbecks and Turkmens are close to their people across the Soviet border. Indeed several thousand of them settled in Afghanistan during the 1920s when Soviet power was imposed in Central Asia. The success of the Dari speakers in trade meant that their language became the language of many city dwellers, including well-to-do Pushtuns. What the Pushtuns and groups like the Tajiks have in common is their adherence to the Hanafi Sunni form of Islam. But just as Afghanistan has more than one people, and more than one language, so there are many of its people who adhere to Shia Islam.

The biggest Shia group are the Hazaras. There are just under a million of them, concentrated largely in the central mountains, which are known as the Hazara Jat. In general the Hazara villages of central Afghanistan are extremely poor, and traditionally many people have left them to work as casual labourers. In Kabul and other cities the Hazaras form a class for menial labour – in the Pushtun-dominated state they were well and truly at the bottom of the social pile. Another important Shia group are the Farsiwans – the Persian people who live in western Afghanistan. There are 600 000 of them. Like the other Shia groups they have been the victims of prejudice by the Sunni majority. In spiritual matters they look to the Immams of Iran.

If the Afghan people lack respect for governmental authority, they have it in abundance for religion. It is a devout society that supports a large clergy: 250 000 spiritual teachers and leaders. These quarter of a million mullahs enjoy a vital leadership role in village and tribal society. They form one of the few literate sections of the community. People look to them to interpret events in Kabul and the world. The mullahs have been a key force for the status quo, resisting the spread of Western ideas and culture. Their immobility on issues such as women's rights and the absorption of new technology undoubtedly inhibits the 'progress' (defined in a Western sense) of the country.

Experts have described religious practice in the country as old fashioned. Afghanistan cannot boast any Islamic scholars or schools of international importance. The Afghan people, led by the clergy, maintained their conservative beliefs and forms of worship throughout the 1970s. They proved as reluctant to listen to those fundamentalist Islamic parties which wanted to revolutionise the faith as they did to the socialists.

Historically Afghanistan is not just an ethnic buffer state, but a buffer state between great powers. Afghan nationalism, where it exists, emerged as a reaction to the unwanted attentions of these foreign states. The country was born between two forms of expansionist imperialism – Tsarist Russia and Victorian Britain. The victory over Britain, achieved largely by the Pushtun tribes rather than the fledgeling Afghan army, gave the country statehood. Since then Afghanistan has found itself under pressure from different forces – the forces of the Cold War. During the 1950s Kabul sat uneasily between the Soviet Union and the USA with their local allies. At first Kabul rejected the offers of both superpowers, trying instead to steer a difficult course of non-alignment. Pakistani membership of CENTO (the British-sponsored Central Treaty Organisation, or Baghdad Pact) meant that they got the backing of the USA over Pushtunistan. And so Kabul looked more and more to the Soviet Union for help with its military needs. Whilst the xenophobic Afghans might not like to admit it, the decisive move towards Moscow was made under King Nadir and Mohammed Daoud's governments. A long cooperation in the supply of weapons and the training of personnel began then.

Paradoxically the very success of the Afghans in resisting British imperialism deprived them of a number of the prerequisites of a modern state. Where the British colonised they left behind an infrastructure, an efficient civil service, an independent judiciary,

an integrated national railway network and well-organised armed
forces. In countries like Pakistan and India the British left the
machinery of state. Had the rulers of Afghanistan inherited such
power their efforts to develop the country would undoubtedly have
met with greater success. Instead they have had to try to finance
their own development with the resources of their desperately poor
country, and to implement their decisions with a completely
inadequate system of government.

The inadequacy of state power in Afghanistan is exemplified by
the financial weakness of its governments. Kabul has never been
able to impose any national system of income tax. Although
agriculture is the livelihood of nearly 80 per cent of Afghans, taxes
on this activity accounted for only 1 per cent of government
revenue. Even in the 1970s almost all government money came
from duties levied on imports and traders. Even these taxes were
widely avoided by smugglers. One consequence of this financial
weakness was a dependence on foreign aid for investment. During
the 1970s, foreign hand-outs accounted for 65 per cent of all
investment in the country. Another result of the dependence on
import duties was that foreign trade, principally by truck through
Pakistan, had to be continuous in order to maintain the stability of
the government.

Afghanistan's exports comprised mainly agricultural products
(such as raisins), animals skins, semi-precious stones, and natural
gas. The poor prices received for these commodities meant that
exports yielded little foreign exchange. Whilst neighbouring Iran
grew rich on petro-dollars, Afghanistan struggled to sell its poor
quality cash crops. By 1977 industrial development had hardly
arrived in Afghanistan – it accounted for only 0.3 per cent of the
country's exports.

Even in the mid-1970s government influence in the countryside
was minimal. Justice was in the hands of religious courts, there was
little regular schooling, and women were still effectively bought
and sold by the payment of bride prices. In some villages
(principally those in tribal areas) there was even exemption from
conscription.

During the last hundred years, different types of government
have sat in Kabul; they have had very little effect on their country.
There was the absolute monarchy of King Abdur Rahman in the
1890s, the constitutional monarchy of King Zahir in the late 1960s,
and the republic of Mohammed Daoud in the 1970s. It would be

wrong to say that these governments achieved nothing for their country, but their record was poor.

An army had been founded by the turn of the century. It was run by Pushtuns, but relied on levies from the ethnic minorities. Even in the 20th century, powerful Pushtun tribes exempted themselves from national service. The civil service was also led by Pushtuns. In time, the educated Dari speakers came to play a vital role in government service. The 1950s and 1960s saw some improvements in education. Whereas there were only 4000 teachers in 1956, there were 13 200 by 1967. There was an expansion in higher education but, despite this, over half the places available were still in Kabul. In the 1970s illiteracy remained at 90 per cent of the population. Among some groups it was even higher – 98 per cent of women could neither read nor write.

It was from the armed forces, the civil service, and the teachers that Afghanistan's educated elite was formed. Within this small 'political nation' there was a high degree of activism; outside it there was virtually none. In the 1965 elections, nine out of ten voters stayed at home. The assembly that was elected aroused so little interest that even its members stayed away – meetings were often inquorate.

Among the intelligentsia there was intense frustration at the slow pace of change. The People's Democratic Party of Afghanistan (PDPA) was founded in 1965. An increasing number of army officers (many of them trained in the Soviet Union) teachers and civil servants were drawn into radical politics. In 1973 Prince Mohammed Daoud siezed power. He dropped his royal title, called himself President and declared a republic. Daoud's government achieved little, and fairly soon the radical intelligentsia were dissatisfied with the royal republican.

Pressures were coming to boiling point for the Afghan Left. If ever a country needed a revolution it was Afghanistan. By the mid-1970s all other forms of government had been tried and had proved themselves bankrupt. Successive governments had failed to make Afghanistan's people literate, failed to improve the lot of minority ethnic groups, failed to gain respect or status for women, and failed to give the country any substantial governmental or industrial infrastructure. In short, they had failed to create a 20th-century state. In April 1978, Afghanistan got its revolution.

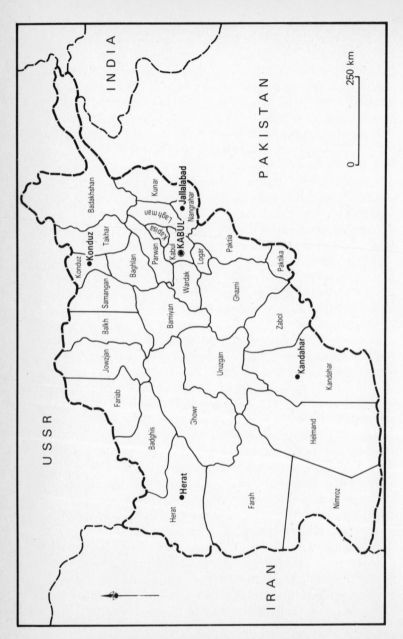

I Afghanistan, provincial boundaries, 1983.

One: 1978

15 April 1978. Mir Akber Khyber, a leading figure in the Parcham faction of the People's Democratic Party of Afghanistan (PDPA) is shot dead. There is outrage among the intelligentsia in Kabul. They believe he has been murdered by agents of President Mohammed Daoud.

19 April 1978. Khyber's funeral turns into a demonstration. A crowd of 15 000 packs the streets of Kabul in a show of grief and anger. The funeral march becomes a display of strength by the Afghan Left. The targets of their chanting: the USA, the CIA, and the Shah of Iran's secret police, the SAVAK.[1] The march is the biggest in years in Kabul. President Daoud, facing a severe economic crisis, views the developments with increasing alarm.

26 April 1978. Daoud's secret police begin to arrest leading members of the PDPA. Among those arrested are the party leader Nur Mohammed Taraki, organisational chief Hafizullah Amin, and the head of the Parcham wing Babrak Karmal. Daoud fails to arrest their most important accomplices in the armed forces. An order for action is issued from the jail cells.

09.00, 27 April. Men of the 4th and 15th Armoured Brigades, based just east of the city at Pol-e-Charkhi, climb into their vehicles. Fifty tanks of the 4th Armoured head into the city. They are led by a battalion commander, Senior Captain Aslam Watanjar.[2] Thirty miles to the north, at the air force's principal fighter base, Bagram, Colonel Abdol Qader takes control of the MiG–21-equipped 322nd Air Regiment based there.

10.00, 27 April. In Kabul's presidential palace the cabinet meet to discuss the fate of the imprisoned leftist leaders.

11.00, 27 April. Captain Watanjar's tanks arrive at the Defence Ministry in Kabul. Meanwhile another group belonging to the 15th Armoured Brigade secures the airport.

12.00, 27 April. Watanjar arrives at the Presidential Palace at the

7

head of a company of nine tanks. He calls upon the occupants to surrender. They refuse and fighting breaks out.[3] The building is held by the 1800 strong Republican Guard Brigade. As the gunfire becomes intense, confused office workers on the streets try to find cover. Reinforcement armour and mechanised infantry arrive at the palace.

15.00, 27 April.   A squadron of MiG–21s makes a series of low-level sorties over the city. They strafe the army Central Corps and 8th Division headquarters.[4] The attacks on army HQs are primarily to deter wavering units from intervening. Other planes launch a more deadly raid: bombing the Presidential Palace where Daoud's guards are still holding out. Several hundred loyalist soldiers are believed killed in the air strike.

17.00, 27 April.   The leaders of the PDPA are released from prison.

19.00, 27 April.   Kabul Radio is seized and a message proclaiming the *coup* is broadcast: 'For the first time in the history of Afghanistan the last remnants of imperialist tyranny and despotism have been ended.'[5]

23.30, 27 April.   Fighting at the Presidential Palace is all but over. The President, his brother, and several other government officials are dead, as are most of the loyalist soldiers who defended them. The final death toll has been estimated at 1000.[6] Armoured units are despatched to Jallalabad where loyalist officers of the 11th Division refuse to accept the *coup*.

28 April 1978.   The new government, whose composition is still unknown to the public, makes its first announcements. Officials are told to report for work by Kabul Radio. The broadcast continues: 'The Revolutionary Military Council is founded on the potential strength of the noble people of Afghanistan; it will make genuine endeavours for the freedom of the people, protection of the homeland and safeguarding of the tenets of the sacred religion of Islam.'[7] The tone of these early broadcasts could be described as Nasserite: the army had seized national destiny; it would enact socialist reforms; but its respect for Islam could be relied upon.

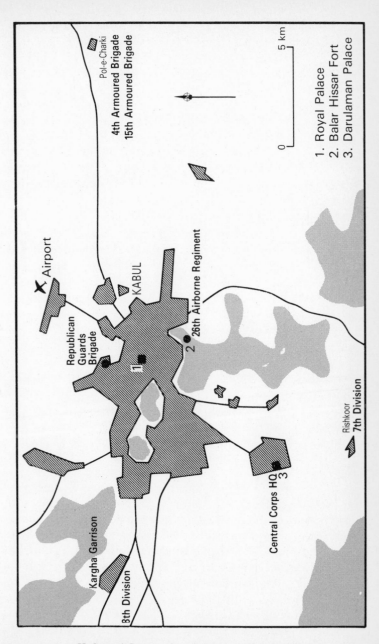

II Central Corps main unit locations, Kabul, 1978.

Resistance in Jallalabad is overcome and the commander of the
11th Division is shot dead.

30 April 1978.   The Revolutionary Council announces Decree
No. 1. Nur Mohammed Taraki is appointed Chairman of the
Revolutionary Government and Prime Minister. The council
announced the formation of the Democratic Republic of
Afghanistan (DRA). The April (corresponding to the Afghan
month of Saur) Revolution was underway.

THE PEOPLE'S DEMOCRATIC PARTY OF AFGHANISTAN

The PDPA were confirmed in power. Around the world
governments tried to find out exactly who the People's Democratic
Party of Afghanistan were. Taraki's party was founded in January
1965. During the spring of 1966 his followers published a
newspaper called *Khalq (Masses)*. Although the paper lasted only
six weeks before it was banned, it had a lasting influence among its
mainly student readership.

Divisions soon emerged in the party and another group formed a
faction around Babrak Karmal. They published their own
newspaper, *Parcham (Flag)*, from March 1968 to July 1969.
Karmal's group was also influential among the students and
members of the mainly Tajik professional class. The PDPA even
had a small following in the armed forces.[8] The elections of the
1960s had confirmed that there was a measure of popular support
for the PDPA. The party had four members (including Babrak
Karmal, who stood for Kabul) elected to the Wolesi Jerga
(National Assembly) in 1965. Hafizullah Amin and Karmal were
elected in 1969.

The question of the degree to which the party should involve
itself with the (highly imperfect) electoral process caused a great
deal of in-fighting. It was one of the issues which resulted in
factionalism and the emergence of groups within factions. A group
called Shol'eh Javid (Eternal Flame) criticised the Parchamis for
involving themselves with the electoral system. Another group,
Settem-e-Melli (National Oppression), which was anti-Pushtun
and dedicated to furthering the interests of ethnic minorities, also
gained ground. Settem-e-Melli survived and developed as a

separate guerrilla organisation. Some party members drifted between groups during the long years of underground political acivity but a solid bloc of Parchamis and Khalqis remained loyal to Babrak Karmal and Nur Mohammed Taraki respectively.

Although both groups claimed the backing of Moscow they received little attention from the Soviet communists who were anxious to maintain good relations with the government of the day in Kabul. The Khalqis were drawn largely from poor rural Pushtuns (like Taraki himself); the Parchamis from better-off Kabul Pushtuns (who spoke the Dari dialect of Persian) and other Farsi-speaking groups. A number of issues divided the groups. Parcham favoured a more cautious approach on the issue of Pushtunistan (the desire to incorporate the Pushtuns of north-west Pakistan into a single state). In general they favoured a more gradual process of change, and there was bitter personal antagonism between Tarkai and Karmal.[9] Parchami cooperation with the government during the 1960s and the early phase of Daoud's republic earned them particular scorn from the uncompromising Khalqis. In 1977, after years of antagonism, the two factions agreed a truce.

The cabinet formed by Taraki and announced on 30 and 31 April (see Appendix III) included men from both factions. It also included key figures from the military who had helped to gain power: Abdol Qader, Aslam Watanjar, and Mohammed Rafi. Watanjar and Qader had also played key roles in Daoud's 1973 *coup* – their following among members of the key military units made them too important to leave out. Some authors have described them as 'independents', but it is true to say that Qader was closer to the Parcham faction, and Watanjar to the Khalq. Taraki involved the Parchamis by appointing Karmal as Deputy Prime Minister (Amin had the titles of First Deputy Prime Minister and Foreign Minister) and giving them ministerial posts such as the Interior, Finance, Information and Planning. Day-to-day running of government was undertaken by this cabinet of ministers. The Revolutionary Council, which was meant to represent a cross-section of Afghan society, quite quickly became little more than a rubber stamp. The PDPA Central Committee formed a much more important body, although its meetings and existence were not officially confirmed until later in 1978.

The PDPA relied on a very small constituency of (mainly Kabul) intellectuals. Membership at the time of the April

Revolution was, by some estimates, as low as 5000.[10] Babrak
Karmal subsequently claimed it was 18 000 at this time, the real
figure probably falling between the these estimates at 11 000 to
12 000. Among the members were teachers, army officers and civil
servants. Without a doubt the most important members were those
in the armed services, if for no other reason than that the
90 000-man army was the one institution that could have strangled
Taraki's regime at birth.

THE ARMED FORCES AND THEIR POSTURE

The decisive trial of allegiance had been among units of the
Central (or 1st) Corps based in Kabul itself. The Central Corps
consisted of two divisions (the 7th and 8th), two armoured brigades
(the 4th and 15th), a Republican Guard Brigade, two commando
regiments, and several support units. The 7th and 8th Divisions
were motorised, as were the armoured units; this meant that the
Central Corps contained most of the mobile brigades in the army.
Mobility and their location in Kabul gave the Central Corps
enormous political power. Its officers were often involved in
political intrigues. Because of this governments tried to
concentrate loyal officers in these units. But the PDPA had done its
own recruiting in these brigades. It was in the armoured brigades
that they gained their most important recruits.

The specialist arms tended to attract more officers from the
ethnic minorities, and they also received technical training in the
Soviet Union. In the 7th and 8th Divisions there were a great many
more officers from traditional officer stock – Durrani Pushtuns.
Although some of these men supported Daoud many of them were
discontented with his regime. *Coup* plots against Daoud were
reported in September 1973, August 1974, and December 1976.[11]
Their sympathies however were probably more royalist than
communist. Nevertheless the arrest of key officers and the straffing
by Qader's MiG-21s meant that the *coup* was accomplished with
very little trouble from these two divisions. The only unit of the
Central Corps that did resist was Daoud's Republican Guard
Brigade.

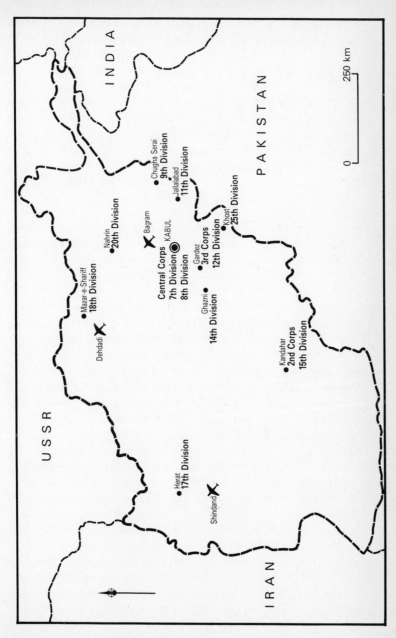

III Kabul forces, main unit locations, 1978.

The army in the rest of the country was divided into two other corps and several independent divisions (see Map III). The 2nd Corps in Kandahar and the 3rd Corps in Gardez had been built up during the 1950s and the 1960s as part of the trial of strength over Pushtunistan. As a result, the army had most of its forces concentrated in the provinces bordering Pakistan. One of these divisions, the 11th in Jallalabad (or at least its officers), did oppose the April Revolution. Its actions were led by loyalist officers. Fighting in Jallalabad is believed to have lasted two days. Officers loyal to the PDPA shot the commander of the Kandahar-based 15th Division when the rising was announced.[12] Among the other scattered divisions (the 17th in Herat, 18th in Mazar-e-Shariff, 14th in Ghazni, and 20th in Nahrin) there was no immediate reaction. Instead they decided to wait and see.

The air force, like the armoured brigades, had a greater history both of political activism and pro-Sovietism. Its units were entirely equipped with Soviet planes and its members formed a large proportion of the 7000 Afghans who had received military training in the USSR and Czechoslovakia in the period 1961–70.[13] Among the air force there were many officers from the non-Pushtun middle classes. Men like Colonel Abdol Qader, a Tajik, bitterly objected to Pushtun dominance of national life. Consequently the air force was to form a solid power-base for the new government.

Afghan airpower had been structured for a possible clash with Pakistan rather than for any internal security mission. It deployed 152 combat aircraft. Ground attack capability was based on 30 ancient IL–28s, 24 Su–7s and 50 MiG–17s. The interceptor force consisted of the 36 MiG–21s of the 322nd Air Regiment. Their main role was to protect the capital. Air force squadrons were grouped into air regiments and these were based at Shindand, Kabul, Bagram, and Dehdadi (close to Mazar-e-Shariff) airfields. The helicopter force – so important in later counter-insurgency operations – was still very small in 1978. It consisted of 18 Mil–4s and three or four Mil–8s[14] which usually operated from Kabul and Bagram in communications and VIP transport roles.

Loyalties among the police and the paramilitary gendarmerie were quite different. Daoud relied on the West German-trained police force as one of his principal instruments of power. The riot police saw action against the PDPA on the streets of Kabul just a few days before Taraki seized power. As a result retribution was swift. Three days after the *coup* a Kabul-based correspondent reported, 'many members of the city's police force have been killed or arrested'.[15]

THE SOVIET REACTION

Soviet recognition of the new regime came quickly – on 30 April. Before the April Revolution, Soviet backing for the PDPA was important but not vital. The Soviets are thought to have sponsored the truce between Parcham and Khalq in 1977. They made efforts to develop party unity but the events of April 1978 (triggered by the death of Mir Akhber Khyber) must have been unexpected. Thus the Soviets (like the People's Democratic Party itself) could have had very little warning of the *coup*.

While Moscow could obviously take great pleasure in the PDPA's victory, it had traditionally kept the party at arm's length. Unlike the other fraternal parties, the PDPA had never been invited to send an official delegation to the Congress of the Communist Party of the Soviet Union (CPSU) in Moscow. Doubtless this was done to preserve Moscow's good relations with the regimes of Nadir Shah and Mohammed Daoud.

THE EMERGENCE OF LOCAL AND REGIONAL OPPOSITION

The fact that the PDPA prior to April 1978 had not been accorded the courtesies that Moscow gave to recognised communist parties did not reassure Afghanistan's neighbours. At the offices of several Afghan exile groups in north-west Pakistan the news of a change of government in Kabul was received with consternation. The larger parties like Jamiat-Islami (Islamic Society) had been waging low-key guerrilla operations inside Afghanistan since 1974 – four years before the PDPA took power in Kabul.

Other guerrilla parties had been fighting even before the republic was proclaimed in 1973. The most important of these was the Hezb-e-Islami (Islamic Party) of Gulbuddin Hekmatyar which wanted to create a fundamentalist Islamic republic. Another group, SAMA (Afghan People's Liberation Organisation) had been operating since 1968. In the light of their subsequent declarations of anti-communism it is worth noting that parties such as Gulbuddin Hekmatyar's were fighting long before the advent of a 'communist' government in Kabul.

The guerrillas had staged a number of important operations during 1975 at the height of the tension between President Daoud and President Bhutto of Pakistan. Bhutto tended to regard the parties in exile as a convenient way of putting pressure on Kabul. When he wanted to improve relations with his neighbour, as in June 1976, he restricted the guerrillas' operations. The strongly Islamic and anti-communist regime of General Zia ul-Haq did not take long to form its own view of events in Kabul. Just five days after the April Revolution the *Daily Telegraph* reported, 'Pakistan and Persia fear new Cuba'.[16] The Chinese were more cautious, granting the new regime recognition on 7 May only after the Afghans had requested it.[17]

THE PDPA'S PLANS FOR CHANGE

The aims of Taraki's regime were soon set out in a document entitled 'Main Guidelines of the Revolutionary Tasks of the Democratic Republic of Afghanistan' (DRA). Despite constant assurances that they would respect custom and tradition it was quite clear that the PDPA wanted to engineer a complete revolution in society. The guidelines set out plans for the redistribution of land, equality for the ethnic minorities, emancipation for women, and education for all. On paper it seemed a laudable and completely necessary plan to bring Afghanistan into the 20th century. Although the People's Democratic Party leadership took great pains to assure their people that they were not anti-religious or pro-Moscow they showed naivety in enunciating their revolutionary programme as candidly as they did. Rural Afghan conservatives became deeply worried at the PDPA's manifesto.

An important first step in the PDPA's programme was taken on 15 May when the Revolutionary Council published Decree No. 4. This set out measures designed to bring ethnic equality to Afghanistan. It also promised newspapers and radio broadcasts in minority languages. There was a consensus between Taraki's Khalqis and their Parcham colleagues over this legislation, but there was trouble ahead.

THE OPPOSITION GATHERS STRENGTH

By late May, rural opposition, stirred up by ultra-conservative mullahs and landowners, was beginning to grow. On 1 June, seven Afghan political parties announced the formation of Jub Najat-e-Milli, the National Salvation Front.[18] The Front contained parties of completely different outlooks. Most important among them was the Jamiat-i-Islami Afghanistan (or ISA) led by Burhanuddin Rabbani, a former Kabul University theology lecturer. Rabbani had been fighting his battle for a nationalist Islamic republic since June 1974 and had succeeded in creating a party organisation by 1978. The fact that Rabbani and many of his followers were Tajiks meant that the ISA were considered unsuitable to lead a federation of Pushtun-dominated movements. Other parties in the Front were, on the other hand, royalist. Another, the Afghan Mellat (Social Democrats) was actually socialist in its outlook.

The Salvation Front did not include Gulbuddin Hekmatyar's Hezb-e-Islami (Islamic Party). This group benefited from very close links with the government of Pakistan under Zia ul-Haq. Zia relied on the Pakistani Hezb-e-Islami (which was affiliated to the Afghan party) for the survival of his own regime. In August 1978 he took five Pakistani Islamic Party men into his government.[19]

Both Hekmatyar and Rabbani had been operating since the early 1970s, and both of them wanted to lead a revival of conservative Islam in Afghanistan. The situation was further complicated by the emergence of an Islamic Party splinter group under Yunis Khalis, another theology teacher. This led to great rivalry. Opponents blame the failure to achieve unity among the resistance parties on Hekmatyar's personal ambitions.

THE PDPA'S IDEOLOGICAL DILEMMA

Taraki's most acute dilemma was establishing a party line on Islam. His early pronouncements, and those of his government, stressed a respect for the principles of Islam. It was even reported that Taraki personally led the Ramadan prayers.[20] Nevertheless, the Marxist-Leninist principles embodied in the PDPA's programme and policies were clear enough. Article 1 of a secret PDPA constitution, believed to be genuine, affirmed the party's belief in Marxist-Leninist ideals.[21] And, for all his conciliatory speeches,

Taraki must have known that the clergy were so closely involved
with the maintenance of the rural status quo that a conflict with
them was inevitable. He told a West German journalist: 'We want
to clean Islam in Afghanistan of the ballast and dirt of bad
traditions, superstition and erroneous belief. Therefore we will
have progressive, modern, pure Islam.'[22]

EARLY RURAL RESISTANCE

In June, fledgeling resistance groups struck at police and army
posts in remote parts of the country. Early areas of activity were in
the provinces of Badakhshan, Bamiyan, Kunar, Paktia and
Nangrahar.[23] The weapons available to the guerrillas were varied:
AK-47s looted from police posts; FN-FALs (provided by Pakistan
some years earlier); Lee Enfields (from the Pushtun workshops in
Darra); and even some left-overs from the colonial wars such as
Martini–Henrys. The guerillas spread alarmist rumours about the
government, and so sowed a growing unrest in the countryside.

In the border provinces there was a long tradition of smuggling
and illicit trading. These caravans of armed (mostly Pushtun) men
carried on a trade in semi-precious stones, guns, and opium.[24] As
the competing guerrilla parties in Peshawar looked for fighters to
sign up, they recruited many of these men. It gave the resistance a
source of fighters and the smuggling bands a form of patriotic
legitimacy. There were also many recruits who joined for higher
motives. A stream of discontented people saw the new government
as a threat to their religion and way of life. A steady flow of
deserters from the Afghan army began.

Traditionally the mission of trying to prevent the infiltration of
guerrillas and smugglers across Afghanistan's borders fell to the
gendarmerie and the Frontier Force. Sometimes when heavily
armed groups of smugglers were contacted, the army was called
in.[25] In general, though, the army was not widely involved in
upholding border security. The arrest and disappearance of many
senior officers in the municipal police and gendarmerie (renamed
the Sarandoy) caused a state of confusion in these organisations
and created an immediate vacuum in parts of rural Afghanistan.

In early July, the National Salvation Front issued a communiqué claiming that they already controlled eight of
Afghanistan's provinces.[26] So began the contention over who

'controlled' what in Afghanistan. While the army was garrisoned in reasonable numbers along the mountainous border with Pakistan, there were many regions in which it was restricted to a single regiment or brigade in the provincial capital. In the Hazara Jat (provinces like Ghowr, Bamiyan, and Uruzgan) and desert (Nimroz, Hilmand) there were areas of the size of small countries where the Afghan army had no garrison and had hardly set foot. Not surprisingly, it was in areas of the Hazara Jat, Hindu Kush and the mountainous north-east (Badakhshan province) that the first rural uprisings were declared. It was relatively straight-forward for the Salvation Front to claim control of a province like Bamiyan: Kabul had never had it anyway.

TARAKI FIGHTS BACK

In the last week of June, against this background of growing rural revolt, Taraki decided to summon tribal and religious leaders from around the country to Kabul. He wanted to allay their fears by giving a careful explanation of government policy. Taraki asked for their cooperation, saying: 'These progressive and national aims of ours can only be attained when the entire patriotic population of the country, whether workers, peasants, toilers or intellectuals, give us help and support and fearlessly defend their people's revo-lution.' Referring to Soviet aid, he said that the DRA reserved the right to seek help abroad, but that this would not undermine their non-aligned status. Taraki restated the theme that his regime was pro-Islamic and reiterated the party's 'profound respect for the principles of the holy religion of Islam'. But Taraki also criticised members of the clergy who had agitated against the regime and said that 'revolutionary methods' would be used against them.

Undoubtedly the main reason in summoning the rural leaders to Kabul was to try to contain the growing rebellion in the countryside. He said, 'Anti-national elements who were against our people's revolution, whether inside or outside the country, have levelled baseless accusations against our people's regime, resorted to wicked plots and propaganda, and have given money to a number of traitorous elements who have provoked you against us.'[27]

As Taraki fought to uphold his position in the country, he also took steps to purge his Parcham partners from the cabinet and the party. The Parchamis under Babrak Karmal were urging a slower pace of reform. In the first week of July, Karmal was dismissed from his post as Deputy Prime Minister and despatched to be Ambassador in Czechoslovakia. The 'old guard' of Karmal's Parchami supporters were removed. Soltan Ali Keshtmand and Nur Ahmad Nur lost their cabinet positions, as did the party's first lady, Anahita Ratzebad, who was sent to Yugoslavia as Ambassador.

Taraki gained support in his anti-Paracham drive from the increasingly powerful Hafizullah Amin. Karmal's removal antagonised his supporters, but this apparently was a risk that Taraki was happy to take. It was the first of a whole series of sackings that was to narrow support for the government, even among the tiny membership of the PDPA. Taraki's dislike of the Parchamis was such that he even refused to acknowledge the existence of the group. He told an Iranian correspondent, 'There was no such thing as a Parcham party in Afghanistan, and there is not now'. Having denied that there were any factions in the PDPA, Taraki went on to threaten, 'Reactionary elements, imperialist hirelings and extremist plotters trying to rise against the revolution will be annihilated decisively.'[28] The meeting of rural leaders and the removal of the cautious Karmal were both undertaken, in part, to prepare the ground for fundamental, and revolutionary, government policies.

On 12 July the Revolutionary Council issued Decree No. 6. This measure was intended to reduce the burden of debt on small farmers. Most poor farmers had to borrow heavily in order to get seed for planting. Year by year these debts accumulated until they were completely mortagaged to the local moneylender or landlord. Decree No. 6 cancelled rural debts incurred prior to 1973. This piece of Khalqi idealism could not have been better calculated to antangonise rural landowners; and of course it positioned this powerful group squarely against Taraki's regime. Naturally the decree provoked disputes about who owed what to whom. Young Khalqi militants were despatched to the countryside to sort out the claims. The intrusion by these leftist city-dwellers into the conservative countryside caused further resentment.

FACTIONALISM AND DISCONTENT IN THE ARMY

Taraki undoubtedly feared the possibility of plots against him by the Parchamis and elements in the army. On 2 August he harangued a gathering of officers with a warning against 'plotting in the guise of faith and religion'. He also told them that plotters would be 'severely punished'.[29] The army became the focus of interest for Taraki's newly formed secret police, known as AGSA. AGSA was headed by a Khalqi hardliner, Asadullah Sarwari. Fairly soon visits from its officers became regular features at the barracks of Rishkoor, and Balar Hissar. Suspects were taken to Pol-e-Charkhi jail for interrogation; many disappeared. The arrival of the PDPA had caused tensions in other arms of government. Khalq party men, many of whom were teachers or writers prior to the revolution, were placed in senior government posts. They found themselves trying to enact sweeping reforms with an old-fashioned and largely uncooperative bureaucracy.

It was the rumour of a military *coup* that allowed Taraki to dispose of the very officers that had brought him to power. On 17 August, AGSA agents arrested the Defence Minister, Brigadier Abdol Qader, his Chief of Staff, General Shapoor Ahmadzai, and several other officers. A few days later other men holding ministerial posts were dismissed: Lieutenant-Colonel Mohammed Rafi, and Soltan Ali Keshtmand. Taraki had further reduced the officer and Parchami elements in his cabinet. Some confusion surrounded the fate of Colonel Aslam Watanjar. At first it was rumoured that he was among the arrested plotters, but he emerged as Army Chief of Staff and early in 1979 became Minister of the Interior.

Having removed a tier of experienced officers in April, Taraki had taken away another group of military leaders in August. It was perhaps at this point that the army's problems began in earnest. Taraki took over the Defence Minister's brief himself and appointed another group of officers whose professed loyalty to the Khalqis outweighed any consideration of competence. Despite this behaviour towards the army, the PDPA had not established any real party organisation in most units. The only significant exceptions to this were the 4th and 15th Armoured Brigades, which soon found themselves with the status of a Khalqi praetorian guard.

In the air force there was a strong Khalqi representation. An Air Force Brigadier, Arab Khan, who subsequently defected, says that there were many more Khalqis than Parchamis in the organisation at this time. According to Khan it was the dominance of the

Khalqis in key units that allowed Taraki to dismiss Parchami
ministers and officers.[30] In most army units however a few
(generally inexperienced) officers who were loyal to Taraki found
themselves at the head of completely unsympathetic units. The
Khalqis failure to establish a widespread party organisation was a
key factor in their inability to control wayward regiments, notably
in the provinces.

Problems of manpower and motivation were critical in the
army's failure to meet the growing crisis in the countryside.
Officers in the large infantry units had a poor level of professional
education and, in many cases, a higher loyalty to the principle of
Durrani Pushtun hegemony than to any government in Kabul.
The enlisted soldiers suffered from an extremely poor level of
training, low pay, and atrocious living conditions. Throughout the
Afghan army there was the problem of allegiances. A 1973 US
Defense Department report described the issue cogently: 'The
population in general regards the armed forces as an instrument of
government, rather than an organisation of citizens in service of
the nation. The individual normally respects authority, but this
respect is shown first and foremost to his own tribal chief or head of
family.'[31]

The allegiances of the Afghan soldier were thus torn between
state and tribe or village. As the mood of the countryside became
more and more hostile towards Kabul this was reflected in a rise in
the desertion rate.

ESCALATION OF RURAL VIOLENCE

In September the government took a bold step against the rural
rebels. It had a religious council in Kabul declare a holy war (or
jihad) against them.[32] By this move Taraki hoped to convince the
average soldier or villager that killing one of the rebels was a
righteous act in religious as well as nationalist terms. The response
of the opposition parties was to make their own declaration of *jihad*.
Their holy fighters (*mujahadeen*) could now go into battle with the
knowledge that if they were killed they would go straight to *djena*
(heaven).

On 17 October the Khalqis promulgated another fundemental
reform – Decree No. 7. This was intended to bring in new era of
equality for Afghan women. It could be argued that they had

suffered under the old order more than any other element of society. Decree No. 7 proclaimed equality for women, banned the paying of bride prices (effectively the buying of a wife), and set a minimum age for marriage of 14. Most Westerners would consider this measure a positive one, yet it deeply offended many Afghans. Perhaps a more graphic illustration of the gulf between Khalqi ideals and the sensibilities of the ordinary Afghan came on 19 October. Kabul announced the unfurling of a new national flag. The new banner disposed of the band of Islamic green and was, instead, an all red one.

Reaction to these new measures was swift and violent. There was an outbreak of fighting in Kunar and Paktia provinces. The guerrillas claimed to have killed 100 Afghan soldiers and four Soviet advisers during this battle.[33] The violence started a movement of refugees into neighbouring Pakistan. By the end of the year there were an estimated 30 000 of them. But the refugee flow does need to be viewed in perspective. The rural violence of 1975, for example, resulted in an estimated 170 000 displaced persons entering Pakistan.[34]

The army found itself trying to cope with this new level of rural unrest. They were under an increased strain because the Sarandoy had virtually ceased to operate. Taraki's response to the army's lack of confidence was to try and recruit more members to the PDPA and to look elsewhere for military assistance. When asked by a foreign journalist whether he would accept more Soviet military aid, Taraki replied ominously, 'every possibility will be utilised'.[35] Increasingly, Soviet advisers were involved in the running of the Defence Ministry in Kabul where the shortage of competent senior officers was accutely felt. Steps were already underway for a major expansion of Soviet–Afghan cooperation.

As the operations of the army became increasingly problematical, and the activities of the secret police, AGSA, became more intense, there was a regrouping of power within Taraki's cabinet. Hafizullah Amin, already First Deputy Prime Minister and Foreign Minister, assumed new responsibilities for security matters.[36] Amin's tough uncompromising style won him increasing influence within the cabinet. The balance of power within that cabinet was now firmly Khalqi. The dismissals and arrests of July and August had removed the key Parchami and officer members. Only a couple of Parchamis remained, and without Karmal's presence they did not hold up the process of reform. The Khalqis

therefore had little cabinet opposition for their next, and most
overly socialistic, decree.

Early in November they issued Decree No. 8. It contained
comprehensive proposals for land reform. Among them was the
breaking up of large estates and the redistribution of land among
those who worked it. The decree was to go into effect in January.
Had the rich and powerful in rural Afghanistan still harboured any
doubts about the hostility of the government in Kabul, Decree No.
8 must surely have dispelled them. The scene was set for a major
conflict in the countryside in the New Year.

A DECISIVE SHIFT IN FOREIGN POLICY

A series of events began to demonstrate a dramatic move towards
Moscow by the Khaqi regime. On 27 November, the PDPA
Central Committee held its first (publicly announced) plenary
session. It became clear that this Soviet-style party organ had a
great deal of power. At this meeting the dismissal of Babrak
Karmal and other key Parchamis was confirmed.

On 5 December, Kabul announced the signing of a Soviet–
Afghan Treaty of Friendship. In one sense the announcement was
not a surprise. Afghanistan had been the subject of considerable
Soviet interest since the time of Lenin. Under Khrushchev,
Afghanistan had been among the top three recipients of Soviet aid.
Major military assistance had been given since 1956, and the
Soviets had also built much of the road network. In another sense,
though, the move was a surprising one. Given the pains Taraki had
gone to to convince people that his government was non-aligned,
and given the real trouble that he was having with rural
conservatives, it was strange that he decided to make so public a
demonstration of his regime's pro-Sovietism.

The treaty itself was composed mainly of standard clauses.
Article 4 for example stated, 'in the interest of strengthening the
defence capacity of the high contracting parties [i.e. the USSR and
DRA] they shall continue to develop cooperation in the military
field on the basis of appropriate agreements between them'. The
treaty did contain one important new proposal. Article 10
suggested 'the creation of an effective security system in Asia on the
basis of joint efforts by all the countries of the continent'. While the
idea of a collective security system was not a new one, the

recruitment of Afghanistan to such a plan caused concern, especially in Peking. This public alignment of Kabul and Moscow in Asian geopolitics was of grave concern not just to China, but also to her principal regional ally, Pakistan. The Afghan–Soviet friendship treaty marked the beginning of deep Chinese antagonism towards the Taraki government.

The Chinese took practical steps against Kabul remarkably quickly. By late December there were reports of major Chinese arms shipments to the Afghan rebels.[37] Some weapons were apparently supplied to the *mujahadeen* direct through the thin strip of land that connects Afghanistan and China called the Wakhan Corridor.

By December 1978 there had been a pronounced and important change in south-west Asian political relationships. Afghanistan had moved decisively towards the USSR and was encountering the hostility of China and Pakistan – which was host to a growing resistance movement. Afghanistan's other neighbour, Iran, was undergoing a revolutionary process of its own. Under its new leader, Ayatollah Khomeini, it too was to align itself decisively against Kabul.

As 1978 drew to a close the upheaval in the Afghan countryside continued. The army stood close to collapse. The PDPA, a tiny party trying to change a whole society was itself split. The *mujahadeen* were gathering strength to give Kabul a major trial in 1979; it was to be a trial that Taraki's Khalqi regime did not survive.

Notes

1. Fred Halliday, 'Revolution in Afghanistan', *New Left Review*, no. 112, November–December 1978.
2. Account of 4th Armoured Brigade's role broadcast on Moscow Radio (home service), 16 January 1980.
3. *The Guardian*, 28 April 1978.
4. Ibid.
5. Kabul Radio, 27 April 1978.
6. Louis Dupree, *Afghanistan* (Princeton, 1980). Some Western estimates of the casualties ran as high as 10 000 (*Daily Telegraph*, 2 May 1978); Taraki's own claim was that less than 100 had died.
7. Kabul Radio (home service), 28 April 1978.

8.   Halliday, op. cit.
9.   Thomas Hammond, *Red Flag Over Afghanistan* (Westview Press, 1984).
10. Louis Dupree, 'Afghanistan Under the Khalq', *Problems of Communism*, no. 28, 1979.
11. For plot details see *Keesings Contemporary Archives* (see indexes for 1974 and 1976).
12. *Daily Telegraph*, 2 May 1978.
13. A. Hyman, *Afghanistan Under Soviet Domination* (Macmillan, 1984).
14. IISS, *The Military Balance 1976–77* (London, 1976).
15. *The Observer*, 30 April 1978.
16. *Daily Telegraph*, 2 May 1978.
17. *Daily Report*, 8 May 1978.
18. *Middle East Economic Digest*, 7 July 1978.
19. Kalim Bahadur, in *Afghanistan In Crisis* (Vikas, 1981).
20. Moscow Radio, 5 March 1979.
21. Contained in Hammond, op. cit.
22. *Die Zeit*, 9 June 1978.
23. *Middle East Economic Digest*, 7 July 1978.
24. US Department of Defense, *Area Handbook For Afghanistan* (Washington, DC, 1973).
25. Ibid.
26. *Middle East Economic Digest*, 7 July 1978.
27. Taraki's meeting with tribal elders, reported on Kabul Radio, 26 June 1978.
28. Interview with Nur Mohammed Taraki, broadcast on Iranian Radio (home service), 20 July 1978.
29. Taraki's speech reported in *Keesings Contemporary Archives*, 20 October 1978.
30. Interview with Brigadier Arab Khan in *Afghanistan Information Centre Bulletin*, no. 12, 1982.
31. US Department of Defense, op. cit.
32. Reported in *Keesings*, 1 June 1979.
33. *Daily Telegraph*, 31 October 1978.
34. Estimate of refugees contained in *Keesings Contemporary Archives*, 23 July 1976.
35. Kabul Radio, 18 November 1978.
36. Fred Halliday, 'War and Revolution in Afghanistan', *New Left Review*, no. 119, Jan.–Feb. 1980.
37. 'Afghan Communist Regime Facing Chinese Threat', *Daily Telegraph*, 30 December 1978.

Two: 1979

RESISTANCE IN THE PROVINCES GROWS

The first few weeks of January saw an expansion of the rural revolt. Reports of the fighting were confused and incomplete. Government sources published very few details of the trouble, perhaps hoping that things might quieten down. But press reports compiled from rebel sources indicate the principal areas of *mujahadeen* activity for the early part of the year.

Paradoxically it was those areas of the country where oppressed ethnic minorities lived, i.e. those that could have expected to benefit most from a 'progressive' government in Kabul, where the counter-revolution raged most intensely. One reason for the strength of the revolt in the north was the peasants' deeply hostile image of their Soviet neighbours. They were despised as communist *kafirs* (non-believers). Certainly there was a wealth of anti-Russian, anti-communist folklore among the Tajiks, Uzbecks and Turkmens, some of whom had emigrated to Afghanistan to escape the Sovietisation of Central Asia in the 1920s.

There was insurrection in the central provinces – the Hazara Jat – where local people took advantage of Kabul's traditional weakness. In January guerrillas claimed to have killed 700 government soldiers in fighting in the Hazara province of Uruzgan.[1] There was also trouble in the north-eastern province of Badakhshan where the Maoist group Settem-e-Melli (National Oppression), as well as some of the fundamentalist groups, had made headway recruiting amongst the local Tajik population.[2] The Tajiks of Nuristan were also in revolt, constituting one of Kabul's biggest problems in the east of the country.

Nuristanis in Laghman and the north of the Kunar valley had revolted in the autumn of 1978. Their activities, and the government response to them, led to a growing insurrection among the Pushtun population of the Kunar. Early in January a large guerrilla force set out to capture the provincial capital of the Kunar and headquarters of the 9th Division, Chugha-Serai (also known as Asadabad). Press reports estimated that guerrilla strength in the area was 5000 men.[3] This was to be the first of many attempts to take this town. Kunar's popularity with the *mujahadeen* stemmed from its mountainous terrain, and its close proximity to sources of supply across the Pakistan border. The revolt among rural Pushtuns was, by early 1979, still confined to Kunar and parts of Paktia provinces. There had been little trouble amongst the very large Pushtun population of the Kandahar plain.

The indifference of many rural Pushtuns came to an end with Kabul's attempts to implement its land reforms. It was in the largely Pushtun areas south of the capital that attempts radically to change the pattern of land ownership were begun. The government was to claim that 132 000 families received land by August 1979. But the share-out caused a great many problems. There were disputes over ownership and the Khalqi militants sent to arbitrate these had little grasp of the realities of rural life. In many cases peasants refused the land, or handed it back to their landlords. In these cases, ties of servitude, debt and custom – or simple coercion by the landlords – prevented the scheme's successful implementation. On the landowner's side the patchy nature of the reforms heightened their sense of injustice.

The land reforms had a profound effect on rural opinion and served to rally forces against Kabul. New parties emerged in response to the outcry from landowners and middle-class men of property. Among them was the National Islamic Front of Afghanistan (NIFA) led by Pir (meaning descended from a follower of Mohammed) Sayed Gailani. His party backed the traditional establishment, unlike the Islamic militants such as Khalis and Hekmatyar. Gailani was for restoring the monarchy – and if he looked to any outside ideology it was to American capitalism rather than militant Islam. One of NIFA's early successes was setting up a group in Wardak Province, just south of Kabul. It was led by Mohammed Amin Wardak, a former civil servant and something of a local celebrity.

AFGHAN/AMERICAN RELATIONS DETERIORATE

The USA itself was to undergo a profound change of course in relations with Kabul. Matters were brought to a head by the kidnapping of US Ambassador Adolph Dubs. Dubs was taken from his car to a hotel room by terrorists of the Settem-e-Melli group. They demanded the release of three activists from jail. In an attempt to prove their resolve the Kabul government ordered the storming of the hotel and Dubs was mortally wounded in the shooting. Washington expressed outrage, saying that they had asked the Afghans not to storm the hotel and alleging KGB involvement in the operation. Moscow dismissed these claims as 'absurd stories' but the damage had been done.[4] Following the incident, Peace Corps workers were withdrawn and US government aid to Afghanistan was slashed.

The new hostility of the Carter administration was accomplished by an escalation of covert operations. Although there were (surprisingly) few Soviet/Afghan allegations of Central Intelligence Agency (CIA) supplies to the *mujahadeen* at the time, they have subsequently claimed that these were underway from mid-1979. According to a Soviet source, a freighter called the *Al-Kasum*, laden with arms, arrived at the Pakistani port of Karachi in June 1979.[5] These weapons, many of which were Soviet-made had apparently been bought by the CIA for the *mujahadeen* on the open market.

AMIN VERSUS TARAKI

Within the Afghan cabinet there was an increasingly bitter power struggle between Hafizullah Amin and Nur Mohammed Taraki. Amin relied on the support of men like Shah Wali (who became Foreign Minister on 31 March) and Information Minister Bariq Shafie. Taraki's supporters included Interior Minister Sherjan Mazduryar and Chief of Staff Aslam Watanjar.[6] Amin gained cabinet support by consistently maintaining an uncompromising line towards opponents of the regime. Cabinet tensions were to be brought into full relief by events in the hitherto peaceful western city of Herat.

The months leading up to the first anniversary of the April Revolution were marked by the launch of a major literacy campaign. The aim was to teach a million people to read and write in the first year of the campaign. Illiteracy was a particular problem amongst women, in fact almost none could read.[7] This constituted a major social disadvantage for Afghan women, but attempts to teach them to read provoked enormous hostility from conservatives. It was the campaign to teach women to read and write that sparked off the biggest challenge to Kabul's authority to date.

THE HERAT REVOLT

Demonstrations against the literacy campaign began on 15 March. What turned the situation from a minor local disturbance into a national crisis was the use of soldiers from the army's 17th Division to break up the riot. This was unwise because the 10 000-man division was barely under government control. According to a former officer of the 17th, there were only 15 Khalqis in the formation.[8] Senior Captain Ismael Khan, of the anti-aircraft battalion, and Captain Alladin, a signals officer (both of them Tajiks) organised the defection of almost the entire division. Literally thousands of men went over to the rebels.

As the soldiers deserted to the rebels they looted government arsenals and distributed hundreds of automatic weapons to the mob. The government faced an unprecedented situation. Indeed they have not had an entire division, and an entire city, out of their control since then. In the ensuing mayhem several (estimates vary from 28 to 200) Soviet citizens (advisers, their wives and children) were cut to pieces and their remains paraded around the city. Attempts to rally army units in the city were unsuccessful and the town remained out of government control for several days. Subsequent reaction was harsh.

The 4th and 15th Armoured Brigades were dispatched from Pol-e-Charkhi. Because this journey would take several days, Amin called on Major-General Sayed Mukharam (commander of Kandahar garrison) to form a mobile force and recapture the city. The general accepted his orders, and moved north with a column of loyal troops. They surround the city, and prepared to take on the rebels. There was then an air strike by IL–28 bombers from the 355th Air Regiment at Shindand.[9] Areas of the city, including the 17th Division HQ, were subjected to repeated bombing. The armour moved in afterwards, by which time most of the resistance had subsided. Western sources estimated that 5000 people died in the fighting.[10]

Events in Herat shook the government. The defection of so many officers and soldiers during the revolt raised serious questions about the reliability of the army. The scale of the trouble also signalled that the Khalqis had a major problem in an area of the country that had hitherto been relatively peaceful. News of the events galvanized local resistance. Ismael Khan and Allaladin, the two officers who led the rebel soldiers, formed a guerrilla front and pledged allegiance to Burhanuddin Rabbani's ISA. Khan was over-all leader of the front, with Allaladin as his military commander. The men and weapons that they brought with them fuelled local resistance for several years. Using their knowledge of tactics, organisation and the region, they formed an effective band. Their activities have undermined government authority in the area ever since.

Hafizullah Amin used the trauma of Herat to advance his own position in the cabinet. On 27 March it was announced that Amin had been appointed to the post of Prime Minister. The government then announced the formation of the Homeland High Defence Council. It was intended to use this council to coordinate a new security offensive. Its members included Amin, Taraki, Aslam Watanjar, Mazduryar (the Interior Minister), AGSA chief Assadullah Sarwari, the Chief of Staff and heads of the air force and air defence forces.[11] The council was perhaps also intended to contain the growing factionalism within the Khalq. Amid the bitter recriminations over Herat there was a fresh wave of arrests among army officers and party workers suspected of disloyalty.

THE SOVIETS ESCALATE

The most serious long-term result of Herat was the marked change in the attitude of the Soviet Union. On 6 April Army-General Alexei Yepishev arrived in Kabul with a high-level military delegation.[12] Yepishev, as Chief of the Main Political Administration of the Soviet Army and Navy, occupied an important position of trust with both the Military Council of the USSR Ministry of Defence and the Central Committee of the Communist Party. In this capacity he was obviously considered the ideal person to asses the military/political consequences of a deeper Soviet commitment in Afghanistan. It is interesting to note that Yephishev made a similar fact-finding tour of Czechoslovakia in 1968, shortly before the Warsaw Pact intervention there.

Following the Yepishev visit there was a marked increase in all types of Soviet aid to Afghanistan. The most urgent requirement was for help in defeating the rural insurgency. Just weeks after Yepishev's return to Moscow, the USSR delivered large quantities of weapons. The package reportedly included 100 T–62 tanks, half a dozen MiG-21s and 12 Mil-24 helicopter gunships.[13] Deliveries were also prepared of Su-20 fighter-bombers, and Mil-6 helicopters. Several of these systems, such as the Mil-24 and Su-20 had not previously seen service with the Afghan air force. This required the commitment of pilots and technicians to operate the new equipment. The total number of Soviet advisers grew quickly. The number serving in Afghanistan early in 1979 was about 1000.[14] By August the number (including civilian advisers) was estimated at 5000.

The increased military commitment reflected a resolve on the part of the Soviet political leadership to come to the aid of the beleaguered PDPA regime. The theme of a revolutionary state trying to resist the forces of world reaction became the dominant one in the Soviet media's increasingly frequent reports on the situation in Afghanistan. *Izvestia* reported events in western Afghanistan: 'in the last few days foreign agents and mercenaries have been put into Afghan territory and have, together with gangs of counter-revolutionaries who are active in the areas of the country which border on Pakistan and Iran, staged an anti-government uprising in Herat'.[15] Next day Radio Moscow laid the blame firmly at the door of the country's neighbours: 'Afghanistan has found itself the target of the subversive acts launched from Pakistan, Iran, and China . . . Chinese instructors take part in training bands for subversive and terrorist actions.'[16]

The increase in reports from Afghanistan and the change of tone reflected the new commitment of the Soviet political leadership to the regime in Kabul. In a speech to mark the ratification of the Afghan–Soviet friendship treaty on 20 April, Leonid Brezhnev drew parallels with the Soviet experience of revolution: 'The aims of the Afghan revolution . . . are familiar and comprehensible to us. The fulfilment of these tasks is no easy matter. We know from our own experience that it demands the overcoming of opposition by internal and external foes, persistence, endurance, solidarity. But we are firmly convinced that the new democratic Afghanistan will pass through all tests successfully.'[17] This new commitment by the Kremlin was accompanied by contingency planning by the General Staff for a takeover of Afghanistan by the Soviet Army.[18]

THE DEMORALISATION OF THE AFGHAN ARMY

The arrival of more Soviet advisers, though viewed as essential in

Kabul, may well have contributed to the fall in morale in the army. The increasing reliance on the Soviets was a controversial policy, even among the Khalqis. The army's conduct of operations in the countryside was fairly straightforward. In most places the garrisons lacked the mobility and the offensive spirit actually to go out on operations. In these areas isolated army posts were attacked by bands of rebels an the soldiers gave themselves up relatively quickly.

But in some cases troops behaved with incredible brutality – allowing the resistance to flesh out their anti-government propaganda with gruesome fact. On 20 April 1979, the village of Kerala in the Kunar valley was razed, and over 1000 of its inhabitants killed.[19] The massacre only exacerbated the army's difficulties in that long, hostile valley.

The only real capacity for conducting mobile offensive operations lay with the Central Corps. Armoured and motorised units from the Central Corps became involved in increasingly frequent 'fire brigade' deployments to areas of unrest. During the second week in May, a motorised brigade of the Central Corps 7th Division was despatched from Kabul to fight the rebels in Paktia Province.

On 17 May it set out from Gardez on the road to Khost and made contact with a rebel force. But the disillusioned brigade commander surrendered his entire unit to the *mujahadeen*, apparently on the condition that they be able to keep their army uniforms and weapons and join the fight against the government.[20] The defection of an entire brigade of perhaps 2000 men together with its armoured vehicles and heavy weapons was a serious blow to the government. Even by May, desertions to the *mujahadeen* must have amounted to thousands of troops. A Western report that 10 000 had deserted by the end of May could well have been an underestimate.[21] Among the deserters were senior army officers who established themselves quickly in the resistance. One of the key commanders in Sayed Gailani's National Islamic Front was the former army officer, Colonel Esmatullah Achadzai. He was one of six senior ex-army officers with Gailani's group, and in April 1979 claimed to command forces totalling 7500 men across southern Afghanistan.[22]

A further deterioration of the security situation occurred in June with the spread of unrest to central Kabul. On 23 June, violence broke out in Kabul old city following anti-government demonstrations by Hazaras. Soviet radio reported these events and commented: 'the Afghan revolution has encountered strong resistance from its enemies'.[23]

In the Hazara Jat itself the rebels were increasingly well organised. In September 1979 the Shura-ye Ettefagh (Council of the Union, usually known simply as Shura) was set up as an umbrella for various groups. This body, under Sayed Ali Beheshti, established systems of administration, taxation and even a limited form of conscription. The Shura established the Hazara Jat as a 'no-go area' for the army.

Combat losses and the desire to expand fighting capabilities meant continued arms shipments from the Soviets. Late in June, an American paper quoting 'intelligence sources' said that the Soviets had stepped up deliveries of war *matériel* by air to Bagram. They reportedly delivered a further 18 Mil–24 helicopters as well as more MiGs and Sukhoi bombers.[24] Early in July, Bagram became the target for a guerrilla attack. Incidents like this resulted in the Soviets committing several companies of troops for airfield defence in September.[25]

In Kabul the worsening security situation resulted in more operations by AGSA and the Sarandoy. Following the removal of many officers from the Sarandoy just after the April Revolution, the organisation had been re-built as a solid Khalqi force. Increasingly the Sarandoy and AGSA were used against soldiers whose loyalty the government distrusted. On 5 August, AGSA and Sarandoy men staged a joint raid on the 444th Commando Battalion's barracks at Kabul's Balar Hissar Fort.[26] They went to round up officers who were suspected of disloyalty to the government, but their arrests triggered a gun battle between the commandos and the police. As the situation became serious the government had to rely once more on the armoured brigades to go in and suppress the mutiny.

THE SITUATION IN THE KUNAR VALLEY

As if the problems of factionalism and bad morale in the army were not serious enough, Kabul was confronted with a new spate of guerrilla operations in the countryside. The most serious setback was at Asmar. This town in the Kunar valley was held by the 5th Brigade of the 9th Division, and was under seige throughout the summer of 1979. The brigade was 2000 strong, and it was

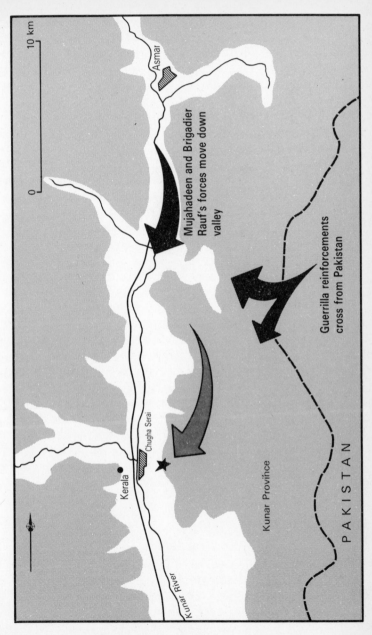

IV Fighting in Kunar Valley, August–December 1979.

surrounded by just 400 *mujahadeen* (mainly Hekmatyar IP and ISA men). In the first week of August the brigade revolted; it was a bloody affair. About 150 suspected government sympathisers from the unit were killed. Asmar fell to the guerrillas, and the commander, Brigadier Abdul Rauf (a non-party man who had survived the blood letting), was allowed to retain authority over his men.

The 5th Brigade then marched down the valley towards Chugha Serai. They were joined by 4000 *mujahadeen*. The force (totalling 6000) pitted itself against a garrison of 2500: favourable odds in a guerrilla war. There was a brief battle as the *mujahadeen* tried to position heavy weapons on a hill overlooking the town. Then the attack collapsed in a series of bitter rows. Brigadier Rauf wanted to pull out, he was afraid there would be reprisals on his village. The resistance parties argued over how they would divide the 5th Brigade's booty. In the meantime the garrison was reinforced and the attack collapsed.

Many of Rauf's disillusioned men deserted the *jihad*, as they had deserted their government, and walked the few kilometres to the Pakistani border. The ISA and IP fighters had a violent confrontation over the booty. Whilst they argued, they lost their chance to evict the communists from the Kunar. Eventually it was the Islamic Party that sold most of the heavy weapons.

The large amounts of cash to be made from selling captured guns and ammunition in the bazaars of Darra (the Pakistani town where a Kalashnikov assault rifle and ammunition could fetch $1000) made the war an increasingly lucrative enterprise for the Pushtun tribesmen of the border area. According to SAS soldier turned film-maker, Nick Downie, who spent four months with the guerrillas of Kunar late in 1979, 'most of them fought for the loot'.[27]

AMIN IN THE ASCENDENT

Hafizullah Amin gained even greater control over security operations when he was appointed Defence Minister on 27 July. Amin seems to have had little idea of military theory but took the job with the conviction that the insurgency could be defeated if sufficiently tough measures were applied. Amin's appointment must greatly have annoyed army men who supported Taraki. The competition for power between them was becoming increasingly intense. The Soviets were believed to oppose Amin in this battle. By mid-August the US mission in Kabul was reporting Soviet plots to dispose of Amin.[28] Pro-Taraki Khalqis published night letters attacking Amin. Amin's power rested on his ability to fill key appointments in the security forces with men loyal to himself.

Amin's determination to step up security operations had several practical results. Preparations were made to establish a national militia organisation and there were attempts to buy the services of Pushtun tribesmen in the border provinces. There was also a new army offensive at the beginning of September. There was an attempt to clear rebels out of the Kunar valley which, it would appear, was only partially successful.[29] There was also an operation by units of the Central Corps in the Panjsher valley. Guerrillas of the Islamic Society were using the valley as a stronghold and base for attacks on Bagram and the vital supply road from Kabul to the Soviet border via the Salang tunnel. Press reports indicated that the Panjsher operation was at least partially successful in forcing the *mujahadeen* into the hills.[30]

The character of rural operations was becoming increasingly destructive. Army sweeps would be preceded by heavy air strikes which resulted in many civilian casualties. The Mil–24 helicopter became the most feared of government weapons. The twin-engined machines used rapid-firing 12.7mm machine guns and multiple fragmentation rockets to terrify as well as to kill. As the death toll rose, the number of people who wanted to take vengeance on the government multiplied.

TARAKI GOES TO MOSCOW

Against the background of warfare in the countryside and intense factionalism in the capital, Nur Mohammed Taraki departed the country for a conference of leaders of non-aligned nations in Havana. On 10 September Taraki interrupted his homeward journey to have talks in Moscow. The speculation is that a plan was hatched to dispose of Hafizullah Amin, although this has never been proved. What *is* known is that Taraki was accorded prime treatment by the Soviets. His picture appeared on the front page of *Pravda*. Moscow Radio said that the Soviet leader had praised the Afghan revolution and 'assured Nur Mohammed Taraki that in this just struggle the friendly Afghan people could continue to count on the all-round disinterested assistance of the Soviet Union'.[31]

Taraki returned to Kabul on 11 September. Amin pre-empted any possible moves against himself by dismissing four pro-Taraki ministers from the cabinet on 14 September. They were spirited out of the country joining other exiles in Eastern Europe and the USSR. Taraki and the Soviet ambassador, Alexander Puzanov, are then believed to have tried to dispose of Amin. They invited him for a meeting at the Presidential Palace. One of Taraki's aides, Major Taroun, informed Amin that it might be a trap, but he agreed to the talks, apparently after assurances from the Soviet ambassador. The meeting turned into a shoot-out. Amin escaped unhurt but Major Taroun was killed. The next day Taraki's retirement 'on health grounds' was announced. It was only on 9 October that Kabul Radio informed the world that the party leader had died. It is thought that Amin's henchmen in AGSA disposed of him.

SOVIET MILITARY PREPARATIONS

In Moscow the news through intelligence sources of Taraki's death was regarded as a serious deterioration of the situation. From mid-September major work began to prepare the army for an operation in Afghanistan. The task facing the General Staff was an enormous one. Within the staff, responsibility for planning the intervention lay with the Middle Eastern section of the Operations Main Directorate. Their preparations for the operation were to take place in three distinct stages: concentration of troops, reinforcement of local air forces and activation of a theatre command structure.[32] The first of these, namely mobilising forces to take part in the operation, began in September.

The Operations Main Directorate faced a very difficult task in putting together their ground force. The formations bordering on Afghanistan were based in the Turkestan and Central Asian Military Districts (MDs). The readiness of these forces was extremely low. Of the five motor rifle (i.e. mechanised) divisions in the Turkestan Military District, none was combat-ready (in Russian, *razvertavie*). In fact this district was suffering the effects of years as a strategic backwater. It had only one *razvertavie* (combat-ready) division, the 105th Guards Air Assault. One of the motor rifle divisions was at about half strength; the other four were simply cadre formations – skeleton units at only about 15 per cent strength.

Readiness in the Central Asian district was slightly better as there had been a build-up there during the Sino–Soviet crisis. Nevertheless, the district's two category I formations (the 8th Guards 'Panfilov' Motor Rifle and 15th Tank Divisions) were deployed primarily to meet a Chinese threat. And that is where they stayed; in the event neither of them was sent to Afghanistan. So in the Central Asian District, too, forces had to be raised from cadre to combat strength.

To maintain the security of the operation it was decided to fill out the divisions by calling up local reservists rather than drafting in too many men from other districts. The men who received the call-up were primarily from local ethnic groups – Turkmens, Uzbecks, Tajiks and Kirghiz. There was an acute shortage of officers, particularly in the technical grades. Many graduates who had done reserve officers' courses found themselves called up to serve as political officers, engineers and in various technical tasks.[33]

Soviet confidence that a local call-up would maintain the security of the operation was misplaced. US intelligence sources detected the unusual movements in the southern USSR almost as soon as they started. On 20 September, in Washington, the US State Department spokesman reported 'increased activity among some Soviet units north of the Afghan–Soviet border.'[34] It was also reported that the 105th Guards Air Assault had gone on a modified alert. The spokesman warned the Soviets against 'any intervention' in Afghanistan's internal affairs.

In the manner of their major operational planning during the Second World War, the General Staff appointed a representative to take control of all the resources that would be involved in the forthcoming operation. This man was First Deputy Defence Minister, Marshal Sergei Sokolov. In his role as a Deputy Defence Minister 'without portfolio' he was ideally placed to undertake the operation. He and the Operations Main Directorate received increasing amounts of intelligence for the forthcoming operation. The Soviets, with extraordinary nerve, had dispatched a team of 60 officers, under the direction of Army-General Ivan Pavlovskiy, to Afghanistan in August.[35]

They had actually travelled about the country deciding where to deploy which units in the event of an intervention operation. There was also a ready flow of information from the Soviet advisory team which was headed by Major-General Gorelov. By September the US State Department estimated that the number of Soviet military advisers in the country was about 2000.[36] These men were able to supply a great deal of information about the morale and readiness of units, and also about the allegiances of particular Afghan officers.

AMIN AND THE SOVIETS

In Kabul, Hafizullah Amin had undertaken a programme of measures to try to gain support for his regime. He announced the disbandment of AGSA, but soon formed his own security police network, KAM. He also announced an amnesty for political prisoners. Amin claimed that 12 000 people had died in government jails between April 1978 and August 1979.[37] While condemning the coercion of Taraki, Amin instituted a new wave of arrests of the ex-President's supporters. One of these men, Distagir Panjsheri (one of the few remaining Parchamis in the cabinet), fled to the Soviet Union where he was publicly greeted. The community of Afghan ex-ministers in Eastern Europe was beginning to look like a government in exile. Amin seems to have been aware, despite official Soviet expressions of goodwill, that they were plotting against him. His Foreign Minister had already claimed that the Soviet ambassador had been involved in a plan to get rid of him. Indeed on the 8 November Ambassador Puzanov's recall, on the insistence of Amin, was announced by the Soviet government.

Amin was never trusted by the Kremlin. He did not have the kind of background that they liked the leaders of 'fraternal parties' to have. Amin had studied for years at US universities (Columbia and Wisconsin) rather than at Moscow's Patrice Lumumba or another Soviet university. He had a command of English but none of Russian. The KGB suspected Amin of deeper, unforgivable heresies. According to KGB Major Vladimir Kuzichkin (who later defected) they 'had doubts about Amin from the beginning. Our investigations showed him to be a smooth-talking fascist who was secretly pro-Western . . . we also suspected that he had links with the CIA but we had no proof.'[38] The belief that Amin was in the West's pocket rather than their own provided another reason for the Kremlin's takeover, and emerged as an important propaganda theme afterwards.

THE SOVIETS ACTIVATE A WAR COMMAND STRUCTURE

In the southern USSR, plans for a military operation were continuing. Heavy transport planes were grouped in the Turkestan District, and Sokolov began to put together a team of senior officers to direct the operation. With him in his Southern Theatre of Military Operations (in Russian, Teatr Voyenikh Deystviy or TVD) HQ was Army-General Valentin Varennikov. Varennikov had been commander of the Carpathian Military District until early October. He was identified on 2 November as having been transferred to the General Staff.[39] It is believed that Army-General Varennikov served as Sokolov's Chief of Staff for the operation. Under Varennikov was a team from the Operations Main Directorate (many of whom had probably accompanied Army-General Pavlovskiy on his visit into Afghanistan in August) which served as a Southern TVD staff cell. Sokolov's Southern Theatre would control two front (army group) HQs for the operation. One was based on the Turkestan Military under the command of Colonel-General Yuri Maksimov, the other on the Central Asian District commanded by Colonel-General Pyotr Lushev. The main ground operation was to be commanded by the Turkestan Military District HQ in Tashkent. An army-level command (the 40th Army in the border town of Termez) would be used as a forward HQ.

Amin's disposal of Taraki simply intensified the discontent in the army. Soon after Taraki's death was announced there was an insurrection by men of the 7th Division.[40] There was further trouble with this unit a month later when it was deployed against *mujahadeen* in the north-eastern province of Badakhshan. The situation was brought under control by the dispatch of the Khalqis loyal armoured brigades to the scene of the trouble.[41] During these months many of those arrested by KAM were summarily executed at Pol-e-Charkhi jail. By Kabul Radio's own estimate (after Amin's ouster) the number of people killed and bulldozed into mass graves at the prison amounted to 'tens of thousands'.[42] On 20 November, the US Chargé d'Affaires telexed the State Department in Washington that there was 'an atmosphere of mortal fear and dread pervading the country'.[43]

THE OPERATION BEGINS

The Soviet army was ready to begin the first phases of its operation to seize Afghanistan. Their objective was simple enough – to replace the regime of Hafizullah Amin with one headed by Babrak Karmal – a regime designed to secure broader support from the people and party. At the same time the arrival of the Soviet army would bolster the Afghans and allow them to renew their rural counter-insurgency. The operation would begin with the seizure of key political and military targets in the capital by a reinforced Air Assault Division. This division, based on the 105th Guards Headquarters, was commanded by Major-General Moussa Yevanov.[44] It gained two additional regiments of paratroops – one from the 103rd Guards Air Assault (a rapid-response formation in the Byelorussian District) and one from the 104th Guards Air Assault Division which was based in the Caucasus. The first regiment of Yevanov's task force (the one from the 103rd Guards) was flown into Bagram on 6 and 7 December.[45] The 40th Army's ground thrust would be two pronged. One force launched from Termez (in the Turkestan District) would proceed down the Salang highway, across the Hindu Kush mountains to Kabul and eastern Afghanistan. The other group would drive from Kushka around the west of the Hazara mountains and secure Herat, Farah and Kandahar. The men allocated to both of these land thrusts amounted to four motor rifle divisions.

The army of four motor rifle and one and a half air assault divisions was small and had limited objectives. By comparison, the force sent into Czechoslovakia in 1968 consisted of around 20 divisions totalling 250 000 men. The good intelligence available from officers inside Afghanistan, the careful work of large teams of staff officers, and the small size of the initial force all support the conclusion that the Soviet force had limited objectives: to dominate key cities and the roads which connected them. Marshal Sokolov had his own contingency plan in case the Kremlin-backed Karmal government ran into serious trouble. He prepared a second echelon of three more formations: the 5th Guards, and the 16th and 54th Motor Rifle Divisions. These would be held in the

USSR in case of a deterioration in the situation. By November the concentration of forces close to the border and the positioning of pontoon bridge sections for a crossing of the Oxus River were underway. US diplomats were refused permission to visit the area.[46]

Soviet army preparations went ahead for an operation in the last week of December. The timing of the final build-up and *coup* would coincide nicely with the Western administrative paralysis of Christmas. Sokolov's intervention force was prepared at the outset for the possibility of conducting conventional as well as counter-insurgency operations. They feared either a Western counter-stroke or a major revolt by the Afghan armed services. To this end, the first wave of 40th Army troops to go into Afghanistan would include units for fighting a full-scale war. Among them were an SA-4 anti-aircraft missile brigade and an army-level artillery brigade. Also included among divisional support elements, and the source of much controversey later, were chemical warfare decontamination units. By mid-December the four motor rifle divisions in the first wave were being brought to their jumping-off points. For most of the troops this was a very short journey. The only formation which travelled any distance was the 201st Motor Rifle Division which came from Dushanbe in the neighbouring military district. Despite having had three and a half months for mobilisation, these divisions were still not fully ready. They reportedly only had two-thirds of their personnel and lacked some support units.[47]

AMIN'S LAST DAYS

Whilst military preparations reached an advanced stage, the Kremlin maintained a courteous relationship with Amin's regime. A telegram expressing fraternal good wishes was sent on 4 December to mark the anniversary of the Afghan–Soviet treaty. The next day Amin launched the National Organisation for Defence of the Revolution, a last attempt to rally popular support for his government. In his speech to the inaugural meeting of the organisation Amin stressed the value of Soviet assistance.[48] Despite the courtesies, Kabul was rife with rumours that the Soviets were trying to form a new party of moderate Marxists and Khalqi dissidents and plotting to oust Amin.

The rumours of Soviet attempts to form a new 'moderate' party, and the knowledge that they already had a PDPA 'cabinet in exile' must have worried Amin. Speaking on 15 December he acknowledged the threat candidly: 'Those who would try to establish a separate party apart from the PDPA have the objective of overthrowing the government because any party's aim is to achieve political power.'[49] Amin addressed the Council of Ministers on 23 December and called on them to 'rally around their party and Khalqi government'.[50] As he was speaking Antonov heavy transports were landing men of the 105th Guards Air Assault Division at Bagram airbase.

'WE'VE COME TO SAVE THE REVOLUTION'

The first regiment of Major-General Yevanov's task force had already left Bagram as the main elements of his formation arrived on 22–26 December. The move was accomplished by Military Transport Aviation Antonov and Ilyushin heavy transports. During the 22–26 December period they flew 350 sorties into Kabul and Bagram.[51] The unit from the 103rd Guards were deployed from Bagram to the Salang pass on 19 December.[52] The Salang pass, with its long road tunnel (built by the Soviets at enormous cost) was the key choke point on the route of advance across the Hindu Kush mountain barrier to Kabul.

Officers loyal to Amin undoubtedly detected these large-scale troop movements but were rendered powerless to do anything about them. There was in any case little will to save the government. On the evening of 26 December the Chief of Staff telephoned Lieutenant-Colonel Alawoddin, commander of the 4th Armoured Brigade. According to Alawoddin: 'He demanded that we should immediately take out the tanks and set off for Kabul to protect the Amin regime. A rather worrying situation arose in the brigade. We immediately called together the party activists and all patriotic officers. It was decided to investigate the situation and not to take any steps which might damage the gains of the April Revolution.'[53] Amin was failed at the critical moment by the hitherto loyal 4th Armoured Brigade. In other barracks Soviet advisers and security men acted to prevent the possibility of opposition. At the garrisons of the 7th Division at Rishkoor and the

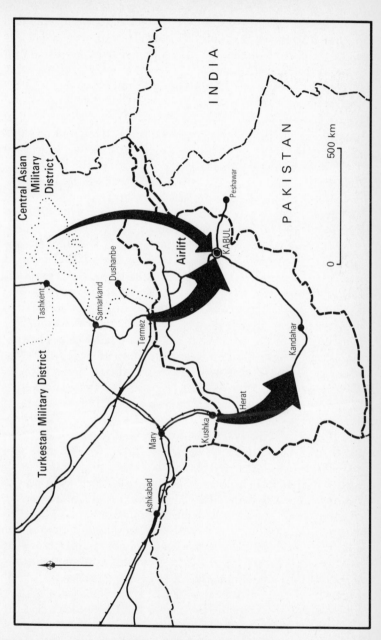

V Main axes of Soviet advance, 1979.

8th Division at Kargha they locked up officers loyal to Amin and immobilised vehicles.[54]

On 27 December the final phase of the operation to seize Afghanistan was launched. Yevanov's paratroops moved into downtown Kabul late in the afternoon. At 19.15 local time they arrived at the Ministry of the Interior and disarmed Khalqi loyalists.

Another force, reportedly made up of KGB Special Forces commandos went to the Darulaman Palance on the southern outskirts of the city. Amin had moved there with his staff only a few days earlier, apparently at the encouragement of the Soviets, 'for safety'. This was doubtless part of their plan as it would keep any fighting out of the city centre, and the Darulaman itself is very close to the Soviet embassy. It is likely that the Soviets wanted to take Amin alive, if only to give him a public trial. However they failed to do this and there was a firefight between commandos and Amin's guards. Amin himself was killed in the battle.

Various theories have been put forward about the presence in Kabul of a close associate of Leonid Brezhnev's – First Deputy Minister of the Interior, Lieutenant-General Viktor Paputin. According to some reports Paputin commanded the intelligence/security aspects of the takeover.[55] Paputin's death was announced a few weeks later. One theory is that he was killed at the Darulaman; another that he committed suicide because of the failure to take Amin alive. Neither explains the fact that Paputin was officially reported to have returned to Moscow on 13 December.[56]

The sound of the fighting at Amin's palace was heard throughout the city. At Kabul Radio, frightened PDPA members, fearing the revolution was over flushed their party cards down toilets or hid them behind radiators.[57] At 20.45 a message was broadcast announcing that Babrak Karmal had taken over the government and requested Soviet military assistance. The station sending the message announced itself as Kabul Radio, but was in fact situated in the Soviet border town (and headquarters of the 40th Army) of Termez. At 21.00 Soviet paratroops arrived at the real Kabul Radio and told staff that they had come 'to save the revolution'.[58]

Pontoon bridges were thrown across the Oxus River and the 40th Army's two-pronged thrust began. The eastern force crossed the river and began moving south, towards the Salang pass. It was led by the 360th Motor Rifle Division. The western force, spearheaded by the 66th Motor Rifle Division and supported by the 357th Motor Rifle Division, began its journey to Herat.[59] Throughout the night an unending stream of vehicles moved across pontoon bridges and into Afghanistan. By the time Karmal's appeal for Soviet help went out, 15 000 to 20 000 of their troops were already in the country.

A NEW PHASE OF THE APRIL REVOLUTION

Through the night hours and into 28 December, details of Karmal's Soviet-sponsored package became known. The aim was to regain the thrust of the bulk of the people and of elements within the PDPA that Taraki and Amin had alienated with such thoroughness. Karmal's policies had to represent a careful balancing act. The new leader wanted to be able to denounce the crimes of Amin, but at the same time not damage further public faith in the PDPA. He wanted to gain the backing of all sections of his party, but knew that radical Khalqis occupied most of the key positions in intelligence and the armed forces.

Karmal's cabinet, announced on 28 December, summed up both his good intentions and his weaknesses. He had brought his staunch Parcham allies into the cabinet, but not given them all the key jobs. Ali Keshtmand became Deputy Prime Minister; Mohammed Dost, Foreign Minister; and Anahita Ratzebad, Minister of Education. A Parchami officer, Brigadier Mohammed Rafi, was made Minister of Defence. But he also brought in old Khalqis like Sherjan Mazduryar (Minister of Transport) and Faiz Mohammed (Minister of Frontiers and Tribes). He even appointed a non-PDPA man to the cabinet. Dr Mohammed Khan Jalalar, a leftist intellectual, was made Minister of Commerce.

But two of Karmal's key Kahalqi appointments reflected his weakness rather than his magnanimity. Khalqui strength in intelligence and the forces under the Ministry of the Interior (Sarandoy and police) was such that Karmal had to proceed very carefully. A Khalqi, Mohammed Gulabzoi, was made Minister of the Interior. The ex-chief of AGSA, Assadullah Sarwari, was made a Deputy Prime Minister, whilst Karmal created an intelligence service of his own. The new organisation Khedemati-e-Dolati (or KHAD as it is widely known) was set up under the control of a staunch Parchami, Dr Mohammed Najeebollah.

Karmal's takeover was accompanied by a determined propaganda drive. The theme was that a 'New Phase' of the April Revolution had begun. Karmal arrived in Kabul at roughly the same time as the 360th Motor Rifle Division, which settled into tented camps on the outskirts of the city. The reaction to this massive intervention was almost wholly negative. Afghan army men and civilians alike felt the pain of national humiliation. The force of their anger was to be felt within days.

On a bitterly cold New Year's Eve, Karmal settled into the Presidential Palace, and the men of the 360th Motor Rifle Division settled into their tents. They received a message of pure optimism from Leonid Brezhnev: 'On behalf of the Soviet leadership and myself personally, I wish you great successes in all your diverse activity for the good of the friendly Afghan people. I am confident that in the present conditions the Afghan people will succeed in defending the April Revolution and the sovereignty, independence and national dignity of the new Afghanistan.'[60]

Notes
1.　*Middle East Economic Digest*, 26 January 1979.
2.　For details of the Nuristani rising, see A. Hyman, *Afghanistan Under Soviet Domination* (Macmillan, 1984).
3.　*The Guardian*, 8 January 1979.
4.　Moscow Radio, 15 February 1979.
5.　Vladimir Efros, *Afghanistan: US Terrorism in Action* (Novosti, 1984).
6.　Fred Halliday, 'War and Revolution in Afghanistan', in *New Left Review*, no. 19.
7.　*Kabul Times*, 19 June 1979.
8.　Commander Allaladin, 17th Division rebellion leader, military commander of Herat ISA front, interviewed by the author, 7 April 1986.
9.　*The Guardian*, 31 March 1979.
10.　Ibid.
11.　*Kabul Times*, 2 April 1979.
12.　*Kabul Times*, 7 April 1979.
13.　*RUSI Newsletter*, 15 February 1981.
14.　*New York Times*, 24 March 1979.
15.　*Izvestia*, 20 March 1979.
16.　Moscow Radio (world service), 19 March 1979.
17.　Leonid Brezhnev's speech to the Supreme Soviet, reported on Moscow Radio (home service), 20 April 1979.
18.　John Erickson, the West's leading authority on the Soviet Army provided details of the run-up to the intervention in testimony to the British House of Commons Foreign Affairs Committee.

19. Edward Girardet, *Afghanistan: The Soviet War* (Croom Helm, 1985).
20. Agence France Presse, 27 May 1979.
21. *Daily Telegraph*, 26 May 1979.
22. *International Herald Tribune*, 17 April 1979.
23. Leonid Levchenko in commentary on Moscow Radio (Pushtun service), 25 June 1979.
24. *Washington Post*, 29 May 1979.
25. *Foreign Broadcasting Information Service*, (USA), 25 September 1979.
26. *International Herald Tribune*, 13 September 1979.
27. Nick Downie, eyewitness at Asmar and Chugha Serai. His superb film of these events was transmitted on British ITV in 1980; more detail has been obtained through subsequent interviews by the author.
28. Cable No. 199533, Kabul to State Department, 11 August 1979.
29. *Daily Telegraph*, 5 September 1979.
30. *International Herald Tribune*, 13 September 1979.
31. Moscow Radio, 10 September 1979.
32. Erickson, see note 18.
33. Ibid.
34. *International Herald Tribune*, 21 September 1979.
35. *Washington Post*, 2 January 1980.
36. *International Herald Tribune*, 21 September 1979.
37. Kabul Radio, 23 October 1979.
38. Vladimir Kuzichkin, interview published in *Time Magazine*, 22 November 1982.
39. National Foreign Assessment Centre, *Directory of USSR Ministry of Defence and Armed Forces Officials*, August 1983.
40. Thomas Hammond, *Red Flag over Afghanistan* (Westview Press, 1984).
41. *Daily Telegraph*, 19 November 1979.
42. Kabul Radio, 5 January 1980.
43. Cable 8073, Kabul to State Department, 20 November 1979.
44. *Sunday Times*, 6 January 1980.
45. *Sunday Times*, 20 January 1980.
46. *International Herald Tribune*, 17 December 1979.
47. Erickson, see note 18.
48. Kabul Radio, 7 December 1979.
49. Hafizullah Amin, speech to education officials, Kabul Radio, 15 December 1979.
50. Hafizullah Amin, speech to Revolutionary Council, Kabul Radio, 24 December 1979.
51. *The Times*, 14 January 1980.
52. *Washington Post*, 2 January 1980.
53. Lt. Col. Alawoddin, interviewed on Moscow Radio (home service), 16 January 1980.
54. *Los Angeles Times*, 10 January 1980.
55. R. D. M. Furlong and Theodore Winkler, 'The Soviet Invasion of Afghanistan', in *International Defence Review*, no. 2, 1980.
56. Kabul Radio, 13 December 1979.
57. Sayed Faz Akhbar, Director of Kabul Radio 1978–80, interviewed in *Afghan Realities*, no. 6, July 1982.

58. Ibid.
59. Furlong and Winkler, op. cit.
60. Leonid Brezhnev, message to Afghan leaders, Moscow Radio, 31 December 1979.

Three: 1980

The Soviet introduction of massive military force into Afghanistan was accompanied by the launch of a new political initiative. Throughout the first months of 1980 the Afghan and Soviet media repeated the theme that the change of government in Kabul had been so significant that it marked a 'new phase' or a 'new stage' in the April Revolution. Underlying the Karmal package was the belief that the Khalqis had alienated the population because they had tried to push the pace of change too quickly. As far as the Kremlin was concerned, Amin had been precipitate in declaring Afghanistan a socialist state. The PDPA did not have the membership, nor the government the right mechanisms for harnessing public support for this to happen. As the director of the Soviet Institute of Oriental Affairs, Yevgeniy Primakov, was to state later, revolts erupted because Amin and his colleagues 'did not take objective reality into consideration'.[1]

The Kremlin wanted to assure the world that, while the Khalqi's claims to have created a genuine socialist society had been premature, there was now a regime in Kabul that might, slowly, be able to move towards this. Soviet ideologists downgraded the Afghan revolution to one in its 'national–democratic' phase rather than its socialist one. As Moscow Radio put it, 'genuine people's power has been proclaimed in the country, which will struggle for the final victory of the national–democratic, anti-feudal, and anti-imperialist revolution, and for the creation of a free and independent Afghanistan'.[2]

Following the announcement of his new cabinet on 28 December, Babrak Karmal prepared his package of measures designed to win support within the country. On 3 January he appeared at a conference of the world's press to present his 'new phase'. Attempting to cope with contradictory aims of trying to win widespread popular support while at the same time maintaining the confidence of all sections of the party, including radical Khalqis, required a display of ideological gymnastics – and that is what Karmal produced.

Karmal said that he intended to restore freedoms that had been taken away by the 'fascist' Hafizullah Amin: 'The aim of the new phase is to give freedom to all the people of Afghanistan to live a democratic life while enjoying extensive liberties of speech, assemblies and freedom of political parties and social and people's organisations'. These freedoms would be guaranteed by a new constitution. In an attempt to win back popular support, Karmal told the journalists that this constitution would 'respect and adhere to the sacred religion of Islam: this will be the basic point of our new constitution, observance of the principle of private ownership and observance of all political, economic and social rights for the people of Afghanistan'.[3] While on the one hand trying to convince his people that the PDPA had a new respect for the principle of private ownership he also wanted to allay the fears of his own radicals. He made a point of stressing that he had been part of the government which had drafted decrees 6, 7, and 8 – the core of the People's Democratic Party programme.

One of the most important elements of Karmal's campaign for support was his attempt to get backing from the Islamic clergy. On 4 January, Abdul Aziz Saqiq, chairman of a council of religious elders, made a speech of support for the government.[4] On 15 January, a Shia leader from the town of Mazar-e-Shariff, Garf Abdul Gafar, pledged his support. Gafar dismissed claims that the PDPA were anti-Islamic and said 'any honest man who visited our country . . . would be convinced that the government was persistently pursuing a course of freedom of belief'.[5] The vast majority of Afghanistan's conservative clergy took little notice of these speeches; to them Karmal was 'just another communist'.

The drive to broaden support took different forms. There were mass releases of prisoners from Pol-e-Charkhi jail. On 5 January, 2000 were released, on 9 January a further 6000.[6] Many of those released were probably Parcham activists, and Karmal needed their support desperately.

A new propaganda theme emerged: Amin, in collaboration with a monstrous alliance of all conceivable enemies, had planned to dismember the country by ceding its Pushtun part to Pakistan. According to Karmal 'this enormous tragedy planned by the Amin gang in collaboration with the US CIA, the conspiracy of the Peking leadership, the reaction of the region and its constant collusion with the Sadat and Israeli regimes and other reactionary forces, had been drawn up in such a way that its implementation would have eliminated half the population of Afghanistan'.[7] Only pro-Amin Khalqis could be alienated by this line, and by this time many of them were in jail or hiding. There was no criticism of Taraki, the party founder and mentor of many of Karmal's

Khalqi cabinet appointees. In his bed to exercise stronger control over his faction-riven party Karmal appointed new governors to the country's 28 provinces.[8]

Another vital element in the Kremlin-sponsored package was the setting up of mass organisations. These Soviet-style groups were intended to provide a focus for non-party support throughout different sections of the community. Trades unions and professional organisations for teachers and journalists were set up. New energies were put into recruiting for the Democratic Youth Organisation of Afghanistan (DYOA) and the Democratic Women's Organisation of Afghanistan (DWOA). More importantly, Karmal set out to expand the membership of the People's Democratic Party.

AFGHAN REACTION TO THE NEW PHASE

The Karmal package was a comprehensive one, but it was ignored by a large number of Afghans. To them the pledges of freedom, the release of prisoners and the new trades unions were all irrelevant. What was relevant was that Karmal clearly depended on the army of a foreign power – a power that was perceived as godless and anti-Islamic. Within days of the 'new phase' beginning there were widespread displays of hostility. Outraged Afghans demonstrated on the streets, some quit their jobs and went to join the *mujahadeen*, and many deserted the army to do the same. Anti-government demonstrations took place in Kandahar (on 31 December), in Herat (at the end of January), and in Kabul.

Within the civil service there was consternation. Hundreds, perhaps thousands, of key administrators who had served the government up to that point left their jobs. Kabul faced a series of humiliating defections: ambassadors, airline pilots, sports teams and military men denounced the Soviet intervention. The sense of national humiliation and outrage ran through all sections of the community. Above all it was the sense of Karmal's dependence on a foreign power that caused so much hostility. This was displayed by many Khalqis too. The PDPA faced a new eruption of factionalism. Khalqis in the party machine and army tried desperately to cling to power. They obstructed government policies and rallied their own supporters. Parchamis released from Pol-e-Charkhi prison tried to settle old scores with the Khalqis.

While the factions engaged in bitter in-fighting, more and more of the country slipped from government control.

Karmal found his government in a state of seige. Throughout the country 'counter-revolutionary' groups had taken advanatage of the army's weakness. In this desperate situation men of the Soviet 40th Army stepped into the breach.

SECURING KABUL

Even the security of the capital was in the balance. Major-General Yevanov's air assault forces were charged with holding the most vital installations. One paratroop regiment was deployed to Pol-e-Khumri, the vital junction of the roads from the Soviet border to Kabul, Mazar-e-Shariff and Herat.[9] Pol-e-Khumri's position marked it out for development of a key logistics facility. Another air assault regiment held the Salang pass (where it had been since December 19). Robert Fisk of *The Times* ventured to the Salang in a taxi and was captured by these men. He formed a high impression of the men of the 103rd Guards. Fisk wrote of the officer who guarded him, 'Major Yuri seemed a fine professional soldier . . . he was clearly admired by his men who spoke freely to him in a way that most privates might find impossible in western armies'.[10]

The high standards of the air assault troops marked them out for the most vital tasks within the capital itself. They guarded key installations and were reserved as a special counter-*coup* force. The possibility of a Khaqli or dissident officer counter-*coup* within these first weeks of 1980 was a worrying one for the government. Soviet troops were reported to have fought men of the 8th Division at Kargha early in the new year.[11] There was further trouble between Soviet and Afghan paratroops at the Balar Hissar fort in the second week of January.[12] Plotting among units of the Afghan Central Corps was particularly frustrating for Karmal. Like previous governments, Amin had concentrated officers loyal to himself in these units. But the Central Corps also had most of the mobile units capable of waging a mobile war. Consequently it was vitally important for Karmal to secure their allegiance. This kind of dependence forced him to make constant concessions to officers of dubious loyalty and little actual value.

ARMY MORALE SINKS AND DESERTION SOARS

Outside Kabul the security situation was critical. Whole brigades of the army defected in response to the Soviet intervention. The situation was particularly bad in Kunar. The 9th Division had already lost its 5th Brigade at Asmar the previous August; early in 1980 it lost another, the 30th Mountain Brigade.[13] Desertion was such a serious problem that by the summer of 1980 it is unlikely that the 9th Division amounted to more than 1000 men. With the collapse of morale the commanders of the few men who did remain loyal dared not take them out of base lest they desert. *Mujahadeen* (mainly of the ISA and IP) took full advantage of the situation. Weapons and men flowed unrestrictedly to and fro across the border with Pakistan.

From 3 to 5 January, the Soviet Army 201st Motor Rifle Division arrived in Jallalabad.[14] It was hoped that they could stabilise the situation. Their presence may have exacerbated problems within the Afghan army for a further three battalions of the 11th Division surrendered themselves to the guerrillas.[15] The 201st were to be prepared for a divisional offensive at the end of February. This was intended to redeem the situation in the Kunar valley.

In the north-east there was also widespread desertion. A brigade and an artillery unit from the forces in Badakhshan defected early in 1980.[16] In the central provinces of the Hazara Jat the resistance had established a counter-state. The Hazara resistance front, the Shura, had established control over a wide area of Bamiyan, Ghowr, and Uruzgan provinces. They even set up a council to run the region. It had 42 delegates sent by Hazara Jat communities including the Tajiks and Aimaks. The Shura command was established in the town of Waris. As in other *mujahadeen* fronts, ex-army officers and NCOs played an important role. The over-all commander of Shura's military operations was an ex-army major, Sayed Hassan.[17]

The arrival of the Soviets galvanized the resistance and brought them many new recruits. In the days following the Soviet takeover they claimed huge victories. Guerrillas claimed to have wiped out a Soviet brigade in Jallalabad several days before the 201st Motor Rifle Division actually arrived there.[18] Each party tried to outdo the other in tales of how many Russians they had killed. On the ground, Western reporters filed accounts of less heroic resistance.

The *Observer*'s Ian Mather reported from Kabul on 27 January:
'Far from killing thousands of Russians the Afghan rebels have
been sniping at Soviet supply columns'. The colourful accounts of
resistance parties in Pakistan did lasting damage to the credibility
of the resistance, in Western eyes at least.

AMERICAN'S REACTION: COLD WAR RHETORIC

Just as the presence of the Soviet army was far more important
than all of the finer points of Babrak Karmal's policies to the
resistance, so foreign governments could readily agree that the
USSR had committed a gross international indecency. At the
White House, the arrival of the Soviet army in Afghanistan
prompted a complete change of policy. President Carter
denounced the takeover angrily: 'The Soviet invasion of
Afghanistan is the greatest threat to peace since the Second World
War. It's a sharp escalation in the aggressive history of the Soviet
Union.'[19] The Americans mobilised world opinion against the
Soviets. The USSR found itself on the defensive in the usually
receptive forum of the United Nations General Assembly. On 14
January the General Assembly voted by 104 votes to 18 (with 18
abstentions) to call for the 'immediate, unconditional and total
withdrawal' of foreign troops from Afghanistan.

Afghanistan became a vital asset in American's war of rhetoric
with Moscow, and the conflict was fully exploited for its
propaganda value. Nowhere was this more evident than in the
allegation that the Soviets were using chemical weapons against
the *mujahadeen*. The suggestion that nerve gas was being used
against unprotected tribesmen was a highly emotive one.
Newspaper reports that gas had been used began late in 1979. The
role of US 'intelligence sources' in giving these stories to the media
added a measure of authenticity. By 1980 the State Department
was publicising allegations that such weapons had in fact been
used.[20]

Their case rested on a number of facts. The Soviets had arrived
with chemical decontamination battalions: gasmasks and gas
antidote kits were found on Russian corpses; there were reports by
mujahadeen and refugees (some of them ex-army) of the poisons
being used. On the other hand, the Soviet army did bring a great
deal of equipment (such as anti-aircraft missiles) which was
patently useless against the *mujahadeen*. The reports of *mujahadeen*

and even Afghan army deserters are questionable, often hearsay; they are usually sparse on detail and inaccurate (speaking of coloured gases when most nerve agents are colourless). While Soviet deserters have often been prepared to embrace Islam to escape death, none has been able to prove the chemical warfare allegations. In fact several of them have stated that they have never heard of the use of gas in operations against the *mujahadeen*.[21]

The conclusive fact must be that in seven years of war no doctor or journalist has ever been able to bring a single sample of earth or tissue that shows any trace of chemical weapons contamination. In the Gulf War, Western journalists were able to find such evidence (in the shape of unexploded bombs full of mustard gas and casualties treated in European hospitals) within weeks of the first allegations that such weapons were being used. Peter Jouvenal, an ex-British army paratrooper, who has more experience of the country than any other Western journalist (with 25 clandestine trips into Afghanistan to his credit), describes the gas allegations as 'a complete lie . . . a CIA fabrication'.

In recent years the US State Department has shied away from repeating the chemical warfare allegations. Even such doctrinaire US government publications as 'Soviet Military Power' and 'Afghanistan: The Struggle in its Fifth Year' omit them. Nevertheless in 1980 Washington used uncorrobated, entirely circumstantial evidence to launch a major campaign of international vilification.

The White House outrage had a more lethal form. The CIA found themselves with presidential approval to step up covert operations and arms deliveries. Large quantities of Soviet-made weapons were bought from the Egyptians and shipped to Pakistan. Egyptian President Anwar Sadat later confirmed the details of this arrangement on US network television: 'The United States sent me airplanes and told me, please open your stores for us so that we can give the Afghans the armaments they need to fight, and I gave the armaments'.[22] Sadat confirmed that this operation began days after the Soviet intervention.

PAKISTAN'S CONCERN

The arrival of the Soviet army posed a strategic crisis for Pakistan. The arrival of so many refugees posed more mundane but difficult administrative problems in the North-West Frontier Province.[23]

The Pakistani government tried to maintain a display of public propriety, denying that they would allow the passage of arms to the *mujahadeen*. Early in January the government even announced the seizure of US-made weapons by customs men. But it has always been acknowledged 'off the record' by Western politicians that General Zia's regime has allowed large quantities of weapons to be shipped to the *mujahadeen*. Even if the government tried to enforce their pledge not to allow arms to reach the resistance it can be assumed that a system that is so corrupt that it allows the passage of hundreds of tons of heroin per annum could not put a complete stop to gun-running either.[24]

Pakistan's General Zia made the most of the situation. Pakistan, the Americans and the Chinese could all agree that the Soviet invasion had important implications for the balance of power. Zia played on historical images of expansionism, 'if you extend the hammer and sickle over Afghanistan and see from there onwards, which are the areas likely to come under influence. Where is Iran, where is the Gulf and where is the Strait of Hormuz and where is Saudi Arabia and the rest of the Muslim world? . . . if recent events in Afghanistan, because of the Soviet intervention have changed the environment, then Pakistan deserves attention.'[25] And Zia got attention. In January, Chinese Foreign Minister Huang Hua visited Zia; in February came US National Security Adviser Zbigniew Brzezinski. The results: a big US arms package for the Pakistanis and growing Sino–American agreement on security issues.

The weight of international hostility put the Kremlin on the defensive. They sought to justify their actions by saying that they were invited in under Article 4 of the Soviet–Afghan friendship treaty. Pravda stated, 'the Soviet military contingent will be used exclusively to help in repelling the armed intervention from outside . . . the Soviet contingent will be completely withdrawn from Afghanistan when the reason which made such action necessary, no longer exists'.[26] At the root of Soviet policy was the fear that if they allowed the Kabul regime to fall it would be replaced by one deeply hostile to them. Leonid Brezhnev said, 'to do otherwise would have been to allow the emergence of a dangerous situation on our southern border'.[27]

A NEW RESISTANCE FRONT

On 27 January, six parties announced the formation of the Islamic Alliance for the Liberation of Afghanistan in Peshawar. This group received powerful backing from conservative Arab countries: the Saudis gave them an initial grant of $24 million. By March the Alliance had dwindled to five parties (Rabbani's ISA, Gailani's NIFA, Yunis Khalis' Islamic Party, Nabi Mohammedi's Islamic Revolutionary Movement and Sibgatullah Mujaddidi's National Liberation Front of Afghanistan). Disagreements prevented them from electing a leader until April. Abdur Rabdur Rasul Sayaf emerged as the compromise figure. But the rival parties yielded very little real power to Sayaf and the Islamic Alliance. Gulbuddin Hekmatyar's Hezb-e-Islami boycotted the procedures from the beginning.[28] With more money, more weaponry and more foreign interest in their struggle, the rivalry between resistance parties intensified.

Within Afghanistan were many autonomous groups that cared little for the politics of Peshawar and Quetta. One group SAMA (the Afghan People's Liberation Organisation) was making headway within the capital itself. This group, led by Majid Kalakani, had been waging its war in one form or another since 1968. By February 1980 it had an estimated 8000 members.[29] Work by SAMA and other groups early in 1980 created a *mujahadeen* network within Kabul and the other cities – something that had not existed in any strength before. Groups like SAMA mobilised popular resentment against the Soviets, and 1980 saw a rash of demonstrations, strikes, and killings in the towns.

SOKOLOV REINFORCES THE 40TH ARMY

Massive hostility to the 'new phase' presented Marshal Sokolov with a difficult situation. Above all the defection of army units and the bitter factionalism within those that remained meant that the Kabul regime had virtually nothing with which to hold back the growing revolt.

By the second week of January Marshal Sokolov decided to commit his second echelon. The bulk of the new troops went to the west of the country. The 5th Motor Rifle Division went to Farah and the 54th to Herat. Their mission was to seal the Iranian border and protect vital installations in the western provinces. A third formation, the 16th Motor Rifle Division arrived in northern Afghanistan via Termez.[30] This formation was deployed in Mazar-e-Shariff. With the commitment of these additional forces there was a rationalisation of command and control.

The headquarters of the 40th Army was moved from Termez to Bagram (and later to Kabul). The Soviet High Command in Moscow appointed a representative to Kabul to act as chief adviser to Karmal and the Afghan Ministry of Defence. Colonel General S. Magometov held this post until December, when he was replaced by Colonel General Alexander Mayorov. These officers served as strategic advisers to the Afghan regime and a source of information for Moscow, rather than as commanders of operational forces in the DRA.

In Kabul there was an increasing mood of anti-Soviet and anti-Parchami defiance among students and high-school pupils. There was also trouble among the *bazaaris*, the traders. On 21 February there was a call for a general strike in Kabul: many stayed away from work and protested on the streets. There was also trouble at the university, as Moscow Radio reported: 'On 21st February reactionary fanatics tried to stage a pogrom at Kabul university . . . the university's self-defence detachment came out firmly against the bandits.'[31] The Soviet reporter lamented, 'Afghanistan is experiencing a difficult and complicated time'. Following these riots, the resistance suffered a notable setback when Majid Kalakani, the SAMA leader, was arrested.

THE KUNAR OFFENSIVE

In Jallalabad, Soviet officers were preparing for their first major counter-insurgency operation. The aim was to restore government authority to the Kunar valley. The situation here was indeed alarming. The desertion of so many 9th Division soldiers, and the strength of the resistance in the valley, meant that there was a very real danger of the capital (Chugha Serai or Asadabad) falling to the *mujahadeen*. The style of this operation reflected the training and equipment of the Soviet army for conventional mountain operations. The 201st Motor Rifle was equipped with a great many tanks (if full scales of equipment were observed, 265 of them) and a great deal of centrally controlled artillery.

The Kunar operation began in the first week of March, with a large-scale fire preparation of the valley. This heavy shelling naturally spread alarm amongst the local people and forewarned the guerrillas of an attack. Armoured regiments lumbered up the road which runs along the Kunar valley. The Soviets did not use helicopter-landed battalions to block the withdrawal of the *mujahadeen*. The armoured task force made its way up the valley. It took supplies to the beleaguered garrison in Asadabad, re-established authority in Asmar, and pushed on to the end of the valley at Barikot. The operation was largely complete by 15 March.[32] Throughout its advance the division had come under repeated ambush from the guerrillas. The operation eliminated the guerrillas from the valley (for a few days) and did do something to take the pressure off the 9th Division. Its most alarming effect was in the accelerated depopulation of the valley.

FURTHER DIFFICULTIES IN KABUL

In Kabul, Babrak Karmal pressed on with the reforms of his 'new phase'. In his bid to gain party consensus Karmal made increased use of full sessions of the PDPA Central Committee. Whereas there had only been one Central Committee Plenum in the two years to April 1980, there were three in the eight months after it. The 2nd Plenum of the PDPA Central Committee was called on the 13 April. It met to discuss the new constitution that Karmal had promised at the beginning of the year. It also approved the adoption of a new national flag on 21 April.

None of this had any real impact on the public. During the last week of April and the first week of May there were further demonstrations by students and schoolchildren. Kabul Radio broadcast an appeal 'to all students and undergraduates not to be deceived by the provocations of the enemies of the Saur Revolution and the country and to continue their studies'.[33] Rumours spread in the diplomatic corps that fifty students and schoolchildren had been gunned down during these disturbances. An Afghan Interior Ministry statement admitted that children had been involved and that there had been 620 arrests during the riots.[34]

In Kabul there was a growing economic crisis. Trade along the route to Pakistan via Jallalabad had been disrupted by warfare. Strikes by the *bazaaris* had also had an effect. Widespread defections by professionals in industry, the civil service and trade meant that many factories ceased production and severe shortages developed.

THE *MUJAHADEEN* CALL A *LOYAH JERGA*

The resistance, hoping to capitalise on the upsurge in anti-Soviet nationalism called a *loyah jerga* (a grand assembly) of community leaders in Pakistan. They hoped that the 1000-strong assembly could appoint a government in exile to manage the resistance effort. It was an inspired idea. Not only would the endorsement of the *loyah jerga* give added legitimacy to any government in exile but it would also deprive Kabul of it. Perhaps unsurprisingly, the *jerga* did not live up to these high hopes. Instead it became a focus for the increasingly bitter antagonism between the various guerrilla parties.

The conservative Islamic Society and Gulbuddin Hekmatyar's Islamic Party, perhaps the two most important parties, boycotted the assembly. The meetings of the assembly were hindered by the incompatibility of the remaining participants' objectives. The Social Democrats had little in common with Sayed Gailani's National Islamic Front of Afghanistan. It was Gailani's group that perhaps gained the most from the *loyah jerga* due to the clever politicking of Gailani's son Hassan.[35] He gained the endorsement of half the assembly when disagreements split it in two in July 1980.

Hekmatyar pursued a determined and ruthless campaign to become the undisputed leader of the resistance. He went to Iran in a bid to persuade the government to accord his party sole recognition. Hekmatyar's efforts were partly successful, gaining the expulsion of Shaykh Muhsini's Islamic Movement in August 1980.

FURTHER SOVIET OPERATIONS

June saw an intensification of warfare throughout the country. The 201st Motor Rifle Division launched a number of new operations from Jallalabad. Its regiments were sent into Paktia and Kunar as well as operating in Nangrahar.[36] A military disaster in Paktia

Province soon proved the Soviet's poor grasp of counter-insurgency operations. Accounts of the battle on the Gardez–Khost road have become the stuff of *mujahadeen* legend.

Western experts believe that an entire motor rifle battalion may have been wiped out in a well-placed ambush.[37] The Soviet conscripts apparently stayed inside their personnel carriers, firing inaccurately until their ammunition ran out and they were overcome by the guerrillas. In its engagements the quality of both the Soviet army's men (the ranks were still filled mainly with Central Asian reservists) and its machines were found wanting. The guerrillas knew the weak points of the armour on the BTR–60 personnel carriers; their T–55 tanks lacked the gun elevation and depression needed for effective use in the steep-sided mountains.

In June, the Soviet air force played a greater role than in the previous offensive in the east. More helicopters were deployed: in one case a journalist estimated 16–18 of them against a single village.[38] Nevertheless the Soviets had yet to commit sizeable aviation resources to the country. During June the total number of Soviet air force (Vozduyushno Voorezhenie Sil, VVS) helicopters based in Afghanistan was still estimated at only 45–60.[39] Guerrilla operations were becoming more audacious. By mid-June there were frequent attacks on the outskirts of Kabul.[40] The Paghman hills 8 miles to the west of Kabul were established as a *mujahadeen* base.[41]

The government's minimal authority in Bamiyan Province was briefly extinguished when the garrison of Bamiyan (the capital), several hundred men, deserted *en masse*. Authority was reimposed a few days later by Soviet forces.

THE WAR ON THE ROADS

On 19 June, guerrillas attacked the Soviet logistics facility at Pol-e-Khumri. The road from Pol-e-Khumri, through the Salang pass, to Kabul had become the target for raids by *mujahadeen* operating from the Panjsher valley. Ahmad Shah Massud emerged as the most important commander of the Panjsher. Massud, a Tajik, gave up his engineering studies to join the resistance. Like many of the *mujahadeen* leaders his commitment to 'the armed struggle' actually preceded the April Revolution. Massud had been involved with the abortive Panjsher uprising of 1975.[42] His group, part of Burhanuddin Rabbani's ISA, rapidly established itself as the most effective in the country.

Whilst helicopter numbers remained low, the Soviets and their Afghan allies were overwhelmingly dependent on road transport. The ambush became the guerrillas' standard action, and cost their enemy hundreds of trucks. Supply lines were so long (Highway 13 from Kandahar to Herat is 600 km; Highway 2 from the Soviet border to Kabul is 425 km) that they remained extremely difficult to defend. To compound these problems the Afghan army was barely able to supply itself even in time of peace, due to a shortage of transport. In late 1980 hundreds of Soviet- and Czech- donated trucks were formed into the 119th Transport Regiment based at Sherpur barracks in Kabul.

PROBLEMS IN THE 40TH ARMY

The realisation that they were in for a long and difficult time in Afghanistan with an army that was completely unsuitable in training, organisation and tactical doctrine, prompted a massive reorganisation by the Soviets. Marshal Sokolov and his staff had several fundamental problems to put right. The Afghan army had lost a large part of its strength. It was no longer capable of offensive operations above the battalion level. Within its units, effectiveness was further undermined by bitter factionalism among officers.

The Soviet force (known officially as the Limited Contingent of Soviet Forces in Afghanistan or LCSFA) had its own fundamental difficulties. All of the seven motor rifle divisions sent into the country were reserve divisions that had been brought up to operational strength by drafting in local reservists. They were militarily ineffective, they were becoming tired of serving, and there was a danger that they might be corrupted by their Afghan cousins. These men had to be released.

Because of the possibility of having to fight the Afghan army and the shortage of time (which prevented the organisation of special task-organised units), the Limited Contingent had entered Afghanistan with a great deal of equipment that was quite useless against the *dushmans* (the Soviet soldiers' word for the *mujahadeen*, meaning bandit or enemy). The uselessness of much of the armour that they had brought with them had already become apparent. Units needed to exchange the third-rate equipment with which, as reserve divisions, they had been issued, for the best that Soviet industry could give them. The 360th Motor Rifle Division, for example, had arrived in Kabul with artillery that dated from the Second World War, tanks that were 20 years old, and personnel carriers that were 10–15 years old.

Like so many mechanised armies before them, the Soviet army found that the insurgents were able to escape their ponderous thrusts across country. They needed helicopters – and a great many of them – to give them new tactical mobility. They also needed more air support and improved air-dropped anti-personnel weapons.

Underlying all of these (essentially soluble) problems was the deeper and much more worrying issue of organisational and tactical inflexibility. The rigid discipline and the discouragement of independent action by junior officers were well-known aspects of Soviet military doctrine. The Soviet attitude to this was summed up in a standard tactical manual by Lieutenant General V. Reznichenko: 'The success of offensive combat is directly dependent on the level of training of commanders and staffs: the lower that level the greater must be the degree of centralised control'.[43] Yet the Soviets knew that victory in a war against the *mujahadeen* depended on a superior mastery of small-scale operations. This point was stressed by Colonel Yu. Pavlov in June 1980. He wrote, 'it was the skilled actions of small sub-units which often decided the outcome of combat in the mountains'.[44] That skill depended in turn up on the quality of junior officers and NCOs. Counter-insurgency has been described by the British as 'an NCO's war'. In the Soviet army, corporals and sergeants are conscripts with no more experience than the men they are supposed to lead.

As well as its over-centralisation of command, the LCSFA was over-centralised in organisation. Its operations against the guerrillas had to be carried out at the battalion and regimental level or very occasionally at the divisional level. The formations that entered Afghanistan had most of their combat support resources (like artillery, engineers, and signals) organised at the divisional level. Other support elements (including aviation) were grouped at an even higher level of organisation – the 40th Army. This was entirely unsuitable for a guerrilla war where battalion commanders need instant, dedicated support rather than having to go through regimental, divisional and even army HQs to get it.

THE REORGANISATION BEGINS

All of these problems meant that the Soviet army in Afghanistan needed a massive re-organisation. This began in June 1980 and went on until mid-1981. It marked the transformation of the 40th Army from a force geared for centrally-controlled high-intensity mechanised operations to one suited to the peculiar requirements of an anti-guerrilla war in Afghanistan.

The first (visible) step of the reorganisation was the rationalisation of the 40th Army itself. Its SA–4 Anti-Aircraft Missile Brigade, artillery brigade, and several other support units were sent back to the Soviet Union.[45] They were among units sent back in the Kremlin's well-publicised withdrawals of 22 June.[46] With the extraction of many of the 40th Army's organic combat support units the nature of the command itself changed. The 40th Army became a forward headquarters for the Turkestan Military District, rather than an army for independent operations in its own right. The First Deputy Commander of the Turkestan District, Lieutenant-General V. M. Mikhailov, was sent to Kabul and placed in command. His presence and job were confirmed by open sources.[47]

New conscripts were brought in so that reserves could be sent home. This accounted for a dramatic increase in the number of flights into Kabul and Bagram.[48] Many of the men had received only their three weeks' basic training (known as the Course of the Young Soldier), and the need to train them in-country sapped the effectiveness of Afghan-based units.[49]

The Soviets took advantage of the large-scale turnover in personnel to change completely the organisation and deployment of their forces. The 105th Guards Air Assault Division was disbanded and its resources re-grouped under the HQ of the 103rd Guards which had been brought from Byelorussia.[50] Its constituent regiments were to be used for heliborne operations, with temporary deployments around the country. The Air Assault Division HQ and two regiments moved to a camp in south-west Kabul, in the Darulaman area.

The poorly equiped 360th Reserve Motor Rifle Division was also disbanded. Resources from the 360th and other units were re-grouped into a new Kabul-based division, the 108th Motor Rifle.[51] This division deployed three regiments: the 181st Motor Rifle at Bagram, the 180th, and another regiment (possibly designated

182nd Motor Rifle) close to the capital at Khair Khana.[52] Forces in the west were consolidated under the aegis of the 5th Guards Motor Rifle Division at the important base at Shindand. The 201st Motor Rifle was restructured and moved to Konduz in the north-east.

In addition to these three motor rifle divisions, resources from the other divisions were re-packaged in newly formed regiments and brigades. Some of their equipment including two tank regiments, some ground-to-ground rocket units and anti-aircraft units were sent to the USSR as part of the 22 June withdrawals.[53] The independent regiments were based at Ghazni (the 191st) and Fayzabad (the 860th).[54] They were deployed with their own combat support resources, for example BM–21 multiple rocket launchers (known popularly as Katyusha's or Stalin Organs) which are normally held at the division or army level. These regiments retained tank battalions, but many tanks were sent back. The number of battle tanks with Soviet forces in Afghanistan decreased from around 1000 early in the year to about 300 by late 1980.[55]

The LCSFA also found itself with two specially-formed motor rifle brigades. The difference between these units (the 70th and 66th Motor Rifle Brigades in Kandahar and Jallalabad respectively) and the independent motor rifle regiments was that they had four rather than three battalions of infantry each, and more support assets. For many operations it is believed that these brigades received their own helicopter units. Certainly the heliborne mission was considered important when they were formed. It has been reported that some men from the disbanded 105th Guards Air Assault Division were integrated into the 70th Motor Rifle Brigade.[56]

During the period June 1980 to mid-1981, the 40th Army was re-structured from a force of seven motor rifle divisions to one of three motor rifle divisions, two independent motor rifle regiments and two motor rifle brigades. The four remaining divisional HQs were withdrawn into the southern USSR where they re-formed. The details of this re-organisation have been gleaned from prisoners of war and intelligence briefings by Western governments and the *mujahadeen*, but they took some years to emerge. In mid-1980 the bulk of Soviet signals traffic was switched to hardened landlines and this meant that Western intelligence agencies were uncertain about many details of the Soviet deployment.

There were major changes to the air force as well. These however involved the introduction of many new units, rather than the re-distribution of those already in the country. There was a massive rise in helicopter numbers. The total climbed from about 60 in June 1980 to around 300 in 1981. This involved the deployment of three complete helicopter regiments (of 40–50 machines each) to centres like Bagram, Konduz and Kandahar.[57] Several independent and detached squadrons were also deployed, under the direct command of army units. Other aircraft types were increased as well. By the end of 1980 there were about 130 jet fighters, mainly MiG–21s, SU–17s and MiG–23s.[58] They flew missions from Bagram, Shindand and Herat. The fighter regimental HQs and support elements remained concentrated in the southern USSR at bases in the Turkestan and Central Asian Military Districts.

The recognition that the Soviets' 'Limited Contingent' was in for a long stay required the development of a logistic infrastructure. Pol-e-Khumri was chosen as army-level support base. Soviet engineers had built a fuel tank farm there within days of the army arriving. As some units left late in June, a pipeline-laying battalion and an engineer regiment arrived.[59] The former was given the task of building a fuel pipeline from Termez to Pol-e-Khumri. The Soviets had already received costly lessons in the vulnerability of fuel tankers on Afghan roads. The pipeline was complete by August 1980. The engineer regiment was assigned to building better positions for the troops. In time, Soviet military engineers started building a permanent bridge across the Oxus at Termez, and improving airbases.

CONFLICT AND MANPOWER PROBLEMS IN THE AFGHAN ARMY

As these major changes began there were more adverse developments in the Afghan army. Karmal's attempts to create a much larger party membership (of Parchamis) and place its members in key positions were being obstructed by Khalqis in positions of power. In mid-July there were rumours of a *coup* plot by the officers of the 4th and 15th Armoured Brigades at Pol-e-Charkhi.[60] Many of the Khalqis in these units and other brigades of the Central Corps remained bitterly hostile to the Soviets and their

Parchami allies. The most serious eruption of army factionalism came at the end of July in Ghazni. Officers led a revolt when Karmal tried to replace their Khalqi commanding general with a Parchami.[61] There was heavy fighting until the 4 August, involving Soviet troops with air support.

The PDPA Central Committee held its 3rd Plenum against the background of this rapidly deteriorating security situation. They are thought to have discussed security issues and the integration of Soviet and Afghan army operations. The most serious problem facing the Afghan army was desertion. Another result of the Plenum was the setting up of zonal headquarters. These consisted of groups of provinces, and the main purpose of the move was probably to improve conscription and military administration, rather than change the operational structure of the forces.

The US State Department estimated that, by September 1980, army strength had fallen to just 30 000 men.[62] This haemorrhaging was depriving the army of any operational capacity. Recruits stayed in the ranks for such a short period that they could not adequately be trained. There were enormous *matériel* losses as well. Each deserter carried off his personal equipment and AK-47 assault rifle. Sometimes they even took tanks and field guns with them. Morale among the conscripts was so bad that they would take the opportunity to desert if they came under any kind of attack. Kabul implemented a package of measures designed to restock the ranks.

On 3 August a new call-up was announced; it included teachers who had not completed their training. The Military Academy started 'crash courses' to train large numbers of officers as quickly as possible. At the passing out parade of such a course on 17 September, Defence Minister Brigadier Rafi gave a frank speech: 'You have completed the crash course at a time when our country is at its sensitive and historic phase and the units of our armed forces are particularly in need of you brave and youthful officers.'[63] Whereas officer courses at the Military Academy took five years before the revolution, some recruits were now being commissioned after just three months on a crash course.

On 6 September, the Ministry of Defence announced a new penal law for the armed forces. Article 1 stated that the new law was needed 'to strengthen revolutionary legality, legal order and discipline in the DRA armed forces, the struggle against encroachment on the security of the DRA, and the struggle against

evading military service'.[64] Jail sentences were set out for a whole
variety of misdemeanours: up to 4 years for ignoring call-up
papers; 2–6 years for being absent without leave; up to 6 years for
feigning illness to avoid service. Punishment of 15 years in prison or
execution was prescribed for a long list of offences: desertion,
insubordination, stealing state secrets, giving weapons to the
enemy, 'conspiracy against the revolution', and 'engaging in
propaganda against the call-up for military service'.

By this time the new intelligence service, KHAD, was beginning
to operate. It had been built up with extensive help from the KGB
and, it was reported, East German security men. This gave
Karmal the confidence to dispose of the Khalqi ex-chief of secret
police, Assadullah Sarwari. He was bundled off to the political
wasteland of Ambassador to Mongolia. Sarwari was replaced as
Deputy Premier by another Khalqi, Mohammed Ziray. Reference
to Appendix III shows that, unlike Taraki and Amin, Karmal did
not reduce the representation of the opposing faction within the
cabinet. Doubtless this was partly due to his dependence on the
Khalqis, but it was also a shrewd policy of compromising leading
Khalqis by involving them so closely in government decisions.

THE NEW SECURITY CAMPAIGN

Early in September, Soviet and Afghan forces launched a military
operation against the ISA *mujahadeen* of the Panjsher valley. The
offensive, probably by a regiment of Soviets and various Central
Corps units also involved a heliborne landing by air assault
troops.[65] Panjsher 1 (as it became known) was complete by the
second week of September. Ahmad Shah Massud's fighters
claimed to have inflicted heavy casualties on the army and to have
shot down 10 helicopters.[66] During the same week, guerrillas
staged a series of attacks within the city of Herat.[67] Film shot in
Kandahar at roughly the same time showed that Afghan/Soviet
troops had little control even over what went on in the country's
larger cities.

Government attempts to stop this infiltration included a drive to
form more Revolution Defence Groups. On 16 September, Major-
General Abdul Qader and Colonel Khalil met religious and village
leaders in Laghman near Kabul. They agreed the setting up of new
Revolution Defence Groups to stop attacks on the Jallalabad

road.[68] The services of tribal militias were as often obtained by the payment of large sums of money as they were by patient explanation of the correctness of the PDPA party line. Hired village militias were used around Mazar-e-Shariff in the north during August and September.[68] The Minister for Tribal and Frontier Affairs, Faiz Mohammed, carried out a campaign to buy the services of tribal militias in the Pakistani border region. He is believed to have achieved some success, but was murdered on 11 September during negotiations with tribal leaders in Paktia.[69]

All of these measures to improve security had some, very small, effect. The Soviet army secured the capital, but even that was subject to guerrilla infiltration. Karmal felt sufficiently confident to leave the country on 16 October. He went to Moscow for talks and medical treatment and only returned on 4 November.

THE CENTRAL COMMITTEE 4TH PLENUM

As the first year of the 'new phase' drew to a close, Karmal was clinging to power, but his regime seemed no closer to gaining broader support amongst its people. The PDPA Central Committee 4th Plenum in November produced a frank and uncompromising evaluation of the DRA's problems:

— The Committee apportioned blame for the economic crisis stating 'satisfactory measures are not being taken by the government authorities, ministries and departments to enhance and strengthen the Afghan economy . . . most institutions perform less work and produce less goods than expected from the possibilities at their disposal'.
— The army, Sarandoy and intelligence agencies were slated for 'inefficient activity in the struggle against counter-revolutionary elements'.
— Veteran (mainly Khalqi) party cadres were giving newly-appointed members trouble. The Committee reported 'mistrust between some candidate and full members of the PDPA'.
— The government itself was accused of 'lack of firmness and concrete instructions'.

The Central Committee recommended a number of measures: increased propaganda to stress the positive value of Soviet aid, the setting up of a new patriotic front to rally domestic support, and the 'elimination of every type of factionalism' within the PDPA.[70]

THE LOGAR RESISTANCE

In the countryside the fighting continued. Ambushes on the Salang road prompted Panjsher 2, a further raid on Ahmad Shah Massud's stronghold. The Soviet launched an offensive in the Logar valley late in November.[71] The Logar (south of the capital on the road to Ghazni) became an operating area for several different guerrilla groups. Hazaras of the Shura party, as well as men of the IP and Islamic Revolutionary Movement. The IRM, headed by Mohammed Nabi Mohammedi, was particularly strong among the Ahmadzai Pushtun tribal groups of the area. Not only was Mohammedi one of these people, but he had become one of their community leaders well before the war, and served as a delegate to the National Assembly for them. Mohammedi's commander in the Logar was Sayed Murtaza, and his men were extracting a heavy toll in casualties among the convoys from Kabul to the south of the country.

The operation against the Logar *mujahadeen* lasted until mid-December. It showed Soviet appreciation of the need to exploit air mobility in their war against the resistance. A series of heliborne landings were made by Soviet air assault troops during cordon and search operations in the Logar.[72] The paratroops also used their BMD armoured vehicles during this battle. The BMD had been specially developed to give the air assault forces a light fighting vehicle that packed a big punch (it carries a 73mm gun, an anti-tank missile launcher and three machine guns, yet weighs just 14 tons) and saw its first combat trial in Afghanistan. Just as the Panjsher was to face repeated Soviet offensives because of its position on the main supply route from the north, so the Logar became the target of operations because it was a haven for men attacking the key road to the south.

Brezhnev had succeeded in putting his chosen leader into power, but that man had been unable to unify the country in the way the Kremlin might have hoped. In the process the Soviets had committed their army to a long stay in a bitterly hostile country. More than any other factor, the arrival of this foreign army had galvanized the resistance and brought it as many new recruits as it could arm.

Notes

1. Yevgeniy Primakov, remarks reported on Moscow Radio, 23 January 1981.
2. Moscow Radio, 28 December 1979.
3. Babrak Karmal's press conference of 3 January, reported on Kabul Radio, 7 January 1980.
4. Kabul Radio, 5 January 1980.
5. Kabul Radio, 15 January 1980.
6. Kabul Radio, reports on 5 and 6 January 1980.
7. Babrak Karmal, speech to AAPSO delegates, 24 January 1980.
8. Kabul Radio, 9 January 1980.
9. *International Herald Tribune*, 7 April 1980.
10. *The Times*, 20 January 1980.
11. *International Herald Tribune*, 4 January 1980.
12. *International Herald Tribune*, 14 January 1980.
13. *Asia Week*, 30th May 1980.
14. R. D. M. Furlong and Theodore Winkler, 'The Soviet Invasion of Afghanistan', in *International Defence Review*, no. 2, 1980.
15. *The Times*, 10 January 1980.
16. N. and S. Peabody Newell, *The Struggle for Afghanistan* (Cornell University Press, 1981).
17. A. Hyman, *Afghanistan Under Soviet Domination* (Macmillan, 1984).
18. Agence France Presse (AFP) 30 December 1979, quoting guerrilla sources.
19. President Jimmy Carter, briefing to Congress, 8 January 1980.
20. US State Department, *Reports of the Use of Chemical Weapons in Afghanistan, Laos, and Kampuchea*, Summer 1980.
21. For example, Sgt A. Peresleni, interviewed by the author, or Pte V. Naumov, Radio Free Europe–Radio Liberty, *Research Paper RL 121/84*.
22. Anwar Sadat quoted in the *Observer*, 27 September 1981.
23. See Edward Girardet, *Afghanistan, the Soviet War* (Croom Helm, 1985) for a detailed account of relief efforts and the refugee problem.
24. For a graphic description of corruption in the Pakistani customs and police see *Sunday Times*, 31 March 1985.
25. *Pakistan Times*, 16 January 1980.
26. *Pravda*, 31 December 1979.
27. Leonid Brezhnev, *Pravda*, 13 January 1980.
28. For details of coalition see Agence France Presse, 22 April 1981; for Hekmatyar's role see *Far Eastern Economic Review*, 23 January 1981.
29. Hyman, op. cit.
30. Furlong and Winkler, op. cit.
31. Moscow Radio (world service), 6 April 1980.
32. *The Economist*, 15 March 1980.
33. Kabul Radio, 6 April 1980.
34. Interior Ministry statement reported on Kabul Radio, 23 May 1980.
35. Hyman, op. cit.
36. *Economist*, 21 June 1980.
37. David Isby, 'Soviet Tactics in the War in Afghanistan', *Jane's Defence Review* vol. 4, no. 7, 1984.
38. *The Guardian*, 12 June 1980.

39. *Jane's Defence Weekly*, 7 July 1984.
40. *The Times*, 10 June 1980.
41. *The Times*, 15 June 1980.
42. Nigel Ryan, *A Hitch or Two in Afghanistan* (Weidenfeld & Nicolson, 1983).
43. General V. G. Reznichenko, *Tactics* (Voenizdat, 1984).
44. Colonel Yu. Pavlov, 'The Commander and Modern Warfare, The Mountain Variant', in *Krasnaya Zvezda*, 1 June 1980.
45. For reports of withdrawals, see *The Times*, 24 June 1980 and *Daily Telegraph*, 25 June 1980; summarised by the author in *Jane's Defence Weekly*, 12 January 1985.
46. *International Herald Tribune*, 25 June, 1980.
47. *Daily Telegraph*, 19 August.
48. *Keesings Contemporary Archives*, 22 May 1981.
49. Details given in interviews with prisoners.
50. Isby, op. cit.
51. Ibid.
52. Private A. Perseleni, soldier of the 180th Motor Rifle Regiment, and Private Yu. Shapaulenko of 181st Motor Rifle Regiment interviewed August 1984.
53. See *Jane's Defence Weekly*, 12 January 1985.
54. Details of independent regiments given by Sergeant N. Movchan of 191st Independent Motor Rifle Regiment, interviewed August 1984.
55. *International Herald Tribune*, 13 August 1980.
56. Jim Coyne, 'SOF Interviews Russian POWs', *Soldier of Fortune*, February 1984.
57. Isby, op. cit.
58. *Jane's Defence Weekly*, 7 July 1984.
59. G. Jacobs, 'Afghan Forces: How Many Are There?', *Jane's Defence Weekly*, 22 June 1985.
60. *Daily Telegraph*, 20 October 1980.
61. *International Herald Tribune*, 28 July 1980.
62. US State Department, *The Soviet Dilemma in Afghanistan*, June 1980.
63. Brigadier Mohammed Rafi, speech to Military Academy reported on Kabul Radio, 17 September 1980.
64. Penal Law, detailed on Kabul Radio, 26 September 1980.
65. *The Guardian*, 5 September, 1980.
66. *International Herald Tribune*, 8 September 1980.
67. *The Guardian*, 9 September 1980.
68. Kabul Radio, 16 September 1980.
69. Kabul Radio, 11 and 17 September 1980.
70. Kabul Radio, 15 March 1982.
71. *The Guardian*, 25 November 1980.
72. *The Guardian*, 19 December 1980.

Four: 1981

By January, 1981 both sides were adjusting to the new realities of the conflict. The Soviet army had arrived and it was reorganising itself for a long stay. The presence of this army had guaranteed the scores of guerrilla parties the interest and support of both Afghan and international forces.

Although the winter generally restricted the operations of all sides, there was fighting in some regions throughout January. In the Logar valley the first casualties of the year fell in heavy fighting between the *mujahadeen* and government soldiers.[1] There was also renewed combat in the Kunar valley, close to the Pakistani border. Guerrillas operating from the Panjsher launched an audacious raid on Bagram airbase in which they reportedly destroyed an Antonov 22 heavy transport plane.[2]

This raid on Bagram triggered a retaliatory expedition into the Panjsher by a joint Soviet/Afghan force. The Soviet element most likely consisted of a reinforced regiment; the Afghan one of an under-strength Central Corps brigade. The three weeks of fighting was classified as Panjsher 3 by foreign experts. Like the previous push (in November 1980) this 'offensive' had the limited objective of disrupting guerrilla infrastructure at the base of the valley for a short period. The response of Ahmad Shah Massud's fighters, as with the previous raids, was to withdraw into the mountains and mount small ambushes on enemy mechanised forces.

KARMAL'S EARLY ATTEMPTS TO BROADEN SUPPORT

The Afghan army continued to experience severe manpower problems. A new law on conscription was announced on 8 January. It contained plans for new conscription boards at the provincial level. These boards (whose membership included representatives from both the Democratic Youth Organisation of Afghanistan and the Islamic clergy) were intended to improve the drafting process as well as add legitimacy to military service. The Conscription Law lowered the age for service from 21 to 20, and also stipulated that recruits could be kept on for a further six months at the discretion of the Defence Minister.[3] No time was

wasted in using this last measure; a Defence Ministry announcement of 21 January extended the service of thousands of men.
Karmal and his Soviet backers were well aware that the army and
other government organs could never work efficiently unless the
People's Democratic Party broadened its support. Early in 1981 a
whole series of measures aimed at doing this began. As Karmal told
a delegation of tribal leaders from Paktia on 4 January: 'the
government cannot build a flourishing new society unless all our
patriotic forces and toiling people cooperate with their government and state'.[4] He extracted pledges of solidarity from these
tribal chieftains.

Aware of the low esteem in which many people held the PDPA,
Karmal wanted to create a new focus for the struggle against the
counter-revolutionaries. Throughout early 1981, there were
preparations for the formation of the National Fatherland Front. It
was hoped that this organisation could be used to rally all sections
of the community on the side of 'legitimacy' and against 'the
bandits'.

On 20 January the Democratic Youth Organisation of
Afghanistan (DYOA) held its first national congress in Kabul.
Government hopes for the creation of a loyal party elite depended
to a large degree on the organisation's success. In the short term,
though, the DYOA had to do its bit for the war effort. On 14
January a DYOA Youth Brigade was formed in Ghazni for
security operations.[5] In April another such force of 300 DYOA
cadres was sent from Khost to fight hundreds of miles away in
Balkh.[6] The number of people involved in these units was not large,
and they did not prove to be particularly effective. The fact that
they were being used was a sign of the desperate manpower
shortage in the armed forces.

Other attempts to extend government support early in 1981
included the 3rd Plenum of the trades unions organisation and the
formation of a department of Islamic Affairs, whose chief had
ministerial status.

THE AILING ECONOMY

A major part of Karmal's task was to try to breath life into the
faltering economy. The war had already caused considerable
damage. Frequent ambushes made the roads unsafe; conscription
and defections had sapped the workforce. The poor condition of

the state textile indutry, one of Afghanistan's few modern enterprises, provides a relevant example. By 1981 only 1800 out of 4000 workers remained at the Bagrame mill.[7] At the Charikhar plant, frequent ambushes had destroyed 18 out of 35 trucks and virtually halted production.[8]

The PDPA's only real option was to ask for more advisers and to trade more with the Soviets. Other Eastrn bloc countries were drawn in and throughout the spring of 1981 a series of trade deals were signed. Hungary sent 70 trucks; the Czechs gave credit for irrigation schemes; East Germany new power plants; and the Bulgarians eight telephone exchanges.[9] Afghan–Soviet trade amounted to $670 million during 1980.[10] It went on increasing; up by 29 per cent to $930 million during 1981.[11] As well as providing thousands of advisers for the economy, the Soviets began major construction projects: expanding Kabul airport and building truck repair depots, hospitals and power stations.

MUJAHADEEN POLITICS AND PAKISTAN

Just as the new year brought attempts to consolidate government support so the *mujahadeen* also struggled for unity. The Islamic Alliance of Afghan Mujahadeen had, to all intents and purposes, collapsed by February. It could not bear the strains of the rivalry between its member organisations. The Islamic Alliance, led by Professor Sayaf, survived this break-up by becoming a party in its own right. Sayaf enjoyed good contacts with conservative Arab governments, the Muslim Brotherhood and the Americans. Like other Afghan parties, Sayaf's also raised money among Afghan immigrant labourers in the Gulf states. He is thought to have received the lion's share of the $39 million sent by supporters in Saudi Arabia in March.

According to United Nations' estimates, the number of refugees in Pakistan reached 1 700 000 by March. A further 400 000 were in Iran. The guerrilla parties entered an unscrupulous competition for recruits among this flood of people. The refugee population is supported by international aid and by the production and traffic of heroin and other narcotics. Indeed the whole local economy has become narcotics-based. According to a leading expert on the drugs trade, Roger Lewis, 'the [opium] poppy is the only crop that functions as a consistent moneymaker on an annual basis'.[12]

From 1979 there was a dramatic increase in the production of heroin in Pakistan's North-West Frontier Province. By 1980/81 there was so much opium in the area that the price per kilo tumbled from £100 to £22. The market subsequently picked up quite briskly and, according to narcotics enforcement officials, the money from heroin production forms one of the principal sources of finance for the purchase of arms. The trade is almost entirely in the hands of the local Pushtuns.

The poppy is cultivated on the plains south of Kandahar, in northern Afghanistan and north-west Pakistan. The growth of production was such that by 1982 heroin produced in this area accounted for 84 per cent of all that siezed by British customs.[13] The transfer of large sums of money from the addicts of London and New York to the Pushtuns of the North-West Frontier Province continues to form one of the most important, albeit unofficial, channels of finance from the West to the Afghan exiles.

Far less important in cash terms, but more so in prestige, was the selling of captured Soviet weapons to officials from Western intelligence agencies. By 1981, the US Defence Intelligence Agency (an arm of the Pentagon which gathers military information) was well established in Peshawar with a 'shopping list' of items it wished to purchase. These included avionics, armour from the Mil-24 helicopter gunship, and scores of other weapons. The men recruited to obtain these items from Afghan battlefields included British ex-servicemen.[14]

THE STRUGGLE FOR UNITY IN THE ARMY

Within the Afghan army factionalism proved a continued problem. On 11 February there was an army officers' and party workers' conference in Kabul. The meeting was addressed by both a prominent Khalqi (Deputy Premier Mohammed Ziray) and a Parchami, Nur Ahmad Nur. Their message to the conference was that unity was vitally important.[15] The same theme dominated the party activists' meeting of the 8th Division held on April.[16]

The tensions within the forces were more complex than simple Khalqi–Parcham rivalry. There were other groups of officers who formed around particular men. During early 1981 it became apparent that the Minister of Defence, Brigadier Mohammed Rafi, was losing his authority. His rival for influence was the former

Defence Minister, and veteran of the April Revolution, Major General Abdol Qader. Although Qader's job as head of the Revolutionary Council Security Committee did not appear to be an ideal power base, there were signs that he was gaining more and more influence. It was Qader rather than Rafi who headed a delegation which toured units in Farah, Herat and Kandahar from 10–15 April. Then, in the first week of May, Abdol Qader led another delegation, around the units of Badakhshan, Takhar and Baghlan provinces. Doubtless Qader was able to count on many friends and appointees from his own time as Defence Minister for support.

With his position becoming less and less tenable Brigadier Rafi's appearances became rarer. On 12 May he went to the USSR on one of several trips that were described as training and medical visits. But Rafi still had some political allies. They secured his appointment to the Politburo during the reshuffle carried out by the Central Committee 6th Plenum on 11 June. But there is no doubt that Qader was skilfully undermining Rafi throughout this period; in September Rafi went back to the Soviet Union for more 'training', remaining Defence Minister in name only.

It is quite possible that competition for support among the officers of the Central Corps 7th Division may have prompted the relocation of this formation. The 7th Division was commanded by a staunch Khalqi, Major General Zia ud-Din, and by July 1981 its HQ had been relocated from Rishkoor (on the outskirts of Kabul) to Moqor.[17] Elements of the 7th Division had conspired against both the April Revolution and the arrival of the Soviet army. It is possible that the move was due to fears about the formation's loyalty, but there were also good security reasons for it. The *mujahadeen* bands of the Logar valley and around Ghazni were increasingly causing problems in supplying the south of the country. From Moqor (about 100 km south-west of Ghazni on the road to Kandahar), the 7th Division would be able to conduct convoy security operations along the southern route.

MUJAHADEEN IN THE CITIES, AND THE GROWTH OF PARAMILITARY FORCES

The transfer of the 7th Division away from the capital came at a time of major re-organisation of security in Kabul. Changes were made essential by the increasingly daring operations of *mujahadeen* around the city. A series of assassinations highlighted government vulnerability. A leading pro-government mullah was shot dead on 27 March, the deputy head of the KHAD on 14 April, and the Kabul Revolutionary Defence Groups commander on 17 April. As well as conducting this policy of assassination, the guerrillas also started attacks on power facilities and the homes of Soviet advisers in the Microrayon district.

The most important force in these attacks was that under Abdol Haq. Haq (who was only 22 in 1981) belonged to the Hezb-e-Islami (Islamic Party) of Yunis Khalis. His involvement in radical Islamic politics preceded the April Revolution, and paradoxically it was under the PDPA that he was released from a long jail sentence for treason. He had been a commander in Nangrahar province (a Yunis Khalis stronghold) during 1978–79 and had moved to Kabul after the arrival of Soviet troops. There he built a new organisation from scratch, which by 1981 numbered several thousand men. Haq soon developed a strategy of assassination and attacks on key targets around the capital. In June 1981 his men bombed the Pol-e-Charkhi power station.[18]

Another commander who could threaten the capital was Shafiullah. His front, affiliated to the largely Pushtun IRM, was based in the Koh-e-Safi area east of Kabul. Here he was in a position to attack Highway 1 (the road to Jallalabad and the Pakistani frontier), as well as the Sarobi power station – one of the capital's main sources of electricity.

By early 1981, it was apparent that the government's response to its security problems included a major expansion of paramilitary forces. This was particularly so in Kabul where Sarandoy (*gendarmerie*) under the Ministry of the Interior was playing a growing role. Responding to the challenge in the capital the ministry set up the Kabul Security Command. This HQ has 12 Security Wards which consist of static defences – observation posts, vehicle checkpoints and so on. It also deploys two mobile units (the 1st and 2nd Standby Regiments) which are used to respond to particular emergencies.[19] The Kabul Security Command also coordinates the activities of the Revolution Defence Groups. These part-time militias were expanded from late 1980 to early 1981. In February, for example, new Revolution Defence Groups were formed in Bagram and Charikhar at the base of the Panjsher valley.[20]

One of the undoubted benefits from the formation of this Ministry of the Interior force to protect Kabul was that it freed Central Corps units for mobile operations against guerrilla bases. The same pattern was duplicated in other parts of the country. Sarandoy provincial commands were given Operational Battalions whose missions included convoy protection and vehicle checkpoints. By 1981 at least eight of these Operational Battalions had been formed. They served the Sarandoy commands of Balkh, Fariab, Farah, Helmand, Parwan, Takhar, Zabol and Herat provinces.[21]

On 10 April, the government announced a new law designed to boost recruitment for these Ministry of the Interior forces. The legislation offered generous rewards for volunteers to these paramilitary units. Pay was to be up to 3000 Afghanis a month.[22] The law also allowed officers to make special payments for exemplary service and heroic deeds.

These Sarandoy and militia forces of the Interior Ministry were not the only new paramilitary forces. Late in 1980 a new Border Force was formed. This consisted of five brigades:

1st Border Brigade at Jallalabad;
2nd Border Brigade at Khost;
3rd Border Brigade at Konduz;
4th Border Brigade at Nimroz;
5th Border Brigade at Herat.[23]

By early 1981 Kabul Radio and other open sources were carrying regular reports of the operations of the Sarandoy, Revolution Defence and Border units. Most of the stories were of unspectacular small-scale actions, but the cumulative impression was one of a comprehensive paramilitary organisation carrying out frequent, albeit small-scale, operations in virtually all of the country's provinces.

Undoubtedly one of the main aims behind the expansion of paramilitary forces was to seal off towns from guerrilla infiltration. Events throughout April, May and June proved that security around the towns were ineffective.

Throughout February–May there was sporadic fighting in the city of Kandahar. Large sections of the bazaar and city centre remained out of government control. The scale of the trouble was however exaggerated. Western newspapers carried guerrilla claims that they had 'seized' the city during the second week in

April.[24] The guerrillas said that it had only been 'retaken' with heavy airstrikes during the first week in May.[25] In fact this period coincided with the visit to Kandahar of General Abdol Qader and his Defence Ministry delegation. Similar tales that the city had been 'flattened' by government airstrikes and artillery emerged following fighting in the town in June. but a trip to the centre of Kandahar a few months later by war cameraman Nick Downie yielded no evidence at all of heavy bombing.[26]

What the visits of Western journalists to Kandahar in 1981 did confirm was that there was a large guerrilla presence in the town and that the government was unable to exert its influence in about half of the city's districts.[27]

One of the main guerrilla leaders in the town was Engineer Esmatullah. He was one of the most remarkable figures in the resistance, being known by several names. To local guerrillas he was also called Esmatullah Moslem, or simply Esmat. Under the name Esmatullah Achadzai he had been an oficer in the royal, republican, and DRA armies. He quit in June 1979 to join Gailani's NIFA party (see Chapter Two). By mid-1981 he claimed to have a force of 5000 men organised into four zonal commands around the city. Esmatullah acted as a NIFA coordinator for the Kandahar Front, which owed real allegiance to a local leader Abdol Latif. The NIFA force was lightly equipped, with a modest complement of heavy weapons including 38 RPG-7s (shoulder-fired rocket launchers) and 8 Dshk 12.7mm heavy machine guns (a favoured weapon in ambushes and against planes).[28]

In Herat, the principal city of western Afghanistan, there was also extensive guerrilla penetration. Heavy fighting broke out there in early June. This followed an outbreak of trouble around Ghazni in May. The Ghazni violence was between the government 14th Division and men of a large independent guerrilla band. This group, under a man called Qari Taj Mohammed, was thought to number around 2000 men.[29] It made and broke several agreements with groups belonging to other parties and pursued a series of actions around Ghazni. At the end of May, a Soviet brigade arrived to conduct operations against this force.[30]

The operational and organisational chaos among guerrilla groups around Kandahar, Ghazni, and in other areas of the country, typified the problems of the resistance. While collectively they had made great progress in the wake of the Soviet intervention, the presence of this foreign enemy did little to resolve the deep inter-group conflicts. At the end of April the fundamentalist parties (IP of Khalis and Hekmatyar, ISA and IRM) tried to form their own alliance. By excluding Sayed Gailani's 'moderate' NIFA and Sigbatullah Mujaddidi's National Liberation Front (NLFA), they hoped to gain a greater consensus.[31] It is at this point that the division between the main fundamentalist parties and those characterised as pro-Western or nationalist attained a clearer definition.

Even so, the categorisation of the *mujahadeen* parties in this way is inadequate. For, among the fundamentalist parties, the rifts between Gulbuddin Hekmatyar's Islamic Party, the Khalis IP and Rabbani's party remained as deep and antagonistic as ever.

THE NATIONAL FATHERLAND FRONT IS LAUNCHED

In Kabul the quest for unity and legitimacy entered a new stage. On 15 June the National Fatherland Front held its first congress in Kabul. In the run up to the congress there had been attempts to stimulate interest in the Fatherland Front by settng up local organisations. These sent 940 delegates to the congress, and Mohammed Ziray was appointed Chairman. The basic idea of the National Fatherland Front was that it would provide an umbrella for organising pro-government (as distinct from pro-PDPA) activities and would thus be more acceptable to people who did not want to be party members. In fact the number of people who fell into this category was well below government hopes, and it fell to party members to organise the Front and to provide its membership, thus lessening its appeal to lay Afghans.

On 20 June the government unveiled a new land reform. It was intended to end some of the confusion caused by the Khalqis' land redistribution of 1979.[32] In a bid to win rural support it offered land to local chiefs and mullahs offering support to the government.

By appointing a well-known Khalqi to run the National Fatherland Front, Babrak Karmal was probably trying to further party unity. It was apparent by mid-1981 that the party factionalism which Karmal complained about in 1980 showed few signs of abating. Karmal was well aware that factionalism within the army was sapping its effectiveness and exacerbating the government's problems.

On 19 August he addressed a conference of armed forces party activists. He outlined plans for stronger party control of the military: 'The PDPA Politburo sees the enhancement of the role of the party in the resolution of military issues, and the raising of the level of Party leadership in all the process of struggle against the counter-revolution, as a first step towards passing on to decisive action against the enemies of the Saur revolution.' But party control of the forces remained tenuous. There was a subsequent admission in *Soviet Military Review* that only one-third of Afghan units had party organisations in 1981.

But Karmal's most emotional exhortations were for unity and discipline: 'Special attention must be paid to the developement of military order, the appointment and election of cadres, the enhancement of their revolutionary consciousness and the preparation and coordination of all state, social and military organisation towards breaking the resistance of our class enemies. In most party organisations these demands of the party have not been observed, and a number of the members of the party due to their links with previous factions, this faction or that faction, have not dispensed with lies, mutual allegations and slander.'[33]

Outside Kabul, the recently reorganised Soviet contingent was ready to undertake a number of important search and destroy operations. In each case a Soviet combined arms force (battalion or regiment) operated in collaboration with Afghan forces. The operations took the form of a retaliatory strike against areas that had been bases for guerrilla attacks.

A NEW OFFENSIVE SPIRIT

On July 4, a Soviet force from the 108th Motor Rifle Division attacked guerrilla bases in the Sarobi valley. The *mujahadeen* had used this base to stage a number of attacks on the Kabul–Jallalabad road. Airstrikes and air-landed troops were used in the operation. According to the *mujahadeen*'s own sources they 'suffered severe losses'.[34] Among the dead was Zabet Khan a local resistance commander.

Several Soviet–Afghan operations followed, but none with as clear cut an outcome as the Sarobi engagement. Government forces at the neck of the Panjsher had suffered several setbacks. In mid-July a battalion of Afghan troops defected from Charikhar to the guerrillas.[35] Then in August a party of *mujahadeen* went into

Golbahar nearby and started shooting government sympathisers.
By the guerrillas' own account they 'executed 70 party members'.[36]
That such a number of party members was at hand to be executed
suggests that recruitment to the government's cause had met with
some success, even in a small provincial town surrounded by hostile
territory.

The incident in Golbahar probably prompted the Panjsher 4
offensive against Ahmad Shad Massud's stronghold a week later.
The attacking force is believed to have consisted of one Soviet and
one Afghan regiment. As with previous sallies into the Panjsher,
the operation was over within two weeks and did only temporary
damage to guerrilla infrastructure. The only important long-term
consequence was that the Soviets established a base at Anjuman, at
the very top of the valley. This base could have little effect on
Massud's operations in the central Panjsher, but did allow them to
control the Anjuman pass which, when clear of snow, provided a
route in or out of the upper valley.

Operations by a commander called Mohammed Shah prompted an offensive in Farah province. Shah claimed a force of 1500
operating from the Sharafat-Koh mountains.[37] His group is
affiliated to the Islamic Revolution Movement of Nabi
Mohammedi. A force believed to consist of one Soviet unit (from
the 5th Guards Motor Rifle Division) and several Afghan ones
(drawn from the 21st Brigade, 4th Border Brigade and Farah
Operational Battalion), totalling nearly 5000 men, launched an
assault on this position on 5 September.[38] The attack went on until
15 September, supported by aircraft from the nearby Shindand
airbase. Both government and guerrillas claimed a great victory,
but it is clear that the offensive did only temporary damage to
Mohammed Shah's forces.

At the beginning of October, government forces staged a series of
search and destroy operations around Herat. These operations
involved one or possibly two Soviet motor rifle battalions as well as
local Afghan forces of the 17th Division and Sarandoy Operational
Battalion. The Kabul media gave particular praise to the
Sarandoy forces involved in these operations.

In a series of sweeps around the villages of Chesht and Band-e-
Salma they claimed to have captured 136 assault rifles, one Dhsk
machine gun, and three RPG-7 rocket launchers.[39] Clearly the
government and its Soviet allies were very pleased with their
operation around Herat. On 15 October, Tass reported that 600

'bandits' had been killed during these sweeps. The next day Interior Minister Mohammed Gulabzoy flew into Herat to decorate soldiers who had taken part in the fighting.[40]

FIGHTING IN BALKH PROVINCE

At roughly the same time, government forces staged an important operation in the north of the country. For some time they had been under pressure from the guerrillas of Zabiullah, a commander of the Islamic Society of Afghanistan, in his twenties. Like their other prominent field commanders (Ismael Khan in Herat and Ahmad Shah Massud in the Panjsher), Zabiullah was a Tajik who had built up a sizeable and, by Afghan standards, competent force of men. Zabiullah launched attacks from a base in the Marmoul gorge, close to Mazar-e-Shariff, capital of Balkh province.

The government offensive against Zabiullah's positions in the Marmoul gorge was triggered by a number of daring raids into the centre of Mazar-e-Shariff in August 1981.[41] The retaliation was well planned and massive. The attack was preceded by a concentration of air assets. A squadron from the 355th Air Brigade at Shindand was flown to Dehdadi Air Force Base near Mazar-e-Shariff. It supplemented two squadrons of MiG-17s from the Dehdadi-based 393rd Air Brigade. These Afghan air force planes were joined by USSR-based MiG-23s.[42] The combined air group spent a week bombing the Marmoul area.

When the planes had completed their fire preparation, a reinforced battalion from the 20th Division staged a heliborne landing on the high plain behind the village of Marmoul. But the Afghan soldiers were unable to fight their way down from the plain into the narrow gorge where Zabiullah and his men held their positions. After several days of fighting and 'scores' of casualties they gave up and were airlifted out.[43]

THE SOVIET TACTICAL APPROACH

By the second half of 1981, Soviet and Kabul forces were demonstrating a new style of coordinated operation. In the Sarobi valley an all-arms Soviet force backed by generous air support had

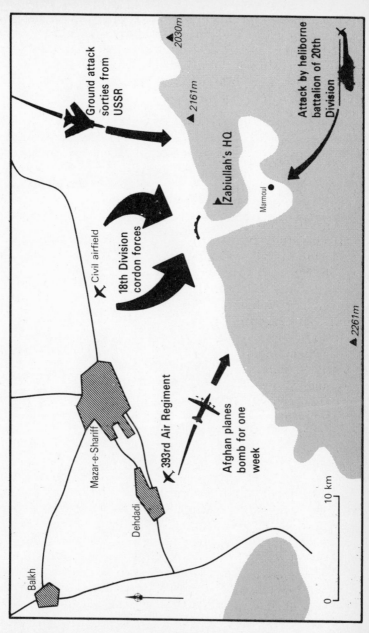

VI Attack on Marmoul Gorge, August 1981.

inflicted heavy casualties on the *mujahadeen*. In the Panjsher, Farah and around Herat, combined Soviet/Afghan task forces had gone into the field. The results were varied, but the very fact of these joint operations at brigade level marked something of a breakthrough. In these battles of late 1981 the basic style of the punitive offensive was practised. Its main tactical features were:

(a) The concentration of air assets, and extensive aerial bombardment of the target.
(b) The landing by helicopter of forces both to stop the withdrawal of enemy forces and to engage them from unexpected directions.
(c) A drive by mechanised forces into areas of guerrilla support, often destroying crops and homes, and often against the 'anvil' of the helicopter-landed party.

These tactics represented a fairly conventional approach to counter-guerrilla operations, but things needed to be simple. The Soviet army was feeling its way as far as such fighting was concerned, and the Afghan army remained barely capable of taking any kind of tactical, let alone operational, initiatives.

This lack of confidence combined with the minimum strategic objectives of the Soviet forces (i.e. the holding of certain key points and the roads which connected them) produced a very low tempo of operations throughout 1980 and the first half of 1981.

The situation in Kandahar in 1981 illustrates this well. Visitors to the city reported that the army made only the most occasional attempts to challenge the *mujahadeen* in the city. The resident Soviet 70th Motor Rifle Brigade remained in its tented camp on the outskirts of Kandahar for much of the time. All of this led one film-maker who went there at the time to conlude, 'the Soviets are making no attempt to fight this war let alone win it'.[44] Another British journalist took the road from Kabul to Mazar-e-Shariff, the Soviets' arterial supply route. He was surprised to see that most convoys were unprotected, that the situation was generally calm, and that there was little evidence of recent fighting.[45]

For many of the Afghan's army's isolated garrisons, the war involved only occasional combat. The officers remained too divided and the conscripts too reluctant for the units to leave camp without the risk of mass desertions. Mike Winchester, a journalist who visited the north-eastern town of Khanabad late in 1981, described the accommodation that the adversaries reached. 'Strictly for appearance a small Afghan army garrison in a small fort on the outskirts maintained the fiction of a government presence. Provided the army and a handful of Soviet advisers stayed behind their walls, an unofficial ceasefire was observed. A regular supply of ammunition from the fort to the *mujahadeen*, and a flow of food in the opposite direction, reinforced everyone's interest in ensuring that this happy state of affairs continued undisturbed. It was slightly surreal but entirely Afghan'.[46]

The *mujahadeen* for their part were interested in using their time to advance their own party interests and to accumulate as much saleable booty as possible without having to throw themselves against the firepower of the Soviet army. During the time (1980 to mid-1981) when the *mujahadeen* clearly held the initiative in much of the coutryside, they were unable to exploit it because of their disunity and poor organisation.

LIMITATIONS OF THE *MUJAHADEEN*

In every valley the competition between parties for recruits and the support of villagers was intense. It resulted in deep antagonism and occasional fighting between groups. During this period the 'successful' *mujahadeen* commanders emerged as those who could mould any kind of fighting force out of the disunited and poverty-stricken peasantry at their diposal. An example of the political skills needed by the guerrilla commander was demonstrated in Logar province.

In mid-1981, the IRM commander in the Logar, Sayed Murtaza made a deal with the other parties operating in the valley. It contained the following elements:

—The setting up of a joint command.

—Each group could levy taxes only on the members of its own party.

—No single group had the authority to tax the general population.

—Villages could decide which party they wished to affiliate to.[47]

This agreement was meant to allow Murtaza to get on with the business of fighting rather than having to devote his time to constant adjudication between squabbling groups and complaining villagers. Men like Mohammed Shah (in Farah), Abdol Haq (Kabul), and Zabiullah (in Balkh province) rose to prominence because they were able, by and large, to strike bargains with other parties in their areas.

Another good example of a *mujahed* who gained prominence by making political deals was Jallaladin Haqqani (IP of Yunis Khalis), best-known commander of Paktia province. Nick Downie, who spent time with Haqqani in 1981, described him as 'a good local politician, but militarily no more able than a platoon commander in any normal army'.[48]

Grass-roots rivalries and squabbles were not the only reason that the *mujahadeen* were unable to capitalise fully on the power vacuum in the countryside. Indeed, cooperation in the field was often much better than in Peshawar where the party leaders pursued their bitter antagonisms. For the fighters in the field there were more basic problems. The poor educational level inhibited the effective use of weapons and, perhaps more importantly, strong local allegiances meant that most *mujahadeen* were not willing to travel any distance from their village to fight.[49] Tactical operations were hindered by the lack of communications, properly organised command structures and clear orders.

On top of all this the *mujahadeen* lacked heavy weapons. While rifles were relatively easy to capture, the supply of ammunition for all weapons remained problematical. A supply train from Pakistan to the Panjsher might take three or four weeks, one to Balkh six weeks, and to the central Hazara Jat eight weeks. The journey would be perilous, not just because of possible Soviet interdiction, but because many guerrilla groups along the way were inclined to 'tax' the shipments.[50]

CUTTING GUERRILLA SUPPLY ROUTES

By late 1981, government forces were making new attempts to stop *mujahadeen* infiltration from Pakistan. The existence of large rebel bases there remained a continuing embarrassment to the Kabul government. Attempts were made to try to frighten the Pakistanis and the refugee population. A whole series of minor air incursions took place: on 4 October, 22 October, 16 November, 2 December, and so on.

These sallies into Pakistani air space were made by jets or helicopters, which frequently flew back without opening fire. When they did make an attack (as on 16 November) the casualties were small. The rash of reports of such incidents undoubtedly owed as much to Pakistan's need to convince the Americans that they needed new fighters as it did to the Afghans' desire to frighten the refugees.

In reality government attempts to block guerrilla supply routes from Pakistan remained largely ineffective. Various methods were tried. Increasing use was made of air-dropped PFM-1 mines. These weapons, referred to in the West as 'butterfly bombs' and among Soviet soldiery as 'green parrots', were scattered, usually by helicopter, in huge numbers along supply routes.

Other measures to stop the *mujahadeen* included fresh attempts to buy the services of tribal groups near the frontier. Tribal Minister Suleiman Laeq visited Nangrahar in October offering cash incentives to local tribes.[51] This tribal recruiting drive met with some success. In several places tribal Revolution Defence Groups were formed. In Paktia province the 300-strong militia group 'Touri' was raised at Mangal, and the 60-man unit 'Tufan' at Khost.[52]

The senior Soviet adviser in Kabul, Colonel General Maroyov, was replaced after less than a year. His successor, Army General M. Sorokin, doubtless arrived with a determination to improve the performance of Afghan–Soviet forces.

Early in December, Soviet and Afghan forces made a number of sweeps in the border province of Nangrahar. Their aim was to disrupt guerrilla infrastructure and supplies. The operations were carried out by Afghan units of the 11th Division and the local Soviet unit, the 66th Motor Rifle Brigade. Their operations involved the use of heavy airstrikes and mechanised pushes, and they brought some results. According to the government, 482 guerrillas were killed in this operation.[53] The haul of weapons included 17 Dshk machine guns and 400 land mines.

In this final operation of 1981, a familiar pattern was repeated – that of the all-arms joint Afghan–Soviet operation at the brigade level. Even if the performance of the Afghan troops in these operations remained very poor, the deployment of these forces for *any* kind of contest remained something of an achievement. The

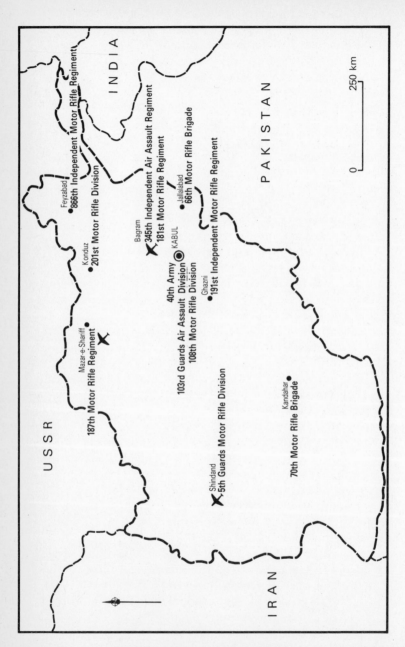

VII Main Soviet unit locations, 1981–83.

Soviet army itself was demonstrating new operational confidence. In 1982 they were to test themselves in the biggest offensive operation of the war to date.

Notes

1. *Los Angeles Times*, 9 January 1981.
2. *The Guardian*, 22 January 1981.
3. Kabul Radio, 8 January 1981.
4. Kabul Radio, 4 January 1981.
5. Kabul Radio, 14 January 1981.
6. Kabul Radio, 21 April 1981.
7. Ali Shah Quyumi, former textiles official, interviewed in *Afghan Information Centre (AIC) Bulletin*, no. 7, November 1981.
8. Yussuf Farand, former textiles official interviewed in *AIC Bulletin*, no. 6, October 1981.
9. Various *Summary of World Broadcasts*, Weekly Economic Reports for the Far East, January–May 1981.
10. Kabul Radio, 18 February 1981.
11. *Bakhtar Report*, 5 May 1981.
12. Roger Lewis, 'The Illicit Traffic in Heroin', *Druglink*, Spring 1984.
13. 'The Illicit Heroin Market in London 1980–83', *British Journal of Addiction*, 3 September 1985.
14. *Sunday Times*, 5 April 1981.
15. Kabul Radio, 11 February 1981.
16. Kabul Radio, 6 April 1981.
17. The move away from Kabul by units formerly based there was reported in Western newspapers around 1 April; confirmation that 7th Division HQ had moved to Moqor was given by Kabul Radio, 13 July 1981.
18. Abdol Haq, IP of Yunis Khalis, commander for Kabul, interviewed by the author, 11 March 1986.
19. Details of the Kabul Security Command given in various Kabul Radio transmissions including 10 October, 26 October 1981.
20. Kabul Radio, 11 February 1981.
21. Details of Operational Battalions given on Kabul Radio in 1981: Balkh (13 July), Fariab (16 January), Farah (15 October), Helmand (24 September), Parwan (10 August), Takhar (12 October), Zabol (4 November), Herat (16 October).
22. Kabul Radio, 10 April 1981.
23. Various Kabul Radio reports, especially 30 September, 15 October 1981.
24. *International Herald Tribune*, 13 April 1981.
25. *The Times*, 4 May 1981.
26. Nick Downie, film transmitted by Thames Television, 14 January 1982.
27. Ibid.
28. *AIC Bulletin*, no. 6, October 1981.

29. *AIC Bulletin*, no. 7, November 1981.
30. *The Guardian*, 30 May 1981.
31. AFP wire, 22 April 1981.
32. Yu. Gankovsky (ed.) *A History of Afghanistan* (Progress, 1985).
33. Babrak Karmal, speech to armed forces party activists, Kabul Radio, 19 August 1981.
34. *Afghan Realities*, no. 2, July 1981.
35. *Daily Telegraph*, 16 July 1981.
36. *Afghan Realities*, no. 3, August–September 1981.
37. *AIC Bulletin*, no. 6, October 1981.
38. Details of Afghan forces, Kabul Radio, 15 October 1981.
39. Kabul Radio, 15 October 1981.
40. Kabul Radio, 16 October 1981.
41. *Afghan Realities*, no. 3, August–September 1981.
42. Brigadier Arab Khan, defector from DRA air force, interviewed in *Afghan Realities*, no. 12, April 1982.
43. Mike Winchester, 'Night Raiders on Russias Border', *Soldier of Fortune*, September 1984.
44. Downie, see note 26.
45. *Daily Telegraph*, 17 July 1981.
46. Winchester, op. cit.
47. *AIC Bulletin*, no. 7, November 1981.
48. Nick Downie, interviewed by the author, 10 March 1986.
49. Abdol Haq, IP of Yunis Khalis, commander for Kabul, interviewed by the author, 11 March 1986.
50. Nigel Ryan mentions Hezb-e-Islami interference with Massood's supply trains in '*A Hitch or Two in Afghanistan*', (Weidenfeld & Nicolson, 1983).
51. *AIC Bulletin*, no. 7, November 1981.
52. Ibid.
53. Kabul Radio, 7 December 1981.

Five: 1982

THE SITUATION IN HERAT

Throughout late December and January there was fierce fighting in Herat. The strength of the resistance there continued to embarrass the government. Only the previous October the Interior Minister Mohammed Gulabzoy had been there congratulating his troops and handing out medals for their 'successful' campaign against the enemy; but 1982 provided Kabul with an unpleasant lesson in the continued power and dynamism of the local resistance.

Herat and the western provinces represent an ethnic patchwork. Amongst the Tajiks, Uzbecks, Aimaks, and Dari-speaking Pushtuns, the Islamic Society of Afghanistan (of Burhanuddin Rabbani) was dominant. The ISA front in Herat, under Ismael Khan, had grown into by far the largest regional resistance organisation. But there were pockets of Pushtuns and Shias who owed their allegiance to other parties.[1]

Among the local Pushtuns the IP (of Gulbuddin Hekmatyar) and IRM (of Mohammed Nabi Mohammedi) were active. However, their activities had been compromised by a number of defections. In March 1981, the local IRM commander, Shirah Khan, deserted to the authorities.[2] In 1982 an IP leader, Turam Gulam Rassool, did the same.[3] There were several parties that recruited among the Shias, including Khair Ahmad Ali's Hezbollah (Party of God).

Defections and in-fighting in the Pushtun and Shia communities combined to strengthen Ismael Khan's position. By 1982 he had established a large, and reasonably well run front, credited with control of 80 per cent of the province's fighters. It had an efficient political organisation, and could mobilise around 5000 *mujahadeen*.[4]

Herat poses peculiar problems for the *mujahadeen*. It is a long way from the ISA supply dumps and camps in Pakistan. Though very close to the Iranian border the ayatollahs tended to save their help for the Shia groups. Around the city, and throughout the western provinces of Herat, Farah and Nimroz, the terrain is flat and open. Enemy airpower makes movement hazardous, forcing the resistance to adopt some unconventional solutions. They moved at night, used tunnels between villages, and sometimes took to the roads in a variety of vehicles including captured GAZ–66 jeeps. The preference is apparently for Toyota pick-up trucks which are smuggled from Pakistan.[5] The openness of the country means the *mujahadeen* have to move quickly from point to point, however obvious the method of transport.

Government forces in the area are small and over-extended. The local military HQ is the 17th Division which is reponsible for Herat, Badghis, Ghowr Farah and Nimroz provinces. Several additional units operate: the 21st Mechanised Brigade in Farah, 5th Border Brigade in Herat, 4th Border Brigade in Nimroz, plus Sarandoy Operational Battalions in Farah and Herat. On paper these units should have totalled 18 000 men; in fact by 1982 it is unlikely that they exceeded with 6000. Ask any military commander to hold an area bigger than Scotland with 6000 men against a larger guerrilla force and he will tell you it cannot be done.

Fortunately for Kabul these forces were not the only ones in the area. In contrast to the Pakistan border area, the Soviet forces in this western zone in 1982 outnumbered the local Afghan troops. The Soviets maintained a major base at Shindand where the 5th Guards Motor Rifle Division was garrisoned along with one helicopter and two fighter squadrons.[6] The total of these forces was over 12 000 men.

By early 1982 the situation around Herat had deteriorated badly for the government. Guerrillas operating in the city executed 60 PDPA officials in January.[7] A string of operations by the 17th Division and 5th Guards Motor Rifle Division were aimed at flushing them out. These took the form of drives by reinforced mechanised battalions into districts of the city and the surrounding countryside. The raids were accompanied by air and artillery support leading to reports of heavy civilian casualties.

There are a few detailed reports of the fighting, but on 21 January the government said 291 guerrillas had been captured in the area.[8] In February, Soviet sources said that 2200 rebels had been killed in this offensive.[9] Undoubtedly the scale of operations was large and a number of Western newspapers reported it as a defeat for the *mujahadeen*.[10] On 7 March, army political chief Brigadier Gol Aqa visited the 17th Division conferring promotions, medals and rewards and praising them for 'eliminating the remnants of the rebel bands'.[11] Aqa's optimism was, perhaps inevitably, premature.

A postscript to these operations occurred a month later when a Soviet unit reportedly crossed into Iran in pursuit of guerrillas.[12] As a result of this the Iranians agreed to restrict *mujahadeen* operations and even handed some *mujahadeen* over to the Afghans on 20 May.[13]

After the fighting, Ismael Khan and his military commander Allaladin re-organised their forces. Their military backgrounds led them to adopt a conventional unit structure. They formed 'battalions' (each of four companies), and 'regiments' (of five battalions).[14]

Two 'regiments' were formed from Allaladin's cadre of 1000 fighters. These men formed the core of the ISA forces, being effectively 'full-time' soldiers. The remaining 4000 or so were generally only prepared to defend their own village or area. The concentration of Allaladin's best fighters into these two large units caused some debate within the Herat ISA front. Despite some commanders' reservations the re-organisation was implemented in the second half of 1982.[15]

FIGHTING IN THE SOUTH AND EAST

In early February, the Sarandoy in Kandahar was reported to have carried out a number of operations with their Operational Battalion in the city centre.[16] At about the same time the local *mujahadeen* were reported to have used some SA-7 shoulder-fired anti-aircraft missiles against government planes.[17] By early 1982 a number of these had found their way into guerrilla hands. Some were captured and others reportedly bought in Beirut. Others were supplied by Egypt and sent by the CIA, along with increasing supplies of Soviet-produced armaments.

Towards the end of March, the Afghan army conducted an operation in Kapisa province. The point of note was that much of the 11th Division apparently left camp to take part in the raid. It therefore marked something of an achievement by the unit, which probably did not number more than 2000 men at the time. According to government sources 220 enemy were captured during this operation.[18]

Kabul Radio reported the return of the 11th division as a joyous patriotic event: 'The people greeted them with decorations and flowers and slogans of "Long Live the PDPA", and voiced their faith in the DRA armed forces...and praised the brave soldiers and officers of Nangrahar 11 Division in routing counter-revolutionary elements, these mercenaries of reaction and imperialism.'[19]

KIDNAP OF SOVIET CITIZENS

As the number of Soviet advisers and technicians grew, so they became easier targets for kidnap attempts. In January three Novosti journalists were kidnapped at Lake Kargha near the capital.[20] An engineering specialist, Olonyuk, was kidnapped soon afterwards and wrote a letter to Soviet Premier Nikolai Tikohonov.

In all cases the Soviets refused to negotiate and the hostages were presumed murdered. It is doubtful that these random kidnappings of civilians did anything but strengthen the Soviets' resolve. This at least has usually been the case in Western countries where such acts are characterised as 'terrorism'. The resistance parties usually executed Soviet prisoners as well; very few were seen by Western reporters until the latter part of 1982.

In January there were reports that a Soviet Lieutenant-General Shkidchenko had been killed in a helicopter crash in Paktia province.[21]

Whilst guerrilla claims to have killed Soviet generals are almost invariably proven to be fabrication or exaggeration (a major being promoted to general by the umpteenth re-telling of the tale), in this case the story was confirmed by 'diplomatic sources' in Kabul.

In all of these cases the Soviets were receiving bitter lessons in the personal costs of their presence in Afghanistan. By 1982 there was a discernible change in the public line on Afghanistan. On 23 February, the Defence Ministry daily, *Krasnaya Zvezda*, published an article which gave a harsh picture of life in the DRA. It catalogued alleged rebel atrocities and told of guerrilla bands thousands strong. It also painted a picture of the problems facing Soviet troops there: 'We won't hide the fact that it's hard there, very very hard.' The article ended with an emotional exhortation to the troops: 'But know friends that you live in every socialist heart. The people are proud of you, they love you, they think of you.'[22]

Slowly but surely there was also a move in the USSR to give more credit and kudos to the men fighting there. In Moscow's Central Museum of the Soviet Army, a place frequented by parties of teenagers nearing conscription, a display appeared dedicated to Senior Sergeant A. Mironenko. A photo of the young paratrooper was on show along with a gold star 'Hero of the Soviet Union', the USSR's highest decoration. A caption informed visitors that Mironenko had received the medal because he fought to the death rather than surrender to the Afghan '*dushmans*'.[23]

THE PDPA NATIONAL CONFERENCE

Early in 1982, various People's Democratic Party organisations began the task of organising a national conference. It was only the second in the party's history, the first being in 1966. The main purpose of the conference was to galvanize the party membership, and instil some new sense of purpose. At the same time it was also hoped that it could be used to unify the PDPA.

Major-General Abdol Qader had taken over as Acting Defence Minister on 4 January. The 'Acting' title was probably a sop to Rafi's remaining supporters; it was dropped in September 1982. Qader's main attractions were his ability to lead the armed forces and soothe factionalism wthin them. Even so, guerrilla sources claimed that Brigadier Ahmad Ali, commander of the 25th Division and a well-known Khalqi, was obstructing the election of conference delegates in Khost.[24]

Whether these rumours were true or not, 866 delegates were elected nationally and they arrived in Kabul for the conference sessions on 14 and 15 March. The conference sessions were chaired alternately by the Khalqi Dr Ziray, and the Parchami Ali Keshtmand. The conference adopted an 'Appeal to the Afghan People' which set out the party commitment to lower unemployment and build new factories; safeguard human rights; provide land and water as well as education for the peasantry; develop light industry; bring equality for minorities; respect Islam; and bring about tranquility by the efforts of the armed forces.[25]

Although this might have seemed no more than a restatement of a programme that had been around since 1978, there were some interesting ideological compromises. The Appeal also pledged a better deal for women, but it stressed that this would only be with their 'voluntary participation'. The party had moderated its stance since the days when Khalqi militants went into villages tearing off veils and enforcing education on peasant women.

There was also some self-congratulation – that the PDPA was growing as a party and extending its influence in the country. Party organisation boss, Nur Ahmed Nur said of the period 1980–82, 'For the first time in the party's history a party apparatus has been set up and numerous professional cadres trained.' By the time of the conference the PDPA claimed a membership of 62 800 in 1656 local organisations.[27] Even allowing for some healthy exaggeration in these figures it was quite clear that there had been an increase in the membership since the days when Hafizullah Amin tried to run the country with only 5000 in the PDPA's ranks.

This expansion coupled with the continued Khalqi representation in the cabinet was also lessening factionalism. The new cadres were swamping the Khalqi contingent and their leaders were being compromised by participation in government. The problem of factional conflict was by no means solved, but it was being lessened slowly.

In April the United Nations Secretary General appointed a special representative: Diego Cordovez. His task was to try to start peace talks between Kabul, Tehran and Islamabad. That spring Cordovez visited each of the capitals for exploratory talks.

OPERATIONS IN THE NORTH-EAST

Like the *mujahadeen* of Herat, those in the north-eastern provinces (Badakhshan, Takhar, Baghlan and Konduz) suffered from their remoteness. It is difficult for them to get arms in and news out. Unlike the Herat guerrillas, these men fought in high mountains where the terrain was far more favourable to their style of war. Rather like the Hazara Jat there were areas of these provinces that remained completely removed from the government and the fighting.

Nevertheless, in April Afghan army units in the north-east carried out a number of operations against the resistance. Elements of the 20th Division were active in Baghlan. The government claimed that they killed 140 enemy during this period.[28] Three weeks later Kabul sources said that security forces in Konduz had killed 75 guerrillas during search and destroy missions.

Further south, at Bagram airbase, preparations had begun for the Soviets' biggest campaign of the war so far. Aircraft were flown in, supplies outloaded to units and warning orders issued. Their target: the Panjsher.

PANJSHER 5

Within the resistance Ahmad Shah Massud had attained the status
of superstar. He played host to foreign film crews, he trained
mujahadeen from other regions, and his men staged daring raids. All
of this rested on his skill as organiser, fighter and tactician. He had
grasped the importance of the key elements of guerrilla warfare:
surprise, organisation, rapid concentration and dispersal of forces.
In these respects Massud was, and by and large remains, far ahead
of the other *mujahadeen*.

By 1982 his forces had been divided into mobile and static units.
His 3000 men were divided into half a dozen 90 to 100-strong
mobile fighting groups (or *motoraks*) and many 25 to 60-man local
defence units (*sabets*).[29] This division between the elite *motoraks* for
mobile hard hitting warfare, and the essentially part-time *sabets*
who defended their own villages was an important achievement.
Most guerrilla movements in the world (for example the Viet
Cong, the FLN in Algeria, or Polisario in the Western Sahara)
have proven that the division of forces into mobile and local
contingents is a vital step. Massud remains one of only a handful of
commanders to have managed it in Afghanistan. The formation of
these *motoraks* required both a dedicated cadre of fighters prepared
to travel away from their villages for long periods, and sufficient
organisation to sustain them in the field.

Massud's own character remained vital to the success of the
organisation. He had been involved in revolutionary politics since
the earliest days of Daoud's regime, and he spent years in exile
studying the classics of guerrilla war – Mao, Guevara and De
Gaulle. His qualities struck visitors: 'There was a speed and
concentration about his movements, as if he needed to dispatch his
business before his enemies could catch up with him. He never
announced his whereabouts in advance or if he did he changed
them; seldom stopped more than an hour in one place; and only the
tiny elite that guarded, cosseted and worshipped him knew where
he slept, which was rarely more than two nights in the same house.'[30]

Massud knew in advance that an attack was imminent. He is
believed to have heard through informers in the Afghan army.[31] In
a bid to forestall it he launched his most daring attack to date. He
dispatched the cream of his forces, several *motoraks* – a battalion-
sized force – to attack Bagram airbase.

Bagram is a well-defended installation and his men breached the
perimeter under cover of darkness on the 25 April. They fired

rockets and mortars, claiming to have destroyed 23 aircraft. A captured Soviet captain subsequently confirmed that the attack had taken place, and that a number of planes had been destroyed or damaged.[32]

This daring raid seems only to have delayed the coming apocalypse for a few weeks. On 10 May it began.

Soviet staff officers had planned by far the biggest offensive of the war to date. At least 15 000 men were involved in the ground operation. The Soviets provided the bulk – around 11 000 men drawn from three different divisions. They were grouped, along with the Afghans, under a single task-force HQ (that of the 108th Motor Rifle Division).

The first wave of the assault force, made up largely of Afghan soldiers (of the 8th Division and 38th Commando Brigade) advanced to Gulbahar and cordoned the neck of the valley.[33] Then the bombing started. Airstrikes were preceded by aerial reconnaissance and target designation by converted An-12 transports. When this was complete Su-25s, Su-17s, and MiG-21s flew in, dropping conventional high-explosive bombs. The photographs taken of the Su-25s were the first to be seen in the West. The new aircraft proved to be highly manoeuvrable and carried a large warload.

This bombing went on for a week, but it was confined to daylight hours. During the night the civilian populace returned to their homes, leaving them at 4 a.m. for their hideaways on the mountainsides. Although heavy damage was done to buildings, many of the bombs failed to explode and they were converted into powerful mines by the *mujahadeen*.[34] Massud's forces remained largely unscathed during the bombardment. They also carried out a number of attacks on the government forces, causing casualties and demoralisation.

On 17 May the bombing stopped and heliborne landings started. The main landings were near Khenj in the centre of the valley (see Map VIII). At least a battalion of air assault troops went there. There were several other landings and the total of Soviet Air Assault Forces involved must have been at least a regiment. These men were drawn from the 103rd Air Assault Division.

These paratroops made little attempt to dig in or conceal themselves until they came under fierce attack. At the same time as they were inserted, a mechanised column of at least one Soviet regiment (believed to be from the 108th Motor Rifle Division) began an advance into the Panjsher.

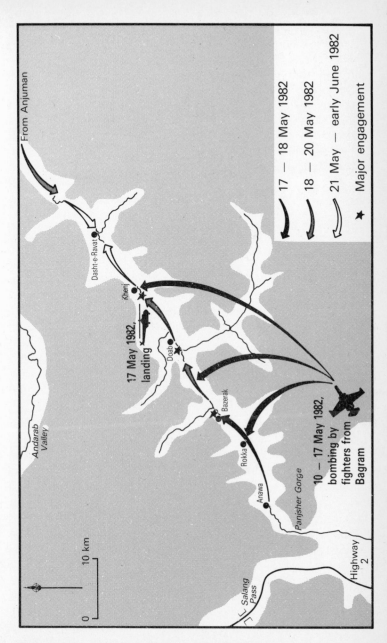

VIII Panjsher 5, May–June 1982.

The mechanised forces made their way up the valley using the single poor road from Rokka. Massud's men were forewarned as a *motorak* was able to observe the advance from its base at Chamal Wadar near Rokka. The guerrillas started landslides in a bid to halt the column.[35] As per standard Soviet battle drills, the mechanised regiment was preceded by a Route Security Patrol (Russian initials, GPZ) of a platoon of T-62 tanks with bulldozer blades for clearing obstacles and some mechanised infantry.

As this GPZ reached the village of Bazerak the motor rifle regiment was subjected to the first of a number of ambushes. Its three T-62s were knocked out in quick succession by *mujahadeen* mines and RPGs.[36] Worse was to come. An even more costly ambush occured near the village of Doab where the Panjsher river crosses a bridge. Here a highly effective ambush knocked out the best part of a Soviet motor rifle company – at least half a dozen BTR-60 personnel carriers and several tanks.[37] The ambushes continued, many from the small tributary valleys that join the Panjsher. The Soviets responded by calling in close air support, almost always Mil-24 attack helicopters. These arrived in teams of six, loitering (in what wartime Soviet pilots called 'the circle of death') before dropping one by one on the instructions of forward air controllers to rocket and strafe targets.[38]

The Soviets' tactical *coup* of the operation was to dispatch a second regiment from the other end of the valley to the north-east. This unit (believed to be part of the 201st Motor Rifle Division) made its way across the Anjuman pass in the north of the valley, where a beleaguered government garrison had been holding out, to Dasht-e-Ravat. Its arrival was a genuine surprise to Massud and his men.

It took the main column three days to travel the 40 kilometres from Rokka to the airlanded group near Khenj – and it was costly: this part of the battle may have accounted for over 100 Soviet lives. While they were getting there the air assault troops remained under intense fire, taking still more casualties. But the pincer was complete; the entire floor of the valley was in socialist hands for the first time since 1978.

The cost to the Soviets was 300–400 dead with perhaps double this number of Afghan casualties. Massud's losses amounted to maybe 100 killed, with several times this number of civilians dead. There were many tactical mistakes in the Soviet operation but the immediate result, the occupation of the floor of the valley, was a success.

Within the Panjsher, Kabul party officials were dispatched to try to hurry a 'return to normality'. Truckloads of Parchami Revolutionary Guard militiamen were sent from the capital to 'explain and propagate the objectives of the Saur Revolution, and to help the toiling people'.[39]

In the valley, the 38th Commando Brigade held a ceremony on 16 June to welcome 'some 820 inhabitants...of the Panjsher district who had left their homes because of the inhuman barbarous actions of the rebels' and who had 'returned to their homes, following the crushing defeat inflicted on these enemies of the people by the heroic DRA Armed Forces'.[40]

The reality was that Massud's forces had withdrawn to the high ground and preserved their fighting strength. They soon began staging new ambushes. The cost of this bitter struggle was expressed by a Soviet private in a letter home: 'Sometimes they descend on us – we are hard pushed things get so bad. From our company four have already been killed and our zampolit Batuyev was blown up by a mine and they hardly found anything left of him...there's practically nothing f——ing left of the third company, they're all either in coffins or the hospital.'[41]

A few weeks after their costly conquest of the Panjsher, Soviet/Afghan forces pulled back to Rokka and Dash-e-Ravat.

NEW DEVELOPMENTS IN THE AFGHAN ARMY

The problem of manpower, or rather the lack of it, remained a fundamental one for the Afghan army. A number of measures were adopted that summer. The age for military service was extended from 35 to 39.[42] Major-General Abdol Qader and Marshal Sergei Sokolov were reported to have met in July to discuss plans for the reorganisation of the Afghan Ministry of Defence.[43] The aim of this was to get more officers into the field.

A more significant boost to army manpower was coming from the newly bolstered Ministry of the Interior Sarandoy forces. They were involved in a growing number of sweeps looking for draft-dodgers. In January these were centred in Kabul, but other cities were searched as well. In some measure the activities of the Sarandoy only increased the resentment of the citizenry, who by and large remained unwilling to risk all for the 'Saur Revolution'. The Sarandoy searchers were called press-gangs and kidnappers. In fact their activities were effective in that from 1982 onwards there

was a slow climb in the numbers of men serving in the Afghan
Army.

Some analysts believe that army strength may have sunk as low
as 25 000 in 1980–81. Whereas the 1981–82 edition of the
authoritative publication *Military Balance* gives an army strength
of 35 000, by the 1983–84 edition this has risen to 40 000.[44] There
was a consensus among intelligence agencies and private analysts
that a slow climb had begun, and 1982 can be regarded as the
turning-point.

Just as the Sarandoy were catching recruits, so the army was
managing to hold on to them slightly better. In 1979 and 1980
there were several confirmed cases of entire brigades defecting. In
1981 there was just one report of a surrender *en masse* – of a
battalion at Charikhar. In 1982, although large numbers of
individuals still absconded from the ranks there is no confirmed
record of a whole unit deserting.

There was also a modest improvement in the operational record
of the Kabul forces. Units in Herat continued their operations – in
July there were reports that they had killed 176 rebels near
Gulrun.[45] But the most interesting operational record was being
notched up by the 1st or Central Corps.

Because of 7th Division's deployment south to Moqor, this corps'
'free' units were the 8th Division, 37th and 38th Commando
Brigades and the two Kabul-based armoured brigades. These
forces were in action throughout the summer of 1982. The 8th
Division and 38th Brigade were in the Panjsher from May to June.
Despite guerrilla claims to have 'wiped them out',[46] the same units
were to return there in August. Even assuming they did lose many
men (deserters as well as casualties), it shows the vitality of the
system that they were back in action only seven or eight weeks
later. The same Central Corps units were also apparently involved
in operations in the first week of July in Paghman where the
government claimed to have captured 200 men.[47]

A few weeks later, Brigadier Gol Aqa, the army political chief,
was fired. He was replaced by Colonel Yasin Sadeqi whose brief
was to tighten the PDPA's grip on the army. Gol Aqa had failed to
establish a party apparatus in the majority of units. The Soviets
and Karmal understood that a comprehensive political machine
was needed to bring wayward officers under control and smother
factionalism. Yasin Sadeqi was to prove markedly more adept than
his predecessor and was promoted to brigadier after a few months
in office.

The performance of the Afghan army in this period was still poor
in the field. Many units remained chronically undermanned. The
7th division had apparently dwindled to just over 1000 men by
mid-1982.[48] For the soldiers of Brigadier Azimi's 8th Division, the
summer still held a major challenge – another fight in the Panjsher.

PANJSHER 6

After the major effort of Panjsher 5, there must have been
considerable frustration among the Soviet generals at the resilience
of Massud's army. The one positive lesson that they could draw
from the previous fighting was that the floor of the valley could be
occupied. If they could do this more efficiently, and attack
Massud's men in their hiding places up the tributary valleys, then
another offensive might finally break the '*dushmans*'.

At the start, at least, the operation was identical to Panjsher 5.
The Soviet and Afghan units involved were the same and the total
of 15 000 was also probably equal. The form of attack, beginning
with lengthy aerial bombardment was also the same.

The bombing began on 25–6 August and once again involved
the modern Su-25 aircraft. About a dozen of these planes had been
deployed to Shindand at the beginning of the year in a
development unit, the 200th Independent Guards Aviation
Squadron.[49] Their flights over the Panjsher were from the
forward operating base of Bagram. Their bombardments were of
suspected guerrilla targets but, once more, Massud's men sat them
out in caves and the main damage was to houses.[50] On 30 August
there was a large heliborne landing near Khenj and a mechanised
column set off from Rokka. This time the air assault troops
conducted themselves with greater urgency and discipline, as did
the men of the ground column. It also seems that Massud's men,
knowing what was coming, conserved their strength by conducting
fewer ambushes than during the previous push.

Within two days the ground forces met up with the air assault
troops and the floor of the Panjsher valley itself was occupied. It
was then that the Soviets began an original, and for the *mujahadeen*
unwelcome, series of smaller attacks. They conducted several mini-
offensives up the main tributary valleys: the Hazara being the
largest, as well as the Chawa and Parende (see Map IX).

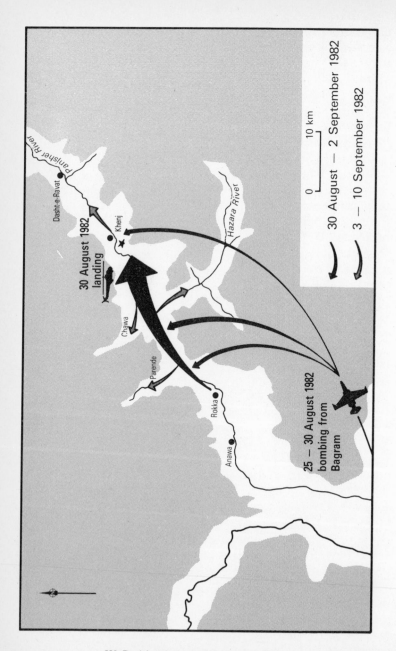

IX Panjsher 6, August–September 1982.

Each of these smaller attacks was preceded by the insertion of a blocking group of paratroops by helicopter. Whilst the *mujahadeen* had taken sanctuary in these side valleys during the previous attack, they were now forced even higher into the mountains. Massud gave the order to 'evacuate the valley'.[51]

According to Girardet, a journalist who witnessed the Panjsher 5 sweep, the total Soviet casualties (dead as well as wounded) in the Panjsher during 1982 amounted to 2000, and Kabul losses to 1200 (including dead, injured and deserted). He estimates that Massud had about 180 men killed and that about 1200 civilians died in the fighting.[52] These figures (which given normal ratios of dead to wounded, suggest 600–700 Soviet fatalities in the valley throughout 1982) are probably accurate.

Soviet/Afghan forces stayed in the valley until 10 September, when they withdrew to Rokka once more. Before they did so, they set about destroying houses, irrigation systems and burning crops. A major refugee flow was triggered. For Ahmad Shah Massud this was the more serious long-term cost of Panjsher 6. By October he was forced to appeal for food for his men. Although Massud himself remained alive and much of his army was intact, Panjsher 6 did cause lasting damage to guerrilla infrastructure in the valley, undoing years of work by the *mujahadeen*. Visitors estimated that the population of the valley had dwindled from 80 000 pre-war to around 45 000.

SYSTEMATIC GENOCIDE OR COLLATERAL DAMAGE?

With the much higher tempo of operations by Soviet and Kabul forces in 1982 as compared to 1980–81, 'collateral damage' to civilian targets by bombing and artillery was correspondingly greater. There was also evidence that Soviet troops had deliberately slaughtered civilians.

One case allegedly occured at Padkhwab-e-Shana village in Logar Province on 19 September 1982. According to refugees from the village, 105 civilians who were hiding in an underground irrigation channel were burned to death when Soviet troops poured petrol into the tunnel and ignited it.[53]

Soviet prisoners of the *mujahadeen* have also spoken about and indiscriminate slaughter of civilians during operations.[54] Houses and farmsteads remain easier targets for pilots than dispersed pockets of *mujahadeen*. For the frightened conscripts (like the French ones in Algeria, or Israelis in Lebanon) searching villages, the hostility of local people makes all operations potentially hazardous.

Their attitude was summed up by a private who served his time in the DRA and returned to his native Estonia: 'It is difficult to get one's bearings there and you never know what you might meet behind the next corner. You must shoot always...the worst thing that happens in these attacks is that many become marauders and become downright beastly, in those instances some seemed to be sadists. Maybe the fact that there is death in front of you and behind you, there are shots, gunbursts, and then in that crazy storm you start shouting as if you had lost your mind – just to encourage yourself.'[55]

It has been argued by some analysts that these acts are part of a centrally organised strategy. If, to borrow the Maoist analogy, guerrillas are fish swimming in the water of the people, then the aim is to 'empty the fishbowl'. Some observers have gone as far as to suggest that the Soviets are conducting systematic genocide by destroying the rural economy.[56] There is ample evidence, not only of the destruction of farms, but of the migration of people – the biggest in Afghan history – abroad or to safer villages.

While the Panjsher does provide an example of deliberate depopulation by the Soviets, and there are others, this does not amount to evidence of a deliberate and centrally organised national policy. There have been many recorded instances where the Kabul government has offered inducements (of cash, land, irrigation) to refugees to get them to return to the land. Indeed there are also accounts from Soviet prisoners of officers who were harshly disciplined for carrying out revenge attacks against civilians.[57]

What was happening was a 'carrot and stick' policy; in *mujahadeen* areas there were scorched-earth operations; in government areas, inducements to farm. In 1982 the Panjsheris experienced both kinds of persuasion: the Soviet army laid waste areas where Massud's fighters had been, but offered cash and land to displaced farmers to settle in the lower part of the valley, which they had cleared (for a short time at least).

It is also true that the bombing in rural Afghanistan is, in terms of the estimated tonnages used, light when compared to the B-52 raids carried out in certain parts of Indo-China. Those were not perceived by most Westerners as a policy of systematic genocide.

The shooting of civilians and bombing of towns has been explained in past guerrilla wars (such as Vietnam) in terms of indiscipline, frustration and a sense of superiority on the part of the soldiers concerned. These failings produced the My Lai massacre in Vietnam; perhaps they were also responsible for the events in Padkhwab-e-Shana.

OPERATIONS IN PAGHMAN AND THE NORTH

Despite the repeated attentions of the Afghan army and the Soviet Limited Contingent, the Paghman hills near Kabul remained a centre for *mujahadeen* operations near the capital. In July there were further attempts to dislodge the guerrillas there.[58]

There was also a series of operations in the north. These involved soldiers of the 18th Division from Mazar-e-Shariff as well as Soviet troops. It appears that there was a further attempt to storm Commander Zabiullah's Marmoul stronghold, which was repulsed in the same way as the attack of the previous July.

Kabul sources reported 18th Division operations throughout November 1982.[59] At the end of the month mobile forces from the formation were operating in the Hazrat-e-Soltan district of neighbouring Samanagan province.[60]

In the Hazara Jat, the hitherto stable rule of the Shura front was coming under pressure. The source of the trouble was an organisation called Nasr (victory). The Nasr party was a vehicle for more radical Shia politics. Its leaders looked to Iran for inspiration and support. Their uncompromising views won them a growing following, but the cost of this was conflict with the Shura.

CHANGES IN MOSCOW

On 10 November, Leonid Brezhnev's death was announced. There were suggestions that the departure of the principal advocate of the Afghan intervention might bring a change in the Soviet position. Whereas Brezhnev had taken several years to consolidate his own position, his successor Yuri Andropov was confirmed quickly in power.

Andropov was keen to revitalize the economy and make broad changes in Soviet society. Under him a rapid change in senior political and military cadres began, although it seemed it was suspended during his illness and the subsequent Chernenko interregnum.

The revelations of a former KGB officer, Vladimir Kuzichkin, suggested that this new leader might want to alter the Kremlin strategy in Afghanistan. According to Kuzichkin, Andropov, as KGB chief, had been vociferously opposed to the commital to Soviet troops.[61] In fact Andropov's arrival did not change Soviet policy in the area at all.

The Limited Contingent's presence had not undergone any significant growth since the reorganisation of 1980–81. Having committed their army the Kremlin was determined not to escalate. In marked contrast to the Western experience of counter-insurgency wars (the Americans and French in Vietnam; the British in Malaya) there was little real growth in Soviet troop numbers during these years. Clearly this meant that the Soviet army could only maintain its level of operations and its minimum objectives.

GROWTH OF KHAD

One of Karmal's most important problems on coming to power was that he did not have a loyal security police network. Naturally Hafizullah Amin had stocked his agency, KAM, with Khalqi loyalists. Throughout 1980–81 the new organisation, KHAD, was built up under Dr Najeebollah.

By 1982, according to defectors, KHAD had a staff of 18 000 grouped into 182 zones.[62] The same report placed the number of Soviet advisers with the organisation at 312. There was evidence that they had achieved extensive penetration of some guerrilla groups. The loss of 120 *mujahadeen* in Fariab in May 1982 was blamed on KHAD informers[63] Tony Davies, a journalist who visited Balkh province in 1982, said there had been 'a marked increase in the number of informants among the *mujahadeen*'.[64]

On the other hand, the evidence of the Panjsher fighting, and that in other areas, was that the Afghan/Soviet troops were still weak on battlefield intelligence. KHAD was probably achieving greater results in the area of political information gathering. Nevertheless their expanded activities led to paranoia among many resistance groups. New arrivals in Pakistani refugee camps, deserting soldiers, and even old comrades, came under suspicion.

One of the organisation's main roles was to improve security in the armed forces. The insertion of agents into army units made the plotting of 'counter-revolutionary acts' a great deal more hazardous and the number of rumoured *coup* plots began to decline.

As a larger organisation, KHAD became newly respectable in Kabul. Its chief, Dr Najeebollah, was referred to more often in open sources. He was even sent on 18 September to try to negotiate a deal with tribal leaders from the frontier provinces – a task that he was to undertake with increasing skill.

For all these modest advances, KHAD was still beset with problems. Its role in penetrating the armed forces, and its largely Parchami membership excited animosity. Relations were particularly bad with the Sarandoy, which still contained a relatively large number of Khalqis.[65] The reliability of some senior KHAD personnel also came under question in December 1982. Then the Chief of Training and a divisional commander reportedly defected to Pakistan.

In all respects 1982 marked a polarisation of the conflict. Large Soviet task forces were deployed in the Panjsher and around Herat. The Afghan army took part in these operations and bore the brunt in many provinces where there was no real Soviet presence (such as Paktia, Kunar, Nimroz and Helmand). Although there was no significant improvement in this army's fighting capabilities, there was evidence of a growth in its numbers and greater stability in the officer corps.

With the intensification of combat activity there was further polarisation among Afghans. The government could claim an expanded (but still largely urban) party membership; the *mujahadeen* more recruits. Caught between the protagonists, an increasing number of people became refugees. By the end of the year there were over 2 million of them in Pakistan. There was also a flow of people into Kabul and the other cities. Depopulation had occurred in areas like the Panjsher and Kunar valleys, but the figures were swollen by many thousands of Pushtuns and Baluchis who traditionally moved into Pakistan in times of hardship.

Nevertheless, in many areas rural communities remained on the land. For example, even after the year's heavy fighting in Herat, much of the local peasantry reportedly remained on the land.[66]

For the Soviet army the year followed a work-up to large-scale combined operations. While the *mujahadeen* held the rural initiative (but rarely used it) for the 18 months after their intervention, the

Soviets had begun to take it for themselves. From the command and logistics point of view the offensives of 1982 were competent but had caused only limited damage to the resistance – at a cost of hundreds of Soviet lives. It was time to take stock.

Notes

1. Olivier Roy, interviewed in *Afghan Information Centre (AIC) Bulletin*, December 1982.
2. Ibid
3. Commander Allaladin, ISA Commander of Herat Province, interviewed by the author, 7 April 1986.
4. Olivier Roy, who spent a month with the Herat ISA Front in October 1982, interviewed by the author, 9 April 1986..
5. Peter Jouvenal, an ex-serviceman who has been into Afghanistan 25 times as a war cameraman, interviewed by the author, June 1985.
6. David Isby, 'Soviet Tactics in the War in Afghanistan', *Jane's Defence Review*, vol. 4, no. 3, 1983.
7. *Keesings Contemporary Archives*, 18 June 1982.
8. Kabul Radio, 21 January 1982.
9. Tass, 12 February 1982.
10. *The Guardian*, 28 January 1982.
11. Kabul Radio, 7 March 1982.
12. *The Times*, 8 April 1982.
13. *International Herald Tribune*, 20 May 1982.
14. Commander Allaladin, interview with author, 7 April 1986.
15. Olivier Roy, interview with author, 9 April 1986.
16. Tass report, 8 February 1982.
17. *The Guardian*, 3 February 1982.
18. Kabul Radio, 23 March 1982.
19. Kabul Radio, 2 March 1982.
20. *The Times*, 12 January 1982.
21. *International Herald tribune*, 24 February 1982.
22. Col. A. Sgibnev, 'We Are Internationalists', *Krasnaya Zvezda*, 23 February 1982.
23. Mironenko display seen by author in Moscow, June 1983.
24. See *ISA Newsletter*, Peshawar, April 1982.
25. Kabul Radio, 15 March 1982.
26. Nur Ahmad Nur, interviewed on Kabul Radio, 16 March 1982.
27. Yu. Gankovskiy (ed) *A History of Afghanistan* (Progress, 1985).
28. Kabul Radio, 6 April 1982.
29. Edward Girardet, *Afghanistan: The Soviet War* (Croom Helm, 1985).
30. Nigel Ryan, *A Hitch or Two in Afghanistan* (Weidenfeld & Nicolson, 1983).
31. Girardet, op. cit.
32. *The Times*, 30 April 1982.
33. Far Eastern Economic Review, 2 July 1982.

34. Nigel Ryan, who arrived in Panjsher shortly after the 5th offensive and witnessed the 6th, interviewed by author, May 1983.
35. Girardet, op. cit.
36. Nigel Ryan, interview with author, May 1983.
37. Ibid.
38. Girardet, op. cit.
39. Kabul Radio, 16 June 1982.
40. Kabul Radio, 14 June 1982.
41. This letter was written by a Soviet soldier known only as Shura. It was taken from his corpse and given to Sandy Gall who was in the Panjsher with Nigel Ryan. It is dated 15 July 1982.
42. Kabul Radio, 2 August 1982.
43. Brig. Mohammed Ayub Asmani, defecting officer of the 7th Division interviewed in *AIC Bulletin*, January 1983.
44. IISS, *The Military Balance 1981-2 and 1983-4* (London 1981 and 1983).
45. Kabul Radio, 6 June 1982.
46. Mohammed Es-Haq, *Jamiat Newsletter*, Peshawar, June 1982.
47. Kabul Radio, 10 July 1982.
48. Brig. Mohammed Brahim, defecting defence ministry official, interviewed in *AIC Bulletin*, December 1983.
49. Isby, op. cit.
50. Nigel Ryan, interview with author, May 1983.
51. Ibid.
52. Girardet, op. cit.
53. For a grim catalogue of alleged Soviet atrocities, see Helsinki Watch, '*Tears, Blood and Cries*': *Human Rights in Afghanistan Since the Invasion, 1979-1984*, New York, 1984).
54. Private Igor Rykov, Soviet prisoner interviewed, *RFE-RL Background Report 220/84*, 1 June 1984.
55. Anonymous Estonian soldier, interviewed in *samizdat* journal, reproduced in *Eesti Paevaleht*, 29 March 1985.
56. Dr Frances D'Souza, report on situation in rural Afghanistan, for Afghanaid of London.
57. Private G. Dzamalbekov, Soviet prisoner interviewed, Radio Free Europe-Radio Liberty, *Background Report RL 270/84*, 12 July 1984. According to this man the commander and senior officers of an air assault regiment were court-martialled for a revenge attack on a village in Balkh in 1983.
58. Kabul Radio, 10 July 1982.
59. Kabul Radio, 12 and 20 November 1982.
60. Kabul Radio, 1 December 1982.
61. Vladimir Kuzichkin, interviewed in *Time* magazine, 22 November 1982.
62. *AIC Bulletin*, no. 7, November 1981.
63. *Afghan Realities*, no. 6, July 1982.
64. *AIC Bulletin*, December 1982.
65. A. Arnold, '*The Stony Path to Afghan Socialism*' (Orbis, 1985).
66. Olivier Roy, interview with author, 9 April 1986.

Six: 1983

OPERATIONS IN THE NORTH AND EAST

The year began badly for government troops in the beleaguered mountain garrison of Khost. Since the early days of the war, this outpost, which is closer to guerrilla bases across the Pakistani border than it is to any Afghan army garrison, had been difficult to re-supply. It depended on one road, which was often raked by enemy fire. It had an airfield which was frequently under fire and when helicopters could not land supplies had to be parachuted in. The permanent garrison there consisted of the 25th Division and the 2nd Border Brigade. Both were under-strength and by 1983 totalled about 2500 men, with around 1500 in Khost itself and others in outlying posts. There were very few Soviets there – perhaps two dozen advisers.

By late 1982, *mujahadeen* strength in the areas bordering Pakistan was growing quickly. Because of their proximity to their supply bases, the guerrillas who operated there were usually well armed. During 1983 operations built up to the point that the survival of some of the border garrisons was in doubt.

The year began very badly for the 25th Division. An outlying post, belonging to the 59th Brigade in Nadershah Kot, fell to the enemy, and 130 government troops were either killed or surrendered in this action.[1] When the base came under attack a party of soldiers rebelled and killed their officers. This gave rise to press reports that the 25th Division had 'mutinied'.[2] In fact, although the fall of the support base was probably due to the rebellion of around 30 men, there is no evidence of a general uprising in the division at this time. Nevertheless, the loss of the base was a serious blow because it allowed the *mujahadeen* to move closer to the city itself.

In the north the Afghan army was, apparently, able to emerge from a difficult situation with some kudos. On 2 January, guerrillas kidnapped 15 Soviet technicians in Mazar-e-Shariff. The men were involved in the construction of a large bakery. They were civilian targets picked at random. The guerrillas produced a statement, signed by the hostages, which called for negotiations.[3] This event touched off large-scale operations by the 18th and 20th

Divisions. The 20th Division operated in Baghlan and Takhar provinces.[4] The 18th Division conducted sweeps around Balkh province.

There were rumours that the Soviets had taken counter-hostages from local opposition leaders.[5] Early in February it appears that the Afghan troops stumbled on the hostages and their captors, and a battle ensued; a number of guerrillas were killed. According to accounts of these events circulating in the Kabul diplomatic circuit, the hostages were freed,[6] but the government would not confirm the rumours.

Nevertheless, a few days after these events, the Kabul media gave great prominence to celebrations in Mazar-e-Shariff on the return of elements of the 18th Division. On 10 February, it was announced, 'a grand rally was held...by thousands of people...to mark the courage and heroism of the security forces of Balkh province in crushing elements treacherous to the homeland and revolution'. The report claimed that 118 'counter-revolutionary elements along with their leaders were crushed'.[7]

Adding to the mood of optimism, the government announced a large increase in armed forces strength during the period March 1982–83. The Defence Ministry claimed a rise of 79 per cent in manpower. The figure does tie in with the modest increases that were being noted by Western analysts at the time.

THE SITUATION IN KABUL

There was evidence of more effective security in the capital. The Kabul Security Command with its Sarandoy and Revolution Defence Group forces had established a ring of posts around the city. Vehicle checkpoints and identity screening were more frequent. All of this forced the *mujahadeen* to adopt different tactics.

Selective assassination was used against key government supporters. The 'holy fighters' also took to planting bombs in public places. In February, there was an attempt to mark the third anniversary of the anti-Soviet demonstrations in Kabul with a series of bombings. In fact most of the bombs were discovered and defused.[8]

On 18 February the Takia mosque in the city was burnt down – according to the government, by an incendiary bomb directed at a pro-regime mullah. The incident at the mosque, the bombings and assassinations allowed the government to launch a new campaign of vilification against the *mujahadeen*. The Soviet press claimed that they had destroyed 1800 schools and 100 hospitals.[9] Guerrilla leaders have admitted that they regard schools where official ideology is taught, and the teachers who spread it, as 'legitimate targets'.[10]

Denied the possibility of large-scale operations within the city, the *mujahadeen* attacked certain favourite targets around it: the Soviet embassy complex at Darulaman; 8th Division headquarters at Kargha; government offices in Paghman; and the hydro-electric plant at Sarobi. Abdol Haq the IP (Khalis) commander regarded the destruction of power installations as a particular objective. Early in March his men blew up power lines near Sarobi again.

THE PANJSHER CEASE-FIRE

The pattern of operations by the Limited Contingent of Soviet Forces in Afghanistan had, since 1980, been dictated by the need to secure certain key roads – in particular, Highway 2 from the Soviet border across the Salang pass to Kabul. The aim of preventing attacks on this road had triggered six offensives against the Panjsher, and now it prompted a remarkable cease-fire.

Many theories have been advanced to explain the peace treaty between Massud and the Soviets negotiated in January 1983. For the Soviets, the security of the road was paramount – the cessation of attacks on it from the Panjsher was one of the most important conditions of the deal.[11] But it might also serve as a model to show how cooperation with the authorities could benefit the local population.

For Massud's part the principal motivation was the need to re-build his infrastructure in the valley. Although the bulk of his armed elements had survived Panjsher 5 and 6, the civilian population had suffered badly. Depopulation and the loss of crops had serious implications; it became very difficult for Massud to support his cadre of full time fighters. By the end of 1982 his position had become quite desperate. He had been forced to appeal for food, and ISA sources justified the cease-fire by the need to 'get out from the prevailing miserable conditions'.[12]

The agreement caused bitter controversy within the resistance. Members of Gulbuddin Hekmatyar's party called it a sell-out and lampooned Massud as the 'King of the Panjsher'. ISA political chief Mohammed Es-haq said that one of the aims of the cease-fire was to 'deceive the *mujahadeen*, and create division and suspicion among them and defame the most capable front and its leadership'.[13] That Massud was prepared to weather the criticism, and that he must have known that the deal would free the Soviets to attack other areas, are signs of how much he needed the respite.

In return for the promise of no attacks from the Panjsher the Soviets withdrew the bulk of their forces from the valley; they left a battalion behind at Anawa. They also agreed to stop bombing the area.[14]

Massud used the cease-fire to improve the training of his men and to rebuild his organisation in the valley. There is evidence that some of his forces were dispatched to other areas. Massud may well have sent some men further south to the Shomali area where they were still in a position to attack the road to Kabul.

There were reports that ISA, IP, and IRM forces were operating jointly out of the Guldara valley in Shomali.[15] On 1 April they launched a major attack on the road to Kabul, causing much destruction.

With a Panjsher cease-fire, the Soviet 108th Motor Rifle Division and Afghan Central Corps were freed for operations against the Shomali, and other enemy bases close to the capital.

SOVIET TACTICAL INNOVATIONS

Through 1978–83 much of the fighting had been directed at the roads. It was the danger posed to these arteries of communication that had triggered successive Soviet strikes into the Panjsher, Shomali, Marmoul and Logar. Although these raids undoubtedly eased the pressure they usually provided only temporary respite from the *mujahadeen*'s ambushes and mines. The Soviet army adopted a number of tactical procedures to try and keep the roads open.

Around major bases and at key junctions, Soviet troops were deployed in bunkers in a static defence role. Generally though, such posts, which could be overrun, were regarded as a drain on manpower; and the task of manning them was left to Afghan troops. Even so the number of men required would have been too great to secure all major routes. The distance along the highway from the Soviet border to Kabul is 425 km; from Herat to Kandahar 600 km; and from Kabul to the Khyber pass 250 km. It was clearly impossible for these major routes, let alone dozens of minor ones, to be secured completely by guard posts.

Mines had claimed many victims; one Soviet correspondent stated, 'there are more bandits' mines than stones'.[16] To cope with this threat, converted T-55 tanks with their turrets removed and anti-mine rollers fitted preceded major convoys.[17] During ambushes in narrow ravines Soviet troops found that their vehicles' weapons could not elevate sufficiently to return guerrilla fire. The 14.5mm machine gun fitted to the BTR-60 PB personnel carrier (the standard vehicle during the first years of the war) could only elevate 30°. The 73mm gun of the BMP (infantry fighting vehicle) was little better having only 33° elevation.

The Limited Contingent received priority deliveries of the new BMP-2. This vehicle had a rapid firing 30mm cannon with 50° elevation. An improvised solution that gained popularity with the troops was the mounting of twin 23mm anti-aircraft guns on the back of trucks. This installation had the great advantages that it could keep up with the other trucks, lay heavy, accurate fire and had very high elevation.

Convoy protection became a great deal more professional and coordinated. Helicopters often accompanied convoys, offering a rapid response to enemy fire. But the *mujahadeen* continued to take a heavy toll on the roads. In 1983 the Soviets donated a further 1500 KAMAZ trucks to the Afghans.[18]

The helicopter provided the answer to many of the Soviet army's tactical transport requirements. By 1983 the number of Mil-8s based in the country was around 150, and Mil-6s around 40.[19] These could be supplemented during operations by others flying from the Turkestan Military District. The growing reliance on helicopters did impose some operational restrictions: the Mil's engine performance in very hot climates and at high altitude is markedly less efficient than under ideal sea-level conditions. This limitation in 'hot and high' performance inhibited operations in some areas during summer. Helicopters also faced icing problems at altitude during the bitterly cold winter. From the tactical mobility point of view this meant that the best time to start a major operation was the spring or autumn.

Whereas the armoured Mil-24s remained difficult to shoot down, the Mil-8s offered softer targets. During the first three years in Afghanistan the Soviets probably lost a few dozen helicopters to ground fire and technical failure. The increased use of infra-red flares (designed to decoy the heat-seeking SA-7 missiles) by Soviet aircraft over Afghanistan in 1983 showed real concern. Yet resistance parties still claimed not to have such weapons.

The VVS (Vozduyushno Voorezhenie Sil or Air Force) continued to base aircraft in Afghanistan on rotation from bases in the Turkestan district. The main parent units were the 27th Fighter Aviation Regiment at Kaka, and the 217th Fighter Bomber Regiment from Kizyl Arvat.[20] This rotation allowed the bulk of support and maintainance to be done in the USSR. These and other Soviet-based units were available for additional missions when required.

During 1983 the VVS made a number of changes in its operations over Afghanistan. Several new types of bomb were deployed following the disappointing results of airstrikes over the Panjsher and other areas. Retard bombs (having a small parachute to slow them down) were introduced for low-level raids. Previously many bombs had failed to arm when dropped at low altitudes (a problem also experienced by Argentine bombers in the Falklands), providing the *mujahadeen* with large quantities of 'free' explosive. In 1983 in the Kunar, the VVS introduced cluster bombs designated RBK–250.[21] Each RBK–250 carries 60 bomblets each one of which is as effective as an 81mm mortar round. The lethal area of one of these bombs is estimated at 200 000 square feet.

There were also experiments in bombing from higher altitudes. Soviet-based planes apparently carried out such raids during actions in Herat in April. During these battles it was reported by normally pro-*mujahadeen* sources that 160 Soviet/Kabul troops and 172 guerrillas had been killed.[22]

PEACE TALKS IN GENEVA

On 11 April, Diego Cordovez's UN peace talks started in Geneva. The aim was to get agreement on the withdrawal of Soviet troops, the repatriation of Afghan refugees, and the resumption of relations between the DRA and Pakistan. The USSR, USA and China were to guarantee any agreement.[23]

After two weeks of talking the delegates left Geneva – without an agreement. They returned in June, but once again they failed to agree. The root of the problem was that all sides (including, one suspects, the Pakistanis) doubted anybody's ability to put a complete stop to *mujahadeen* operations. Resistance leaders let it be known that they would ignore any treaty. Professor Sayaf stated in November 1983, 'any solution that doesn't reflect the will of the *mujahadeen*, that hasn't come from the battleground, has no validity'.[24]

This unpleasant fact influenced the negotiating policies of both sides. The Soviets wanted a phased withdrawal, with the right to suspend the treaty if *mujahadeen* continued to operate across the border. The Pakistanis, precisely because of their limited control over the resistance groups, wanted a rapid Soviet pull-out, to be completed within three months.

GUNS, MONEY AND THE *MUJAHADEEN*

Under President Reagan, the supply of arms to the *mujahadeen* was stepped up. An American newspaper, early in 1983 estimated that aid to the rebels amounted to $30–50 million a year during 1980–83.[25] It also said that the CIA had been supplying SA–7s and other Soviet-made heavy weapons in great quantities since December 1982. Other CIA funds were used to buy Chinese weapons. The usual route for the arms was by ship to the Pakistani port of Karachi and then by lorry to the refugee areas.

The conduit for much of this support was apparently Professor Sayaf's Islamic Unity for Afghan Liberation (IUAL).[26]The IUAL was the product of another attempt at a resistance federation in May 1983. Sayaf used the guns and money to buy himself influence among the Pushtun tribes of the borderlands. In particular it is said that he gave a great deal of hardware to Jallaladin Haqqani, to woo him away from his own IP (Khalis) faction. The other favoured recipients of the US largesse were Sayed Gailani's NIFA. They had established publicity offices in several Western capitals and were regarded somewhat scornfully by the fundamentalist groups as experts in public relations and little else.[27]

Many guerrilla leaders appreciated that the new weapons had to be accompanied by better training. Ahmad Shah Massud used the year to improve the training of his men. Better training facilities were also being established within the camps in mid-1983.[28] Training was confined to a small number and the instructors often had only a rudimentary grasp of modern weaponry.

Supplies by the Chinese continued, going largely to the fundamentalist IP factions and ISA. Their deliveries included 12.7mm Type–54 machine guns (copies of the Soviet Dshk), 14.5mm Type–58 single and twin anti-aircraft machine guns (called Zigouaks by the *mujahadeen*), and some 23mm twin anti-aircraft guns. The equipment was robust, could be broken into man-pack loads, and was identical to that used to such effect by the Viet Cong. Other Chinese deliveries included 82mm mortars, 82mm recoilless rifles and innumerable different types of mine.

Guns, either provided by foreign supporters or captured in battle fuelled the 'alternative economy' of the *mujahadeen*. Weapons would be taken from surrendering government troops, sold in the arms bazaars of the North-West Frontier Province, and then re-purchased by guerrilla parties using money donated by foreign governments. The profit margins of the suppliers, the bazaaris and the middlemen provide a clue as to why the large sums provided by the CIA have not been translated into as much firepower as might have been expected. The big profits to be made in this trade also resulted in a preference among some *mujahadeen* groups for attacking isolated Afghan government posts. These offered the best bargain from the point of view of the low risks involved and the potential booty to be gained. This is why the *mujahadeen* were able to find large forces to besiege Khost and another border garrison, Urgun, during 1983.

Within Afghanistan, the resistance had discovered other methods of making money. The payment of cash to *mujahadeen* by villages and travellers on the roads had become the norm. This could be seen as a patriotic levy or simple protection money. But with several parties active in most areas the peasantry were often having to pay off different commanders. At the senior level, *mujahadeen* leaders were aware of the resentment this caused; one said, 'I went to many villages and talked with the population and I saw in many places that the civilians had suffered a lot under the tyranny of some bad commanders'.[29] He criticised 'all those smugglers, forgers and thieves who, disguised as *mujahadeen*, were only fighting for the booty and looting the civilians'.

But in many areas the money-making enterprises were endorsed by the guerrilla front leaders. *Mujahadeen* operating in the north were hijacking convoys and then re-selling the goods to bazaaris in Kabul at a large profit.[30]

The increase in the supply of arms in 1983 may have exacerbated rather than mollified inter-group tensions. Attempts by one group to interfere with other's arms caravans led to a number of pitched battles between different groups. In the Tagao valley (near Kabul, astride the supply route to the north), men of Gulbuddin Hekmatyar's IP were reportedly seizing other parties' arms. The resultant fighting led to many civilians leaving their homes.[31] In May, a Western journalist reported that 20 *mujahadeen* were killed during clashes between Hekmatyar and Sayaf (IUAL) forces in the Maidan valley.[32]

A more alarming confrontation took place near the end of the year when IP and IUAL fighters were involved in heavy fighting near Ghazni. According to Qari Taj Mohammed, the autonomous local commander, 'in a war between Professor Sayaf and Engineer Hekmatyar groups which lasted 2 months and seventeen days, some 487 men have been killed from both sides. Now Sayaf is entirely wiped out from this area.'[33]

By mid-1983 there was evidence of a new factional contest in the Hazara Jat. Just as Nasr had challenged Shura, so a new group, the Pasdaran (also called Sepah-e-Pasdara, Islamic Revolutionary Party), claimed a growing following. Tehran had apparently lost faith in the Nasr leadership and was backing the Pasdaran (affiliated to the Iranian Islamic Revolutionary Guards Corps) as the authentic Khomeinite front.[34] Nasr retained the right to independence in theological matters. The Revolutionary Guards on the other hand were completely loyal to the Iranian spiritual authorities. Their programme involved the incorporation of the Hazara Jat into a greater Iran. As with the succession of Nasr over Shura, the new contest cost many lives in inter-factional fighting.

THE *MUJAHADEEN* ON THE OFFENSIVE

By the summer of 1983 the *mujahadeen* were pulling the noose tighter around Khost. Forces were being concentrated, there was excitement and talk of a great victory coming. In June, the Afghan army sent Colonel Faruq's 38th Commando Brigade to try to force its way through the blockade, but it failed.[35]

Urgun was a smaller target than Khost. Its garrison consisted of the 15th Brigade. This brigade under Colonel Sayed Rahman consisted, in mid-1983 of about 900 men.[36] About 600 of these were

in Urgun itself and the remainder in outlying posts.[37] The number
of Soviet advisers in the camp was small – it has been estimated at
five. The 15th Brigade had a battery (six) of D–30 122mm gun-
howitzers, five T–55 tanks and several armoured personnel
carriers. The main force of the brigade was billeted at the
polytechnic campus. It was supplemented by a Revolution
Defence Group which apparently included a few dozen local
women.

From July 1983, the *mujahadeen* began to concentrate around the
town. They came from several parties: principally IUAL, IP
(Khalis) and NIFA. The IP Forces were under Jallaladin Haqqani
and had apparently been wooed by Sayaf's inducements, as had a
number of bands of 'freelance' Pushtun tribesmen who also arrived
on the scene.[38]

From the start it was apparent that the forces deployed at Urgun
(and to a degree those at Khost) represented better armed groups
than had been seen previously in the borderlands. Weapons
poured across from Pakistan in what looked a firepower display by
Sayaf and his allies. They could not plead a lack of anti-aircraft
defence: at Urgun alone they concentrated seventy 12.7mm
machine guns, and fifteen 14.5mm Zigouaks.[39] Several BTR–60
personnel carriers were even deployed by Sayaf, and some
captured artillery pieces. Urgun was shaping up as a major fight
between Afghans.

While the concentration of *mujahadeen* from several different
Parties at Urgun was an achievement, there was still evidence of
considerable disunity. In autumn 1983, two tank crews defected
from the garrison, bringing their T–55s with them. Though the
arrival of the armour could have been a boon it actually provoked
an enormous row.

The two tanks were driven to NIFA positions by the crews. The
IP (Khalis) commanders on the scene insisted that the tanks were
theirs. The issue was argued at endless *jergas* between the
commanders. In the end a farcical Afghan compromise was
reached: NIFA got the tanks' front halves, and the Khalis men the
back halves.[40] As a result of this Solomon-like solution neither tank
was used in battle.

In Kabul, the resistance needed to launch a major attack in
order to prove that they could still penetrate the city's defences.
This came on the night of 13–14 August when *mujahadeen* staged an
attack with RPGs and mortars on Balar Hissar fort, home to

various Soviet support units. The fighting continued throughout
the night.

Two weeks later, in Balkh province Commander Zabiullah's
men launched a major attack. They reportedly destroyed some
planes and an ammunition store. With the Panjsher cease-fire in
effect, he received help from Massud's men and a larger share of
incoming arms shipments. Zabiullah's forces had grown to around
6000 by 1983 and their armaments had improved too. Zabiullah's
ISA front had secured several shipments of Chinese weapons. The
Marmoul Gorge was guarded from air attack by four 12.7mm and
several 14.5mm heavy machine guns. His soldiers carried Chinese
produced RPGs (designated Type-69) and copies of the Czech ZB
26/30 'Bren' gun. One witness also saw several ex-Iranian G–3
rifles being used by Zabiullah's men.[41]

KABUL STRIKES BACK

With the situation in the border areas of Paktia and Paktika
becoming critical the Soviet/Afghan command decided to launch
an operation to interdict the guerrilla entry routes. A mobile force
was assembled by the Central Corps, its main elements being a
brigade and artillery unit of the 8th Division as well as the 37th
Commando Brigade. Although supported by Soviet aircraft and
some troops, this appears to have been largely an Afghan effort.

They were sent into Paktia and went into battle on the 13 August
at Khak-e-Jabar where they 'mounted a strong surprise shelling
and bombing strike on positions of the bandits in the gorge area
and went into the attack immediately after the artillery raid'.[42]
The 37th Commando Brigade under Colonel Shahnawaz Tani
acquitted itself particularly well.

Two weeks later Colonel Shahnawaz Tani's brigade was flown
into Khost by helicopter.[43] The situation there had become
desperate. The guerrillas were claiming to have a force of 10 000
men and that the city was 'about to fall'.[44] It is unlikely that
mujahadeen forces at Khost ever exceeded half of this figure, but
even at that they outnumbered the Afghan garrison.

Throughout September there was heavy fighting around Khost,
with the 37th Commando Brigade bearing the brunt. Men of the
25th Division had hitherto proved reluctant to leave their mine-
protected emplacements. The *mujahadeen* pulled back and by
October the pressure on the city had lessened sufficiently for the

37th Commando Brigade to be airlifted back to Kabul.[45] With their departure guerrilla attacks were stepped up again. On 27 October, 22 government soldiers were reported killed in an attempt to capture the helipad. This brought retaliation in the form of airstrikes from Shindand.

While Afghan troops were now clearly bearing the brunt in some provinces, the Soviet army did carry out a number of operations at the battalion and regimental level. In contrast to 1982, though, there was no LCSFA divisional offensive during 1983. Soviet operations that summer were in the Logar, Shomali and around Herat.

During a battalion raid near Kandahar on 2 July, a Soviet column was successfully ambushed. Two Soviet prisoners, Privates Khlaime Lefzhevulevich and Igor Chedikov, were taken.[46] Both men were part of the 70th Motor Rifle Brigade stationed in that city, and they joined a growing number of Soviet soldiers (estimated at the time around two dozen) held in captivity. The testimony of these prisoners revealed important limitations in the Soviet army, and dramatised the miserable service conditions of Soviet conscripts.

PROBLEMS IN SOVIET RANKS

Problems among soldiers and junior NCOs (who in the Soviet military are also conscripts) were serious for an army seeking to win victories by small-unit operations. The need for improved small-unit tactics was stressed again in *Krasnaya Zvezda* in September 1982.[47]

Within Soviet units there was rigid pecking-order among conscripts. 'Old soldiers' who have served more than a year (of a two-year service period) reserved the right to take the best food and to tyrannise newly arrived men. According to Private Vladislav Naumov, 'the question of relations among soldiers between the so-called "old men" and the young ones is the principal scourge as far as the Limited Contingent is concerned'.[48]

An NCO's stripes are no protection against the old men, according to Sergeant Alexei Presleni, a 122mm gun crew leader from the 180th Motor Rifle Regiment. Bullying by 'old soldiers' (most of them privates) was one of the principal reasons for desertion.[49] The weakness of NCO's authority represents a critical problem in an army fighting counter-insurgency operations.

National tensions between ethnic groups are another problem. Official Soviet sources have noted the problem of recruits from one particular area sticking together, and fighting with men from a different area.[50] The existence of grass-roots prejudices is revealed by a soldier who served in the DRA and returned to his native Estonia: 'a Leningrader was much more sensible than a Central Russian. Of course there were Asians, their education is known...a Kazakh hated me especially. And not only me. He cursed me and the Lithuanian I mentioned before – idiots.'[51] Soviet military journals have conceded that national rivalries pose training problems in the Turkestan Military District.[52]

Conditions that were made tough by enemy action and old soldiers' beatings were made even worse by the persistent problem of sickness. Vladislav Naumov describes the situation in the 66th Motor Rifle Brigade in Jallalabad in July 1983: 'The thermometer crept over 60°...we quickly became weak and dried out in the heat. At the time the sick bays were not in a position to accept people with heat stroke. I know of nine cases that proved fatal.'[53] Among the most common diseases are heat stoke, dysentery, typhoid, hepatitis and pneumonia. Sgt Peresleni estimated that half the men in his battery were laid out sick at any given time.[54] Letters from parents in the USSR (taken by the *mujahadeen*) often express concern about poor food and illness.[55]

With these difficult conditions come tales of alcohol and drug abuse:'for the most part they smoke hashish and cocaine. There are also thoses who inject. There are not many of them of course but there are some. The soldiers get hold of drugs by means of sale and exchange. They sell literally everything possible; fat, butter, canned goods, soap, hardware, and arms and ammunition.'[56] The need to get better food and drink leads many Soviet soldiers to looting. According to one:'Along the roads we levied "tolls" for passage. Sometimes there was even robbery. But people took it matter of factly and often gave without threats.'[57]

These problems of bullying, racism, alcohol/drug taking and theft undoubtedly undermine efficiency, and cause further resentment among the Afghans. To be sure though, the Soviet soldiers' desire to buy better food, and occasionally drugs, from the locals must have spawned the emergence of a class of Afghan 'entrepreneurs' who rely on the LCSFA for a living.

More importantly it is vital to remember that these reports have come from men who were so unhappy that they deserted or who have been captured. Either way their survival in guerrilla hands is unsure and may, in their view, depend on them producing suitably damaging revelations about the Soviet army.

The views expressed in the Soviet media and in letters home from Afghanistan are quite different. From these, a story of patriotism and friendships formed in battle emerges. A book of poems written by Soviet Private Vladimir Dodukalov contains a verse entitled 'Faith in the Commander' which ends: 'We were led by our commander and we followed him all the way. It was tough going but we know where he is there is victory. We just have faith in our commander.'[58] Dodukalov's notebook, a rare example of a Soviet soldier's feelings not intended for public consumption, contains themes that are familiar to readers of poetry from other conflicts – of deep ties formed in battle, hatred of the enemy but also of anger with the Soviet 'brass'. From the Russian acronym for the Turkestan Military District (TURKVO), Dodukalov spelt 'Only the dead are allowed by the brass to go back home again'.

SOVIET TRAINING IMPROVED

The Soviet army had not been in Afghanistan for very long before it was realised that conventional training procedures were proving inadequate. Normally Soviet army recruits receive only three weeks of basic training. They are then posted to their units where they get further specialist training. With two call-ups per annum, and soldiers serving for two years, this means that an experienced quarter of the unit is lost and an inexperienced one gained, every six months. Conscripts selected for NCO training go to a training division for six months before arriving at their units with stripes. In normal Soviet military practice it is only NCOs and certain specialist grades who receive any training beyond their three-week induction course before arriving in an operational unit.

Following the replacement of the reservists who filled the ranks of the Soviet units when they first arrived in Afghanistan, this standard procedure was applied. This meant that most Soviet privates were arriving in this hostile environment with only three weeks of basic training. The need to train these men markedly undermined the operational capabilities of LCSFA divisions. Units put together for large operations usually consisted of the most experienced men. In the case of the divisional task force used in Panjsher 5, this meant that regiments were drawn from three different divisions.

For no reason other than historical inertia, it appears that the Soviet army took no major steps to improve this situation until mid-1982. From then on a growing number of men bound for the DRA received training prior to being sent there. The need for this service led to an expansion of facilities in the Turkestan Military District.

The major centre (and home of the 280th Training Division) was established near Ashkabad.[59] Preparing recruits was also entrusted to a Termez-based division (probably the 54th which was withdrawn from the DRA in mid-1980). Another division (the 346th) which had been used in the initial operation was located in Kushka. While the 54th and 346th Divisions have occasionally provided troops for operation inside Afghanistan, the Ashkabad-based formation is a purely training outfit.

Drivers and gunners received 5–6 months of 'pre-Afghanistan' training, as did infantrymen. Exercises were carried out on firing ranges with mock villages. A Soviet private describes the training given in Termez: 'We built models of Afghan villages...under the cover of the infantry's combat vehicles we would raze the village to the ground...We had training during the nights also. Without a sound we would capture house after house, fortress after fortress, we had bayonets and silencers attached to our rifles, and we learned to use them pretty skilfully.' He added, 'at Termez they did not hide from us that we were being trained for Afghanistan'.[60]

There were other training centres in the Turkestan district. For example, one bomb-disposal engineer says he was instructed at Chardzou. There were also cases of soldiers being trained in other military districts, but comparatively few. Clearly the Turkestan region is ideal from the point of view of acclimatisation, and by 1983 a high percentage of the men going to Afghanistan were training there.

The growing role of the Turkestan Military District for training, and as an operating base – particularly for the air force – meant that its commander, Army General Yuri Maksimov, gained much greater importance. He was promoted from colonel-general and awarded the Hero of the Soviet Union in 1982. While officers of Maksimov's stature routinely receive this medal on their 60th birthday, Maksimov got his when he was 58 – a sign of favour.

Although many *mujahadeen* parties claimed to have launched

operations against targets inside the USSR, it is evident that the forces based in Turkestan could operate with relative impunity. Late in 1983, IP (Hekmatyar) forces reportedly attacked the airfield at Pyandzh, just inside the USSR, with RPGs and mortars.[61] But in general such attacks were very risky and, it appears, only undertaken rarely.

FURTHER ATTACKS ON THE SHOMALI

Early in November, the Shomali area came in for more attention from the Soviet army. Attacks by the guerrilla front had continued on Highway 2 – the main road south to Kabul – and retribution came in the form of a heavy bombing raid on 8–9 November. This attack was reported to have cost the lives of around 80 *mujahadeen*.

It was believed that local *mujahadeen* leaders met in the valley on 10 November to plan an attack on Bagram airfield. Perhaps acting on intelligence of this plan, the Soviets launched an attack. Their aim was to flush the resistance out of three valleys (the Istalef, Farza and Shakardara) which penetrate the massif to the west of Highway 2 (see Map X). These defiles were the best available cover for operations against Kabul and the highway north.

On 26 November, elements of the 180th Motor Rifle Regiment (which had also been involved in the year's previous operations in the area)[62] moved to cordon the bottom of the Istalef valley. On 27–28 November, there was bombing of the Istalef, Farza and Shakardara valleys.[63] The ground thrusts, of approximately one Soviet reinforced motor rifle battalion with Afghan support in each of the three valleys, followed. Soviet forces operated there until 6 December when they pulled back. This operation did represent one of a relatively small number of regiment-sized Soviet attacks of 1983.

THE SOVIET INFANTRY GET BETTER EQUIPMENT

In battles like the Shomali that November, fought in narrow populated valleys, the infantry were vulnerable to many forms of attack. New equipment was issued to protect them and allow them to shoot their way out of difficult situations. Flak jackets, designed to stop small arms rounds and shrapnel were issued.[64] Early designs

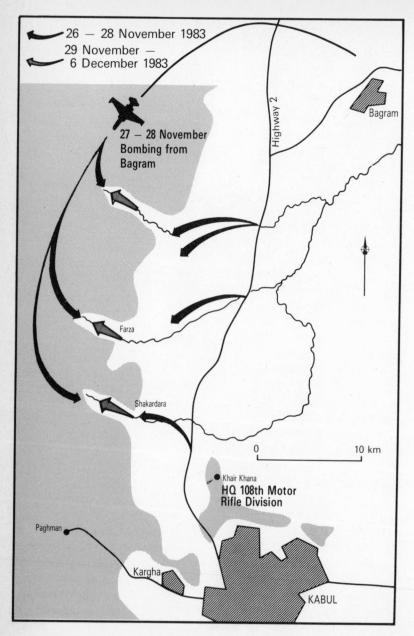

X Shomali Operation, November 1983.

were crudely made with metal plates (rather than advanced fibres as used in Western designs), but did afford better protection and showed concern about casualties. Their firepower was boosted substantially.

The new AK-74 rifle became standard issue. At first it had been carried only by elite troops. The 5.45mm round was much more effective than its 7.62mm predecessor. The round was designed to become unstable in substances denser than air; it tumbled when it hit the body. The horrific wounds proved fatal far more often than those caused by older rounds. The *mujahadeen* dubbed them 'poison bullets'.

The most common form of attack against Soviet soldiers was the ambush. The need to disable concealed snipers prompted a number of measures. Special anti-sniper squads were formed to pin-point their fire.[65] The AGS-17 Plamya (flame) 30mm automatic grenade-launcher found widespread use. Its rates of fire and 800-metre range allowed troops to escape difficult situations by laying a blanket of suppressive fire.

The BG-15 single-shot 40mm grenade-launcher, attached under the barrel of the AK-74, allowed a single infantryman to fire a grenade several hundred metres. RPG-18 rockets were also designed for use by one man. Their design is a copy of the US M-72 LAW, a disposable anti-tank weapon.

The BG-15 and RPG-18 were followed by the RPO and RPO-A (the latter being a lighter version for air assault troops) flamethrowers. This weapon, which looks like a bazooka, fires a round to 200 metres (1000 metres in the case of the RPO-A).[66] When it strikes the target the round explodes into a fireball. It is used against buildings, people and to start fires. With these new weapons even platoons found themselves with extremely good suppressive fire systems – in effect their own artillery.

SOVIET/KABUL OBJECTIVES IN 1983

Whereas 1982 saw two major Soviet offensives in the Panjsher, and one near Herat, 1983 did not witness any such action at the divisional level. Units within the country did conduct a number of operations and the air force was particularly active, but these were carried out at a low level (battalion and regiment). Having secured a truce in the Panjsher, the question arises as to why the Soviets did not launch divisional attacks in the Logar, the Marmoul or some other area.

The simple, logical answer is perhaps that the Soviet command did not consider such attacks necessary in order to continue their mission. Once more, the evidence is that this mission was the limited one of holding key points and maintaining the channels of communication between them. Another lesson to be drawn from 1983 was the critical importance of Massud and the Panjsher to the resistance movement over-all. Quite simply, no other region was worthy of Soviet attentions on the same scale.

The other fascinating development of the year was the growing role of the Afghan army. It is quite possible that the smaller scale of Soviet operations and the use in several areas of mainly Afghan forces for operations was a deliberate strategy to bolster Babrak Karmal's forces in the eyes of the people. In the north in January/February, and Paktia in August, Afghan brigade groups (probably amounting to 1500–2000 men each) were deployed for battle with mixed results. Their performance was often unimpressive and many members of the units concerned took the opportunity to desert. But Afghan army performance in 1983 does present a marked improvement over previous years. Judged against the nadir of September 1979–December 1980, when entire brigades sent to fight would melt into the mountains, their record was an achievement.

The *mujahadeen* gained in strength during the year. They were receiving greater amounts of heavy weaponry from their allies, and better field cooperation was allowing them to deploy quite large forces against Khost and Urgun. At the year's and, both towns remained beseiged. The struggle going on in Paktia was almost entirely between Afghans – no Soviet unit was even based in the province. In the New Year it intensified.

Notes

1. *Afghan Information Centre (AIC) Bulletin*, January 1983.
2. *Daily Telegraph*, 19 January 1983.
3. 'Life and Death on the Afghan Front', *Sunday Telegraph*, 9 June 1985.
4. Kabul Radio, 24 January 1983.
5. *The Guardian*, 3 February 1983.

6. *The Times*, 5 February 1983.
7. Kabul Radio, 10 February 1983.
8. British Chargé d'Affairs (Kabul), Situation Report, 15–21 February 1983.
9. *International Herald Tribune*, 7 March 1983.
10. Abdol Haq, IP (Khalis) Commander of Kabul, interviewed by the author, 11 March 1986.
11. *Kabul New Times*, 9 May 1984 gives an interesting government account of the Panjsher agreement.
12. Mohammed Es-Haq, ISA spokesman, 'Panjsher the Seventh Offensive', *Central Asian Survey Occasional Papers*, no. 1.
13. Ibid.
14. *New Scientist*, 30 June 1983.
15. *International Herald Tribune*, 14 April 1983.
16. *Komsomolaya Pravda*, 4 February 1983.
17. Erik Durschmeid, 'The View From Kabul', transmitted by BBC2 TV, May 1983.
18. Radio Moscow, 15 July 1983.
19. David Isby, 'Soviet Tactics in the War in Afghanistan', *Jane's Defence Review*, vol. 4, no. 7, 1983.
20. Ibid.
21. David Isby, 'SOF Counts Coups in Afghnistan', *Soldier of Fortune*, October 1984.
22. *Daily Telegraph*, 26 April 1983.
23. IISS, *Strategic Survey 1983–84* (London, 1984).
24. Professor Sayaf, interviewed in *Afghan Mujahid*, November 1983.
25. *New York Times*, 4 May 1983.
26. Peter Jouvenal, photographer interviewed by the author May 1985.
27. John Gunston, 'Afghans Plan USSR Terror Attacks', *Jane's Defence Weekly*, 31 March 1984.
28. David Isby, 'Harrassing the Bear', *Soldier of Fortune*, September 1984.
29. Abdol Haq, interviewed in *AIC Bulletin*, August 1984.
30. Commander Nasrat, ISA Balkh front, interviewed in *AIC Bulletin*, June 1983.
31. *AIC Bulletin* May 1983.
32. Bernd de Bruin, interviewed in *AIC Bulletin*, May 1983.
33. Qari Taj Mohammed, interviewed in *AIC Bulletin*, January 1984.
34. Edward Girardet, *Afghanistan: The Soviet War* (Croom Helm, 1985).
35. *The Guardian*, 8 June 1983.
36. Shyam Bahtia, 'Afghan Fighters Plot New Dien Bien Phu', *The Observer*, 14 August 1983.
37. Peter Jouvenal, photographer eyewitness to the siege of Urgun, interviewed by the author, May 1985.
38. Ibid.
39. David Isby, *Strategy and Tactics*, January/February 1985.
40. Jouvenal, see note 26.
41. Mike Winchester, 'Night Raiders on Russia's Border', *Soldier of Fortune*, September 1984.
42. Tass, 18 August 1983.
43. *AIC Bulletin*, November/December 1983.

44. NIFA spokesman, *Daily Telegraph*, 15 September 1983.
45. *AIC Bulletin*, November/December 1983.
46. Jim Coyne, 'SOF Interviews Russian POW's', *Soldier of Fortune*, February 1984.
47. Major V. Bogdanov, *Kraznaya Zvezda*, 9 September 1982.
48. Pte V. Naumov, interviewed in Radio Free Europe-Radio Liberty, *Background Paper RL 121-84*, 19 March 1984.
49. Sgt A. Peresleni, interviewed by the author, August 1984.
50. Lt V. Kovalev, *Krasnaya Zvezda*, 7 February 1986.
51. Anonymous Estonian soldier, interviewed in *samizdat* journal, reproduced in *Eesti Paevaleht*, 29 March 1985.
52. Col G. Ivanov, *Krasnaya Zvezda*, 14 February 1986.
53. Naumov, op. cit.
54. Peresleni, see note 49.
55. 'With Love From Moscow', *Sunday Telegraph*, 16 June 1985.
56. Naumov, op. cit.
57. Anonymous Estonian soldier, op. cit.
58. 'Life and Death on the Afghan Front', *Sunday Telegraph*,9 June 1985.
59. Pte S. Busov, interviewed in RFE-RL, *Background Paper RL 205-84*, 24 May 1984.
60. Naumov, op. cit.
61. Gunston, op. cit.
62. Pte S. Zhigalin, former soldier of 180th Motor Rifle Regiment, interviewed by the author, August 1984.
63. British Chargé d'Affairs (Kabul), Situation Report, 25-30 November 1983
64. Jouvenal, see note 37.
65. Isby, op. cit. note 19.
66. *Voyennye Znaniya*, no. 11, 1985.

Seven: 1984

CHANGES AT THE MINISTRY OF DEFENCE

Early in 1984 a number of changes were made at the Afghan Ministry of Defence. Major General Nazar Mohammed was appointed Chief of Staff. Nazar Mohammed's previous job had been Commander of the Air Force and Air Defence Forces. Also on 7 January, Brigadier Mohammed Nabi Azimi was appointed First Deputy Defence Minister. This post had been vacant for two years. Colonel Shahnawaz Tani, whose 37th Commando Brigade had performed well at Khost the previous year, was promoted to brigadier and made commander of the highly important Central Corps.[1]

All three men were reportedly Khalqis, and the appointments (in particular of Azimi and Mohammed) were regarded as undermining the influence of Defence Minister Abdol Qader. Throughout 1984 there were rumours in the Kabul diplomatic circuit that Qader was about to be dismissed.[2] That the newly promoted men were all Khalqis may or may not have a wider significance. The previous incumbents of these posts had also been from this faction, but it is quite possible that Karmal and the party leadership were using a Khalqi/Parcham rivalry between Qader and Mohammed to displace the minister.

The power of forces political chief, Brigadier Yasin Sadeqi, continued to grow. In April 1984 he was promoted to major-general. By 1984 he had succeeded in establishing party organisations in over half the army's units. The existence of PDPA cells in units encouraged good behaviour by previously fractious officers.

In mid-Janury there was a mysterious development with the departure for Moscow of Nur Ahmad Nur. A long-time close associate of Karmal's, he was assumed to be in some kind of disgrace. Nur stayed in the USSR for most of the year.

SIEGE ENDS AT URGUN

On 22 January, the Kabul government announced that the siege of

137

Urgun had ended. Soviet sources claimed that 600 *mujahadeen* had died there during the previous year. The collapse of this guerrilla operation did represent an achievement by the Afghan army. The figure of 600 casualties needs to be treated with caution, but an eyewitness has confirmed that *mujahadeen* losses there were unusually high.[3]

In the end, the 15th Brigade with about 600 men, and a further 150-200 militia had held off a force of about 2000 guerrillas (of whom only around a quarter were in close proximity to the town at all times).

The oft-used guerrilla excuse that enemy air power prevented victory is inapplicable. Air support for the garrison was minor by the standards of that which accompanied Soviet operations. The guerrillas had in any case deployed a considerable amount of anti-aircraft armament at Urgun. Unlike Khost the previous year, there was no major reinforcement of the garrison by helicopter.

The prolonged length of the siege and the onset of winter were undoubtedly important. Many of the tribesmen who had turned up in the expectation of a quick surrender and plenty of booty simply wandered off. The 15th Brigade's positions were surrounded by dense minefields which prevented the *mujahadeen* from storming them. They also stopped less enthusiastic elements in the garrison from deserting. But some credit must go to Colonel Rahman and his men for maintaining some sort of morale in a seemingly hopeless situation.

The *mujahadeen*'s failure to dominate highlighted certain basic faults in the resistance's structure. Urgun was very close to guerrilla supply dumps across the border and this allowed them to bring in considerable firepower. But politics and rivalries prevented the *mujahadeen* from employing the heavy weapons to any real effect. Had agreement been reached for the use of the armour and heavy guns it is still doubtful that they would have been enough to win the battle. Guerrilla knowledge of modern weapons remained pitiful. As a frequent companion and friend of the *mujahadeen* put it, 'you could give an Afghan a cigarette lighter and he wouldn't know how to use it'. Whereas other guerrilla movements around the world have learnt the value of specialisation, the idea of having dedicated anti-aircraft troops or sappers (to remove the mines around positions like Urgun) remained alien to the *mujahadeen*, with the exception of Ahmad Shah Massud.

TRIBES IN SERVICE OF THE PDPA

Since the earliest days of the war tribesmen of some areas had transferred their allegiances between government and resistance quite regularly on a cash basis. The bands open to such deals included ethnically heterogeneous 'freelance' groups as well as Pushtun ones. The PDPA's attempts to buy up this sort of support centred on the provinces bordering Pakistan: Paktia, Paktika, Nangrahar and Kunar. Other areas for tribal recruitment were around the capital and certain key roads. The tribal leaders of these areas received regular visits, often from cabinet ministers trying to woo them.

Early in 1984 the government enjoyed several successes in this campaign. In January they announced the formation of the 1st Tribal Regiment.[4] This unit was made up of Pushtun warriors from the Rud-e-Ahmadzai area of Paktia province. Another tribal group that made a deal with the PDPA was led by Hassan Khan Karokhel.

Karokhel's group lived in the Sarobi valley, near Kabul. They were taken on to protect the power station and pylons that had become one of the guerrillas' favourite targets. The danger of attacks on electricity-generating facilities was underlined on 14 January when *mujahadeen* hit the Pol-e-Charkhi power station. It appears that Karokhel and his men were successful in preventing attacks through January–August 1984.[5]

Another group to join the government's cause during this period was the one led by Joma Khan. He went over with 507 men in the Andarab valley.[6] This new tribal regiment was in a position to interdict Ahmad Shah Massud's contacts with the north and give some protection to the Salang road. But Massud also sufferred problems from groups that were still, nominally at least, loyal to resistance parties. Within the Panjsher he had problems with IP (Hekmatyar) groups such as the one led by Commander Niazi.

In the atmosphere of bitter inter-party rivalry it was often claimed that groups like Niazi's were operating under the instructions of the KHAD. Whether these rumours were true or not, it is just as likely that many groups decided that looting other guerrillas' supply trains was an infinitely preferable way of accumulating saleable booty than actually fighting the Soviet army. One commander who claimed to be on the resistance side but certainly was acting on Kabul's behalf was Esmatullah

Moslem. Moslem had been a NIFA commander in Kandahar and the south-east. Having deserted the government in 1979, he later deserted the resistance. Early in 1984, his men in southern Kandahar province started interdicting rebel supply columns.[7] A large-scale battle was fought between Moslem's band and *mujahadeen* from other groups. Moslem and many of his men (estimates range from 300 to 800) chose to enlist in the government militia. Having once turned poacher he was able to play gamekeeper to greater effect. Moslem's defection was the government's biggest *coup* in years of trying to improve security in Kandahar. The man who had once proclaimed himself resistance commander of the city was now its militia commander. In the following months his forces accounted for several hundred enemy casualties.

SOVIET MEDIA COVERAGE: A NEW BREED OF HEROES

Soviet media coverage of the duties of the Limited Contingent of Soviet Forces in Afghanistan (LCSFA) had developed in certain well-defined phases. From December 1979 to late 1980. Soviet papers, while printing some quite sobering accounts of *mujahadeen* strengths, portrayed the role of their troops purely in terms of peaceful construction. A typical story read: 'When the bandits destroyed a school in the village of Chaugani, Senior Lieutenant A. Zaitsev and a group of Soviet soldiers offered their help. The Soveit handicraftsmen made 100 tables and 130 benches.'[8]

This type of coverage clearly lacked credibility, even to the Soviet consumer. During 1981 and 1982 reporting developed and Soviet soldiers were shown to be dying heroically. Nevertheless, LCSFA units were almost invariably shown in a support role. In 1984 there was a significant increase in both the number of Afghan stories and the frankness of their content. Soviet newspapers began to tackle the issues that cause discomfort in any society, writing of young men crippled for life and of bereaved parents.

In February 1984, *Komsomolaya Pravda* published a remarkably frank account of a former conscript called Alexander Nemtsov.[9] Nemtsov returned from Afghanistan as a paraplegic, but met little sympathy or understanding from the local communist party bureaucracy. This official indifference to Nemtsov's suffering so annoyed his neighbours that they contacted the paper. The story triggered a huge response. *Komsomolaya Pravda* received 500 letters and printed several including one from the parents of a soldier who had been killed in the DRA. In a follow-up the following month they announced, 'those at fault have been severely punished'.[10]

Nemtsov's story was not an isolated one. In March, *Krasnaya Zvezda*, the Defence Ministry daily, published another. It concerned Senior Lieutenant Valery Radchikov. Radchikov, an Air Assault Forces officer, was trying to defuse a mine in the Panjsher valley when he set off another: 'He tried to lift himself off the ground on his elbows. His arms obeyed him. He saw the bones of his demolished legs sticking out of his trousers. Later he could not forget the eyes of the boys in his reconnaissance party.'[11] Radchikov's journey through the medical system was followed in painful detail: 'Valery was suffering from septic fever now. He had been transferred to still another hospital for still another operation. He had several blood transfusions. More of his infected limbs had to be removed.'

Radchikov's rehabilitation was portrayed as a true story of Soviet courage, and as greater detail emerged there were certain themes which united different stories: the Soviet soldier's selflessness, the value of initiative in 'complex' battle situations, and the necessity of their 'internationalist mission'. Comparisons were made with the Soviet troops who served in the Spanish Civil war and in Mongolia in the 1930s.

KARMAL AND THE ARMED FORCES

In a series of speeches in spring 1984, Babrak Karmal showed a frank appreciation both of the regime's limited achievements and of the problems that remained for the security forces. On the positive side he noted that the armed forces had 'multipied in numbers, have become more powerful and are in a very good shape compared with the past'.[12] He also stressed major achievements in the field of PDPA unity.

Karmal declared: 'We have emerged victorious from this horribly difficult period after the second stage of the Saur Revolution . . . I say to you now that our party is following and must follow the process of organic unity step by step at a high level.' He did not pretend that factionalism was dead: 'We must struggle against factionalism . . . we must also struggle against conspiracies, adventurism and foil the propaganda of reaction and imperialism against Afghanistan.'[13] Despite the insistence of *mujahadeen* sources to the contrary, there is considerable evidence that the party had made some headway in its attempts to reduce factionalism.

In the first place Karmal's suggestion that the party had been 'victorious' in the matter contrasted with his desperate pleading for unity during 1980–81. Though factionalism clearly did continue to sap the effectiveness of the army, it had not produced the spectacular consequences (such as the officers' revolt in the 14th Division) that it did in 1979–80.

But in his speech to army party workers on 17 January, Karmal had also listed many defects that still affected the forces:

(a) He criticised ill-treatment of conscripts saying, 'I am seriously requesting that your behaviour towards new recruits should be altered to an exceptionally sympathetic, more fraternal, more humane attitude'.

(b) There was still ethnic persecution and indiscipline; according to Karmal, 'laws regulations and provisions exist which ought to be consistently and seriously implemented'.

(c) Karmal highlighted conflicts between party and military authorities at local level saying, 'all party and government organs at local areas and provincial level must cooperate fully with headquarters. The implementation of headquarters decisions is obligatory and essential'.

(d) He told the party workers that the army, Sarandoy and KHAD had not been cooperating well enough at local level.

Following Karmal's speeches over the years it is apparent that by 1984 the strong inter-service rivalry between these three large security organisations ranked alongside 'traditional' Khalqi/ Parcham factionalism as a major concern. The need for better coordination was stressed again by Karmal during a speech to Sarandoy party workers in April.[14] Attempts were made to lessen this rivalry by the use of local joint HQs for coordinating activities. Within the Politburo it was believed that Dr Najeebollah had taken over all responsibilities for security matters, giving him influence over the army and Sarandoy as well as his own KHAD.

What these limitations in the security forces added up to was that the government was still unable to control much of the country, and was still heavily dependent on the Soviet army. Speaking on the anniversary of the April Revolution, Karmal honestly conceded the regime's inability to control large areas of Afghanistan: 'It is important now to broaden the expansion of revolutionary sovereignty in the localities and to secure their consolidation. It should be stated explicitly that so far not much success has been achieved and no fundamental transformation has taken place in this regard.'[15] He added, 'Most of this results from inexperience among Party, government and military cadres.'

FIGHTING IN THE NORTH

During the 1983 Panjsher cease-fire, the Islamic Society of Afghanistan (ISA) forces under commander Zabiullah had been built up. A system of alliances with guerrilla groups in neighbouring provinces allowed the Zabiullah front to claim a membership of 20 000.[16] The Soviet army and government forces launched several major operations as spring came to the north.

The 18th Division conducted several sweeps against Islamic Movement (of Sheikh Muhsini) forces in the Fariab province. The IM was a largely Shia party which had its main strength on the northern fringes of the Hazara Jat. The 18th Division's 35th Regiment, based in Sheberghan, was supplemented for these operations by a mountain battalion sent from Balkh. Their main aim seems to have been to flush out a pocket of IM guerrillas near Andkhoy on the Soviet border. Kabul sources said that 50 IM fighters under a commander called Zabet A'bad surrendered there on 28 March.[17] A further 31 were reported killed and 13 captured on 15 April.[18]

On 18 April, *mujahadeen* near Konduz in Badakhshan captured 12 Soviet soldiers from the nearby 201st Motor Rifle Division, but the prisoners were all 'shot while trying to escape'. These killings triggered a Soviet counter-stroke in the Gor Tepa district. According to *mujahadeen* sources, 133 fighters (including their commander) belonging to the Islamic Party (Khalis faction) and 250 civilians were killed in the battle.[19]

THE PANJSHER CEASE-FIRE CRUMBLES

The Panjsher cease-fire lasted about one year. During that time the Soviets were able to forget about their major tactical headache. But by 1984 the cease-fire was crumbling. According to Kabul, Massud refused to extend the agreement when offered the chance in March 1984.[20] In any case, many people suspected him of exploiting its terms (a halt to operations in the Panjsher valley) to his own advantage, and of sending his troops to fight in the Shomali valley and Balkh during 1983.

By April the Salang road was regularly under attack once more. Journeys on this route had become so dangerous that it had attained an awesome reputation among Soviet drivers. An account of a convoy's journey down the road was published early that year. ' "Sergeant Khomovskoi's vehicle has stopped," someone reported. When they opened the door the whole cab was splashed with blood. The sergeant had been wounded in the side, leg and arm ... The worst point – the Salang pass – was still ahead. Something just has to happen there.'[21]

PANJSHER 7

The decision to launch a seventh major offensive against the Panjsher valley was probably taken shortly after Massud's refusal to extend the cease-fire. Soviet forces for the attack were probably drawn together under the HQ of the 108th Motor Rifle Division, this time under Major-General Saradov. They amounted to several motor rifle regiments, an air assault regiment and a further air assault battalion detached from the 345th Independent Air Assault Regiment at Bagram.[22] The Afghan force was drawn together under Brigadier Shahnawaz Tani's Central Corps. Their contingent for this operation was larger than that for Panjsher 5 and 6. It consisted of the bulk of the 8th and 20th Divisions and the 37th Commando Brigade. Total forces committed amounted to perhaps 10 000 Soviet and 5000 Afghan troops. Part of the task-force was used for a sweep in the neighbouring Andarab valley. The tribal regiment of Commander Jom'a Khan was reported in action against the *mujahadeen*.[23]

The plan that was drawn up for Panjsher 7 was quite different from that used previously. It contained a number of innovations and tactical changes. The experience of the previous offensives, that Massud's men could take to the side valleys and if necessary leave the Panjsher altogether through high passes, had been learnt. The new plan involved widening the area of operations considerably.

During the second week in April, the Soviet air force moved 36 Tu–16 bombers from other areas of the USSR to bases in the Turkestan Military District. This movement was detected by US intelligence.[24] These bombers were intended for high-level carpet-bombing of the valley. The use of USSR-based heavy bombers would prevent the need for an obvious build-up of air assets at Bagram. They might also achieve greater tactical successes by bombing from such great heights that they would be invisible and inaudible, and might thus catch more enemy fighters in the open.

As with other major LCSFA operations, the task-force was to be made up of elements drawn from several different formations. On 17 April, two columns left to take part in the operation, each one of approximately battalion strength. One came from the 66th Motor Rifle Brigade near Jallalabad, the other from the 191st Independent Motor Rifle Regiment in Ghazni.[25] A few days later the 180th Motor Rifle Regiment left its camp at Khair Khana in northern Kabul.

Massud was probably aware that an offensive was imminent and he had done much during the previous year to prepare his forces for it. The ISA Panjsher front had expanded, possibly to as many as 5000 men. It had also acquired many more anti-aircraft heavy machine guns – by some claims as many as 200.[26] Massud's stock of heavy weapons included captured tanks (one T–62 and several T–55s) and three D–30 122mm gun-howitzers.[27] It is quite possible that he intended to make some kind of stand with these forces. Shortly before Panjsher 7 began, Massud ordered the mining of key roads in the valley.

Although Massud was expecting an offensive, the actual timing and the form of it seem to have surprised him. He dispatched a strong force amounting to several *motoraks* (nearly 500 men) to attack the Salang road in a pre-emptive strike.[28] They struck on 19 April, destroying many trucks. But they were surprised by the response that they triggered. A large heliborne force was dispatched with alarming speed from Bagram and several landings were made in a bid to encircle the attackers. They apparently suffered many casualties.

On 20 April, Massud launched a second pre-emptive attack on Anawa at the mouth of the valley. On the same day the Tu–16s began their heavy bombing. Ground forces pushed off the next day, with a 'rolling barrage' of bombs continuing up the valley. It is not known how many *mujahadeen* were killed by the high-level bombing, but added to the shock of the swift heliborne operation near the Salang, its effect was to unnerve Massud. According to ISA spokesman Mohammed Es Haq, 'it was decided that since the relative size of the enemy force was too big, that new plans were

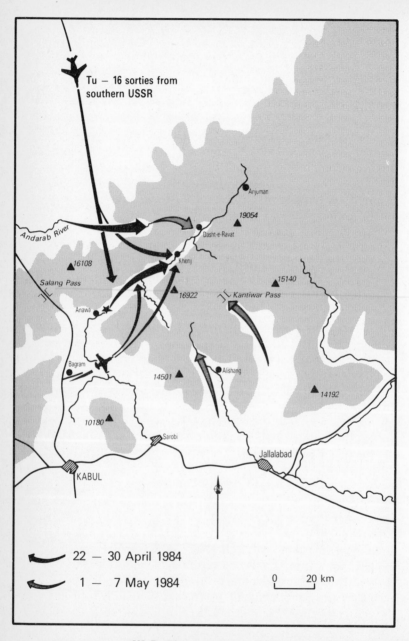

XI Panjsher 7, April–May 1984.

being introduced and that there was the possibility of chemical weapons being used, we should avoid direct confrontation with the enemy inside the valley'.[29]

With Saradov's force having to retake ground given up in the cease-fire, it took the Soviet mechanised column until the 24 April to reach Rokka. The armour pressed on towards Bazerak, its pace slowed by the many mines planted by Massud's men. The motor rifle forces advanced until they reached Khenj. They did not make attacks up the Panjsher's tributary valleys during the opening phase of the operation; this may well have been a ploy to lull the *mujahadeen* sheltering in them into a false sense of security. Progress beyond Khanj became impossible for the mechanised force because the snow had not yet thawed. A battalion heliborne landing was made further up at Dasht-e-Rawat.

According to a guerrilla source, the casualties in the first five days of the offensive amounted to 200 Soviets and Afghan army, and 150 of Massud's men killed.[30] These figures represent a far higher loss rate for the the *mujahadeen* during the opening phase of operations than during the previous two offensives.

The next and most innovative phase of the operation took place during the first few days of May. Several battalion-strength forces were placed at key passes out of the Panjsher. Then a large heliborne landing was made in the upper Andarab valley, and a further force was despatched from Jallalabad to block the Alishang valley.[31] As this was done the force occupying the valley floor began pushing up the tributary valleys. These attempts to block the *mujahadeen's* routes of withdrawal forced them higher into the mountains than they had been previously. Groups were scattered as they tried to avoid being trapped by heliborne landings.

Even before the operation was complete, Kabul radio announced, 'We bring you good news that the criminal band of Ahmad Shah no longer exists. We invite you and all noble inhabitants of the Panjsher wherever you are to return to your home dwellings and resume your tranquil life.'[32] On 6 May, a high-level government delegation, led by Babrak Karmal himself, visited Anawa, Rokka and several Afghan units in the valley .[33] Evidently it was considered safe for them to travel into the Panjsher – for the first time since 1979. there was a further visit two days later by army political chief General Yasin Sadeqi. Several important ISA prisoners were taken, adding to the government's sense of triumph.

The most famous of the prisoners was Commander Abdul Wahed, who was subsequently shown to the world's press. He had been in charge of a 25-man logistics column that had been captured. Wahed's capture represented a humiliation for the resistance; in the past he had travelled the world to argue the *mujahadeen's* case, even appearing on the British TV programme, 'This is Your Life'. In captivity Wahed said what was required of him, denouncing his former comrades: 'They get foreign help, they murder innocent people, and abuse them indecently. They claimed Islam was in danger. I changed my mind because it was not in danger as far as I was concerned.'[34]

Rather than withdrawing from the valley as they had done previously, the occupation force began to build a system of forts and posts. They relinquished control of the side valleys, but remained in the main valley as far up as Pechgur, just below Khenj. Clearly they had decided that garrisoning the lower valley might prevent further attacks on the Salang. With a force remaining in the Panjsher, the guerrillas found themselves with more attractive targets closer to home. Fighting continued throughout the summer.

Although the *mujahadeen* claimed that Panjsher 7 was a failure, their adoption of a new strategy suggests that it caused them considerable operational problems. They announced that 'by fighting outside the valley the presence of enemy troops inside the valley will prove useless'.[35] They also said that 'nearly all' of the valley's inhabitants had been evacuated by them at the start of the operation.

The government for its part said that 'revolutionary sovereignty' had been restored and that citizens who had formerly been 'deceived' by the *mujahadeen* were returning to their homes and resuming a normal life. A measure of confirmation of the government story comes from the unlikliest of sources: the British Chargé d'Affairs. In a routine telegram to the Foreign Office it was revealed that 'in the lower valley life is going on fairly normally under government control – e.g. food is available and cheaper than Kabul'.[36]

AIR ASSAULT OPERATIONS

Panjsher 7 highlighted new enthusiasm among Soviet commanders for heliborne commando raids. According to Massud's spokesman, 'units composed of Soviet and DRA troops numbering from 500 to 2000 were airlifted by helicopters and landed to encircle villages with aerial support...It is a new challenge and it requires a highly organised village defence system.'[37] Other resistance leaders noticed the increase in operations by Soviet elite forces. Abdol Haq's group lost over 40 men in an ambush near Paghman.[38]

As these operations increased there was growing official recognition in the Soviet Union for the men of the Air Assault Forces (Vozduyushno Desantniki Voisk or VDV). Early in 1984 the press announced that another young paratroop sergeant, Nikolai Chepik, had been posthumously awarded the Hero of the Soviet Union medal.[39] As a corps the VDV seemed to be winning the bulk of these decorations. A magazine article revealed later in 1984 that there were at least nine living VDV personnel who had won their country's highest decoration in Afghanistan.[40] Whilst these awards were not officially gazetted, it is likely that at least half of the 30 or so Hero of the Soviet Union medals awarded for exploits in the DRA (by early 1984) had gone to the Air Assault Forces.

Often a reinforced regiment from the VDV group was deployed, for several months at a time, in the regions, During 1983 there was a deployment to Shir Khan near Mazar-e-Shariff.[41] In general most operations were carried out at the reinforced battalion or regiment level. Often units were landed in remote areas by fleets of helicopters. On other occasions the VDV troops would act as mechanised infantry, driving into the mountains in scores of BMD armoured transporters. Several new versions on the vehicle appeared in the DRA. An open-topped BMD carrying an 82mm 'Vasilek' automatic mortar was followed into service by one with a 120mm mortar in a new turret. Both variants provided rapid, flexible firepower. The requirements of the Afghan mission also prompted the introduction of certain items not normally issued to these troops. A divisional multiple rocket launcher battalion with BM–21s was identified in Darulaman, near the Soviet embassy and the formation's main base.

The requirement for these special troops was such that in 1984 a new Soviet air assault brigade was identified in Gardez. Battalions of troops are sometimes flown from the USSR and placed under the direct command of this HQ for limited periods. The new brigade was one of the few combat units formed in the DRA after the 1980–81 reorganisation.

The deployment of VDV units in Afghanistan was proportionately much higher than for other branches. In addition to the 103rd Air Assault Division there was an air assault brigade (possibly the 56th), the 345th Independent Air Assault Regiment and several other battalions. This commitment represented about 15 per cent of the VDV's total strength. By comparison the Ground Forces troops in the DRA amounted to $2\frac{1}{2}$ per cent of their service total. The practice of rotating entire USSR-based battalions and sometimes regiments through Afghanistan has meant that a significant proportion of the VDV total manpower receives combat experience.

Within Afghanistan there were also operations by highly trained commandos of the General Staff Main Intelligence Directorate (GRU). These included several companies of reconnaissance troops attached to other units and 'special designation brigades', in reality battalion-strength elements. These so-called *Spetznaz* units were based in Kabul, Kandahar and Shindand.[42] The main missions of these forces have been the gathering of information, ambushing of guerrilla bands, and the spreading of disunity in rebel areas. There are several reports of *Spetznaz* troops adopting 'pseudo-gang' tactics like those employed by the SAS in Malaya and the Selous Scouts in Rhodesia. This involves attacks on villages and armed groups by Soviet Commandos dressed as *mujahadeen*, thus spreading both fear and inter-group tension.[43]

Even the comparitively secretive GRU announced its own war hero. Captain Igor Ploskonos, a reconnaissance company commander, won a hero's gold star 'for courage and valour in performance of his internationalist duty on Afghan soil'.[44] Among his deeds, Ploskonos had saved the life of an Afghan Lieutenant-Colonel. The GRU *Spetznaz* troops soon gained a fearsome reputation among the *mujahadeen* who called them the 'black soldiers'.

A WIDER OFFENSIVE

While large forces were still in the Panjsher, the Soviets and Afghans conducted other regimental attacks on guerrilla strongholds. There were several sweeps across the Herat plain.[45] During the summer of 1984, probably for the first time since its arrival, the capabilities of the Soviet army in Afghanistan were stretched by simultaneous large-scale actions.

Early in June, a Soviet regiment, apparently without the usual presence of Afghan units, was dispatched up the Logar valley. Guerrillas of Sayed Murtaza's IRM front conducted a series of ambushes on them. According to *mujahadeen* sources there were around 100 Soviet casualties in this battle.[46]

During the last week of June, there was a joint Soviet/Afghan operation against the men of Commander Shafiullah's Koh-e-Safi front. The Koh-e-Safi plain to the east of Kabul was not only a base for operations against the city, but also a vital through-route for guerrillas going to the Panjsher and further north. The attacks there during 25–29 June may well have been part of General Saradov and Tani's series of blocking actions against routes to and from the Panjsher. Indeed the stepping up of operations in Koh-e-Safi and around Bagram that summer forced guerrilla caravans to find new routes. Many went to the west of Kabul via the Paghman hills.

NEW *MUJAHADEEN* TACTICS IN KABUL

Compared with early 1980, *mujahadeen* capacity to act in Kabul had declined considerably. Whereas large-scale civil disobedience and armed attacks could be organised by the resistance parties in February and March of that year, the gradual improvement of security around the capital had forced the *mujahadeen* to abandon such high profile activities, and to confine their operations to night time. By 1984, the government said it had 10 400 Revolution Defence Group militia in the Kabul area.[47] This figure seems reasonable given the size of the population (about 1.5 million) and is actually corroborated by guerrilla accounts. They supplemented a large force of Ministry of the Interior Sarandoy and several Central Corps units that were available for defence of the city. The construction of large numbers of fortified posts was, by 1984, on the guerrillas' admission, posing 'problems' in getting forces into Kabul.[48] Further afield the presence of tribal groups like Hassan Khan Karokhel's in the Sarobi valley was also preventing them from attacking certain key targets.

As security around Kabul became more effective so the *mujahadeen* adopted new tactics. During 1981–82, assassination by gunmen operating alone or in pairs became more frequent. RPG and bomb attacks on barracks and housing complexes for Soviet advisers were also stepped up. From August–November 1984, the *mujahadeen* markedly increased their activity, and adopted a number of new tactics. The IP (Khalis) front commander, Abdol Haq, probably the most influential guerrilla leader in the area, persuaded Hassan Khan Karokhel and his followers to abandon their task of protecting the Sarobi power station.[49] They left for Pakistan late in August after Abdol Haq had threatened to wipe them out.

Other responses adopted by Abdol Haq's fighters were to prove far more controversial. On 3 September, a bomb went off at Kabul airport killing 31 and injuring 200 people. Abdol Haq subsequently claimed responsibility.[50] Although the guerrillas said they killed party activists on their way to the USSR, it was quite clear that there were many youngsters and bystanders among the casualties.

But the major tactical change was the use of unguided rockets. Although these had been fired before August 1984, it is from then that their use really increased dramatically. The main weapons used were Chinese-made 107mm rockets. They have a range of about 8 km and rely on a high-explosive fragmentation warhead for their anti-personnel effect. Occasionally the *mujahadeen* also used Chinese-made 122mm rockets, and sometimes even captured Soviet-built 122mm 40-barrel BM–21 rocket-launchers (called '*Grad*' or 'hail' by the Russians). But because they were light and easily portable, the 107mm rockets remained the firm favourite. Mainly single rockets were used, but by late 1984 some Chinese-made 12-barrel Type-63 107mm rocket launchers began to appear in guerrilla hands.

Lightness and simplicity made the 107mm rockets a preferred weapon of the Viet Cong, but they devised ingenious ways of aiming them. Many *mujahadeen*, on the other hand, were happy to lean them against a rock, so long as they were pointing in the general direction of the target. The guerrillas have made incredibly specific claims (based, they say, on informants inside garrisons) on the effects of these rocket attacks but it is clear that they are often inaccurate and indiscriminate.

On the night of 13 September, for example, guerrillas fired a total of 14 rockets into Kabul. One salvo of six aimed at the Soviet embassy complex in Darulaman, apparently landed near their target, but the rest fell all over the city including one which hit the Iranian embassy.[51] By the end of the year they had succeeded in hitting the Pakistani embassy and scoring a near miss on the US mission – surely the most inconceivable deliberate targets. The guerrillas were so keen on this new form of warfare that by mid-September ISA forces around Kabul had run out of rockets. their commander, Nabi, went to Pakistan to obtain more.[52]

Despite this poor accuracy the *mujahadeen* believe that the rockets are useful as a constant reminder of their presence to the populace, and can be launched at little risk. On the question of the morality of using them, their logic is less persuasive. Abdol Haq defends their use: 'Their target is not the civilians...but if I hit them I don't care. I feel sorry for them but I don't care.' To Abdol Haq, and commanders like him, the widespread bombing of villages by government planes justifies any retaliation – and he expects others to share his zeal: 'If my family lived near the Soviet embassy I would hit it. I wouldn't care about them. If I'm prepared to die, my son has to die for it and my wife has to die for it.'[53]

Government re-organisation of security around Kabul had in turn prompted a guerrilla shake-up. Abdol Haq re-grouped his men into nine zonal commands surrounding the city. Co-ordination between these forces remained minimal. As late as 1986, Abdol Haq told the author that there was no radio contact either between these zones or between his own HQ and the party leaders in Pakistan. Instead he relied on attacks launched at agreed times and organised some way in advance. Such an attack was made on the night of 24 September.

The main target, an old guerrilla favourite, was the Balar Hissar fort. Between 40 and 60 mortar bombs were fired into this camp at around 21.00 hours that evening. Simultaneous attacks were launched at Bagrame, the airport and the Darulaman district. By 23.00 Soviet reinforcements had arrived at the Balar Hissar and there was heavy fighting as they tried to trap the *mujahadeen*.[54]

The Soviet response to the increasing use of rockets was to reply in kind: they drafted in more BM–21 battalions. Fairly soon it became common for *mujahadeen* rocket fire to be answered by shattering salvoes from these Katyushas. Although the BM–21 is considerably more accurate than the 107mm rocket it is doubtful whether these retaliatory barrages could have found their targets very often. But firing them probably made the frustrated Soviet troops feel better anyway.

THE BATTLE FOR ALI KHEL

The garrison at Ali Khel (also called Jaji) in Paktia province, like so many others in rural Afghanistan, was in an area of high resistance activity. It lay on the route between the Pakistani town of Parachnar and Kabul. Throughout 1984 the town had come under siege from a combined guerrilla force, drawn largely from the Khalis Islamic Party. Several Afghan columns were beaten off in attempts to re-supply the base.

In August the Soviets launched a major joint operation with the Afghans to break the siege. It was the largest Soviet operation in Paktia up to that point. The 70th Motor Rifle Brigade came from Kandahar and an air assault regiment was brought in. But because air assault forces were already so heavily committed in the Panjsher and elsewhere, the Soviet High Command took the unusual step of flying in a regiment from the 104th Guards Air Assault Division from Kirovabad, Transcaucasus Military District. This formation had provided a regiment for the orginal operation to seize Kabul, but this had been withdrawn by June 1980. The Afghan army element consisted of the 38th Commando Brigade and some elements of the Gardez-based 12th Division. According to *mujahadeen* and diplomatic sources this force totalled at least 12 000 men.[55]

The operation, carried out at the end of August, succeeded in driving the guerrillas back. The scale of the Soviet force came as a surprise to the *mujahadeen*, given their comparatively minor role in the province up to that point. Following the operation, the air assault regiment flew back to the Transcaucasus Military District.

THE SITUATION IN THE HAZARA JAT

During August there was also heavy fighting in the fortress of Qala in the Hazara mountains. There were reports that a guerrilla force had taken the town and that government troops had subsequently launched a counter-offensive. They succeeded in re-taking the town and reportedly inflicted heavy casualties on the *mujahadeen*.

The feuding between parties continued, Commander Rahim Ali from Bamiyan province reported 'increasing disunity' among the populace. He blamed the Nasr group for making matters worse.[56]

Nevertheless, whatever the relative strengths of the Nasr and

Pasdaran, Kabul's influence in the vast mountainous centre of the country remained very small. A few months later an *Izvestia* article confirmed that the army was limited to just a few bases in the Hazara Jat.[57]

REVERSES FOR THE ISLAMIC SOCIETY OF AFGHANISTAN

By 1984, Burhanuddin Rabbani's ISA had established itself as one of the most effective resistance organisations in the country. Its three principal fronts – Massud in the Panjsher, Ismael Khan in Herat and Zabiullah in the Marmoul – commanded thousands of fighters and operated over large areas. But late in 1984, all three suffered blows.

Fighting in the Panjsher continued throughout the summer, with Massud trying to re-group his scattered forces. There was additional high-altitude bombing. At the beginning of September, the Soviets launched Panjsher 8. According to diplomatic sources the guerrillas suffered heavy losses during a raid on Eid-e-Qorban on 5 September. Estimates of their casualties range from 200 to 300. This eighth offensive was not comparable to the seventh. When the bombing was complete there were several heliborne raids and small (battalion) operations. The aim was to relieve pressure on government forts in the valley. The result was that Massud's forces were damaged at a time when they needed to recover.

Ismael Khan's Herat front had been built up to about 12 000 men.[58] During 1984, high-level bombing and a greater frequency of Soviet and government operations combined to accelerate rural depopulation. This posed a number of problems for Commander Allaladin's military operations. As rural supporters left, so food, information, money and recruits declined. A British professor who visited the area reported that the resistance was 'completely isolated and under heavy enemy pressure'.[60]

If the Herat ISA front was suffering operational inconvenience, then the Marmoul one was about to face a much more serious problem. On 3 December, Commander Zabiullah was killed. He died when a jeep in which he was travelling hit a landmine. He was by far the most important resistance leader to be killed since the outbreak of the war. He had forged a working arrangement between several parties in the northern provinces that, according to some estimates, deployed 20 000 fighters. He had built an enormously strong base in the Marmoul Gorge, which had survived repeated attacks.

Several theories have been advanced to explain Zabiullah's death. According to one, the mine was command-detonated by Soviet *Spetznaz* troops. Other accounts say it had been planted by men of the Islamic Movement. The rumour caused much bad feeling between ISA and IM forces in the north. Whoever was responsible had succeeded in depriving ISA and the resistance of one of their most capable leaders.

STRIKE IN THE EAST

Following August's fighting around Ali Khel, the Soviet command embarked on a new series of operations in the east. The aim was to interdict guerrilla supply lines from Pakistan. *Mujahadeen* caravans were bringing in an increasing amount of sophisticated weaponry.

There was an increase in the use of SA-7s, particularly near Kabul. On 28 October, a Soviet An-22 heavy transport was shot down. Early reported indicatd that 240 troops were killed in the crash, but later ones stated the plane was carrying cargo and that only 12 flight crew were lost. A major tragedy was narrowly avoided when an Afghan Airlines DC-10 returning from Mecca was hit by SA-7. The plane managed to land safely, its 300 pilgrims unhurt.

The timing of the eastern offensive, coinciding with the onset of winter, must have come as something of a surprise to the *mujahadeen*. There were two principal sweeps: in Paktia near Khost, and up the Kunar valley. In both cases regiment-sized Soviet air assault contingents were flown in.

The Paktia operation, which was launched on 18/19 November, reportedly involved five squadrons of heavy-lift Mil-6 helicopters.[61] Some of these had been flown down from the Turkestan Military District. They conducted sweeps around the Khost plain, but apparently did not seriously threaten the major guerrilla bases of Jaji and Zhawar which were close to the border itself.

A month later, the Soviets turned their attention to the Kunar valley. The Soviet force concentrated there was larger than for any operation since the one in March 1980. It reportedly consisted of 10 000 Soviet and 7500 Afghan troops.[62] These were made up of the

66th Motor Rifle Brigade, an air assault regiment, a *Spetznaz* battalion, the Afghan 9th Division, elements of the 11th Division and a commando battalion.

The operation took some pressure off the garrisons of Asmar and Barikot higher up the valley. Nevertheless, quite soon afterwards, the situation of Barikot and some smaller posts near the Pakistani border became critical again.

THE PLIGHT OF REFUGEES

The campaign in the border areas also had the effect of slowing down the flow of refugees into Pakistan. The almost continuous operations in these provinces in 1984 meant that it was unsafe to attempt the journey. The number of displaced people already in Pakistan was 3 500 000 and in Iran possibly up to 1 500 000. In summer 1984, the United Nations High Commissioner for Refugees succeeded in establishing a mission in Tehran. The UN relief effort in Pakistan had been underway since 1980 and in 1984 amounted to $500 million.[63] Although there had been some attempts to re-settle the refugees in the Punjab (a few thousand also went to Turkey), the bulk remained in western Pakistan. Although driven from their homes with few possessions they managed to establish, by the standards of world refugee misery, an acceptable base there.

Relief organisations have succeeded in providing for them adequately. There has been no famine or epidemic disease. Some help has come from sympathisers abroad. The Committee for a Free Afghanistan (in Washington) and the Afghan Support Committee (Afghanaid, in London) are just two groups which have campaigned on behalf of the refugees, and the resistance in general. The Afghan Support Committee benefits from close connections with the Conservative Party, and the Foreign and Commonwealth Office.

Inside Afghanistan, medical care remained poor. French volunteer medical teams provided help in rebel areas. Other victims had to make the journey to relief agency hospitals in Pakistan. Eastern bloc doctors and nurses serving Kabul provided the PDPA with one of its more subtle weapons. Many people chose to move into government territory and accept land and health care rather than face continued bombardments on their ancestral lands. These people provided a new constituency for the government. During the siege of Khost in 1983, for example, most of the population ignored resistance orders to leave. They stayed put, even in the face of death threats.[64]

THE SOVIETS' TACTICAL LESSONS

As the year progressed the treatment of the conflict in the Soviet military press became more candid. On 10 August, *Kraznaya Zvezda* published an intriguing account of inefficiency in air force units based in the DRA. The article, written by a lieutenant-colonel, contained a degree of criticism which would be hard to find in the newspapers of any country whose army was at war.

The *Kraznaya Zvezda* correspondent found himself waiting in the scorching heat for six hours with some other Russians because the helicopters could not be reloaded: 'There's no point getting irritated,' Captain S. Bazunov, the helicopter commander, explained. 'Until the storekeeper gets back from base let's do some sunbathing.'[65] He pointed out that the wait was by no means exceptional. 'Once, for example, a loaded An-12 could not take off for two and a half hours – that's how long it took to find the driver of the refuelling truck'. He asked, 'Who benefits from this apology for a time schedule?'

The *Kraznaya Zvezda* report confirmed the suspicion held by some analysts that simple Soviet inefficiency posed a significant operational limitation. A rather more straightforward and authoritative account of the tactical lessons being learnt in the DRA, and in the preparation of troops across the border, appeared three months later.

In an article called 'Mountain Training', Army General Yuri Maksimov listed the main tactical lessons that had been learnt during the previous four years. Throughout that time he had commanded the Turkestan Military District and, late in 1984, assumed over-all control of the Southern Theatre of Military Operations (TVD). The article set out the principal tactical lessons of the conflict to that point:

(a) The vital importance of small unit actions: 'Combat operations in mountains are characterised by a number of features conditioned by the nature of mountainous terrain, such as its extremely rugged character, scarcity of roads and their poor trafficability and a great number of natural obstacles. All this forces troops to operate sometimes in comparatively small sub-units and in seperate sectors. Besides, these peculiarities make it more difficult to coordinate, control and manoeuvre the resources at hand.' Having explained the need for independent small-unit actions he added: 'Even a small sub-unit can decide the whole battle by unexpectedly manoeuvring around the defenders' flank or capturing a dominating height.'[64]

(b) The need for a high level of combined arms cooperation, down to the lowest levels: 'Even a motorised rifle company operating as a bypassing detachment or an airborne party, i.e. fulfilling an independent mission, should by all means include an artillery officer and an air controller. The lack of close cooperation among the motorised infantry, artillery and aviation in mountainous areas may result in the failure to fulfil the combat mission assigned'. He also stressed the particular importance of combat engineers.

(c) The requirement for special training. General Maksimov wrote about the setting up of a special 'district mountain training centre' – almost certainly the facility at Ashkabad. He stated that the use of this base had made possible 'the successful solution of a great number of such versatile and complicated tasks'. Maksimov described the instruction that went on there: 'After the recruits finish the course of basic mountain training and acquire practical training skills in observing safety precautions, they are trained to advance to the assault position and deploy there, conduct defensive and offensive operations, execute marches along steep mountain roads and operate in bypassing detachments and tactical airborne parties'. He stressed that officer training required 'particular consideration' given the importance of small-unit operatons.

The year 1984 saw the most dramatic escalation of the conflict of any year since the commitment of Soviet troops. The increased participation of Afghan units and the stepping up of Soviet combat activity resulted in several major offensives. Panjsher 7, effectively a corps-sized operation, and joint forces of divisional size were used in Herat, Paktia and the Kunar valley. In addition, the Soviets may have launched up to a dozen regiment/brigade strikes. The growth

in heliborne and *Spetznaz* operations reflected a new aggressiveness
on the part of Soviet commanders.

On the resistance side there was escalation too. There was a
growing sophistication in their armaments, with SA–7s, Western-
made plastic-cased mines and the 107mm rocket being more and
more widely used. Over-all, though, it was a very bad year for the
resistance. Rural depopulation had acclerated in some areas,
forcing them to organise their own food distribution. The scope of
the Soviets' summer offensives had come as an unwelcome surprise
to many commanders. At the end of an unpleasant year there had
been another serious blow with the loss of Commander Zabiullah.
The *mujahadeen* began to adjust to the new tactical realities.

Notes

1.   Kabul Radio, 2 March 1984.
2.   British Chargé d'Affairs, Kabul Sitrep, 1–5 April 1984.
3.   Peter Jouvenal, eyewitness at the siege of Urgun, interviewed by the
     author, May 1985.
4.   Kabul Radio, 24 January 1984.
5.   Edward Girardet, *Afghanistan: The Soviet War* (Croom Helm, 1985).
6.   Kabul Radio, 18 October 1984.
7.   *The Guardian*, 12 January 1984.
8.   Col. V. Izgarshev, 'At The Bidding of Internationalist Duty', *Soviet Military
     Review*, 11/1980.
9.   *Komsomolaya Pravda*, 26 February 1984.
10. *Komsomolaya Pravda*, 14 March 1984.
11. Major A. Oliynik, 'The Soviet Character', *Soviet Military Review*, 2/1985;
     story first printed in *Kraznaya Zvezda*, 12 January 1984.
12. Babrak Karmal, speech to Armed Forces and Party Officials, Kabul
     Radio, 12 January 1984.
13. Ibid.
14. Babrak Karmal, speech to Sarandoy Officers, Kabul Radio, 3 April 1984.
15. Babrak Karmal, speech at April Revolution Anniversary Meeting, Kabul
     Radio, 25 April 1984.
16. *Afghan Information Centre (AIC) Bulletin*, February 1985.
17. Kabul Radio, 30 March 1984.
18. Kabul Radio, 5 April 1984.
19. *AIC Bulletin*, May 1984.
20. *Kabul New Times*, 9 May 1985.
21. Col. V. Filatov, 'Cement', *Soviet Military Review*, 10/1984.
22. David Isby, 'Panjsher VII', *Soldier of Fortune*, February 1985.
23. *Foreign Report*, 5 July 1984.
24. *International Herald Tribune*, 18 April 1984.
25. British Chargé d'Affairs, Kabul Sitrep, 15–22 April.

26. Isby, op. cit.
27. Peter Jouvenal, interviewed by the author, May 1985..
28. Anonymous diplomat, interviewed by the author, October 1984.
29. Mohammed Es-Haq, 'Panjsher The Seventh Offensive', *Central Asian Survey*, Incidental Paper no. 1.
30. *AIC Bulletin*, June 1984.
31. British Chargé d'Affaires, Kabul Sitrep, 6–10 May 1984.
32. Kabul Radio, 24 April 1984.
33. Bakhtar News Agency wire, 6 May 1984.
34. Abdul Wahed, interviewed on 'Kabul Autumn', transmitted on British TV Channel 4, December 1984.
35. Es-Haq, op. cit.
36. British Chargé d'Affaires, Kabul Sitrep, 11–17 December 1984.
37. Es-Haq, op. cit.
38. Abdol Haq, interviewed in *AIC Bulletin*, August 1984.
39. *Daily Telegraph*, 3 August 1984.
40. *Voenniy Vestnik*, 9/1984.
41. Pte G. Dzhamalbekov, interviewed in Radio Free Europe–Radio Liberty, *Research Paper RL 270/84*, 12 July 1984.
42. David Isby, *Russia's War in Afghanistan* (Osprey, 1986).
43. Commander Daulat, interviewed in *AIC Bulletin*, February 1984.
44. Lt-Col V. Sukhodolsky, 'Reconnaisance Company Commander', *Soviet Military Review*, 12/1984.
45. *The Times*, 25 July 1984.
46. *AIC Bulletin*, July 1984.
47. Kabul Radio, 30 December 1984.
48. Abdol Haq, IP (Khalis) Commander of Kabul, interviewed by the author, 11 March 1986.
49. Girardet, op. cit.
50. *The Guardian*, 7 March 1986.
51. British Chargé d'Affaires, Kabul Sitrep, 11–17 September 1984.
52. British Chargé d'Affaires, Kabul Sitrep, 30 December 1984–7 January 1985.
53. Abdol Haq, interviewed by the author, 11 March 1986.
54. British Chargé d'Affaires, Kabul Sitrep, 25 September–1 October 1984.
55. *AIC Bulletin*, December 1984.
56. Commander Rahim Ali, interviewed in *AIC Bulletin*, June 1984.
57. *International Herald Tribune*, 28 December 1984.
58. Olivier Roy, interviewed by the author, 9 April 1986.
59. Professor Nick Danziger, interviewed in *AIC Bulletin*, October 1984.
60. Commander Allaladin, ISA Commander of Herat interviewed by the author, 7 April 1986.
61. *Times of India*, 8 January 1985.
62. British Chargé d'Affaires, Kabul Sitrep, 11–17 December 1984.
63. Girardet, op. cit.
64. Peter Jouvenal, interview with author.
65. Lt-Col V. Skrizhalin, 'While Helicopters Stand Idle', *Kraznaya Zvezda*, 10 August 1984.
66. Army General Yu. Maksimov, 'Mountain Training', *Soviet Military Review*, 12/1984.

Eight: 1985

RAISING THE STAKES

Early in 1985, a number of stories appeared in the Western media about the stepping up of US aid to the *mujahadeen*. Whereas the White House had, in the early years of the Soviet presence, maintained a knowing silence on the subject there was now an increasingly open debate on how best to destabalise the Kabul regime.

Reports in January indicated that the USA would provide the Afghan rebels with $250 million during the year.[1] Estimates also appeared that total US aid to the *mujahadeen* up to 1985 had reached $400 million.[2] The cash came from various departments but was channelled through the CIA.[3] Most of the weapons were shipped to the Pakistani port of Karachi. Following the death of President Sadat, Egyptian stocks of Soviet-type weapons were closed to the CIA. A new supply came from Israel. They provided hundreds of tons of brand new Soviet-made hardware that had been captured during the invasion of Lebanon in 1982.

The congressional debate on Afghan funding brought into the open a number of important issues. Several congressmen highlighted the inefficiency and corruption of the supply system. It was claimed that only 10 per cent of the aid was reaching the front. There was general agreement that the rebels' most urgent need was for an effective anti-aircraft defence. Until then the CIA had been careful to purchase Soviet-made or Chinese-built copies of Russian weapons; it was now felt that such anonymity was no longer of vital importance.

It does not appear that the USA supplied advanced Stinger anti-aircraft missiles until 1986. Instead the CIA and British intelligence collaborated in a plan to send Blowpipe missiles, made by Shorts of Belfast. An initial shipment of about a dozen launchers was arranged in late 1985 through Saudi Arabia. The US and British authorities then agreed the order of a special batch of 300 Blowpipes, the first of which arrived in Afghanistan in early 1986.

Congress was in a bullish mood throughout these months. One of the leading lights in the *mujahadeen* fund-raising campaign, Representative Charles Wilson, stated, 'there were 58 000 dead in

Vietnam, and we owe the Russians one'.[4] Driven by this argument, Americans have given the plans to donate large sums to the *mujahadeen* an uncritical reception, even though the voting of appropriations one-tenth as large for the Nicaraguan contras provoked intense public debate.

Pravda claimed that a further $200 million was coming from an unholy alliance of Israel, Saudi Arabia and China. In presenting the news to Soviet readers they also stated that the war had already cost Afghanistan 1814 schools, 35 hospitals, and 14 000 km of telephone lines.[5]

THE FIRST EASTERN OFFENSIVE OF 1985

From mid-January there was a string of search-and-destroy operations by Soviet and Afghan forces in the centre and east of the country. The general purpose of the operations, like those of late 1984, was to damage guerrilla infrastructure in the borderlands. In some areas the resistance threatened the government presence. Khost and the outposts at Jaji and Tani were constantly under siege. High in the Kunar valley the garrison of Barikot was also cut off from supply – except for the occasional courageous helicopter pilot.

Garrisons like the ones at Barikot and Jaji were only a few kilometres from the Pakistani border. Maintaining them was an expensive business, justified in terms of interdicting guerrilla supply routes and sealing the border. In fact they did little except stay in their emplacements. Attempts to dislodge them, on the other hand, did occupy a disproportionate amount of the *mujahadeen's* time and effort. If you could make your contribution to the *jihad* a few hours away from the refugee camp why bother to walk to Kabul?

The offensives that started from late 1984 do mark a change in strategy by the Soviet/Afghan command. Evidently General Sorokin, the chief strategic adviser in Kabul, was able to advocate more aggressive campaigns aimed at evicting the enemy from previously safe areas. They involved large forces and seemed to be directed at breaking guerrilla power, and establishing more government posts along the border and elsewhere, rather than just assuring the continued survival of a few isolated garrisons.

In mid-January, a force attempted to fight its way through to

Jaji. A fortnight later heavy fighting was reported in the Shomali valley, just north of Kabul, and near Barikot on the border. There was also fighting in Nangrahar during which an important IP (Khalis) commander, Qari Samad, was reportedly killed.[6] Samad had commanded a force of 800 men.

Elements of the Afghan 8th Division participated in a number of operations. In January they were in Shomali, and by mid-February in action in the Logar valley.[7]

The operations were mostly conducted at the brigade level except the one in Kunar. This involved a task-force under the 9th Division commander, Colonel Gholam Hazrat. It consisted of brigades from his own and the Jallalabad 11th Division supplemented by the 10th Engineer Regiment and the 46th Artillery Regiment.[8] The Soviet contribution was a single air assault regiment. A guerrilla source estimates that there were 2000 Soviets, 4000 Afghan army and 5000 *mujahadeen* in action in Kunar during January.[9] This estimate tallies with the order of battle of the forces involved. Another guerrilla source gives casualties for the operation as 100 Soviets, 450 Afghan army, with 66 *mujahadeen* killed.[10]

The operation is interesting because the force was predominantly Afghan, and because of its size. The *mujahadeen* were scathing about it, and claimed to have prevented them reaching Barikot. In fact this may not have been their objective. Colonel Hazrat's main mission was probably to clear the single road that runs up the valley while the engineers improved it for a bigger offensive later in the year. Their achievement was to deploy a comparatively large Afghan force up the Kunar and back again from the same garrisons that had witnessed mass desertions in 1979/80. Certainly Kabul's verdict was favourable – Gholam Hazrat was promoted to brigadier two months later.[11]

KABUL REMAINED VULNERABLE

Despite some success in sealing off the capital from rebels, it remained under attack from rockets, mortars and bombs throughout spring 1985. On the night of 22 February, the airport was attacked. Security forces apparently thwarted an attempt to attack the power station at Sarobi.[12]

Although they had little military effect on the regime, these continued attacks undoubtedly damaged morale. The Soviets and Babrak Karmal became convinced that the PDPA could not achieve much until there was broader popular support for the government. Karmal, unlike Amin, understood that programmes to broaden the appeal of the government were an integral part of the military campaign.

Speaking on 20 March, Karmal stated, 'the completion of this formidable task [defence of the revolution] is linked with major socio-political work among the people and the need to raise the social awareness of the masses'.[13] The PDPA had prepared a major package of initiatives for 1985 which were aimed at widening government appeal and fostering local consensus.

As if to underline the need for these measures there were more attacks on the capital and key installations. The strategic Salang Highway 2 came under intense and repeated attack. Ahmad Shah Massud's forces claimed to have destroyed 300 trucks on the road during that spring.[14] On 12 April, there was a rocket attack in Kabul. This triggered a series of sweeps through the city during which female Sarandoy officers were apparently used for the first time. Hitherto, many Afghan soldiers had refused to search women and there was great resentment when it was done by Soviet troops.

The vulnerability of the capital to rocket attacks prompted a series of operations to attack guerrilla bases around the city.

OPERATIONS IN CENTRAL AFGHANISTAN

The Maidan valley, south-west of Kabul, was an important centre of resistance. In its lower part, NIFA guerrillas under Rahim Wardak operated. But the Maidan was also an important through route to the Hazara Jat. In the upper part of the valley, Shia Hazara groups were active.

In the first week of April there was fire preparation for an operation into Maidan. Targets around Jelez at the mouth of the valley were bombed by aircraft including Su–25s and Mil–24s.[15] The major ground operation was launched on 9 April. The forces involved were probably not very large – the Soviet contingent was estimated as a reinforced battalion. What made the operation important was the Soviets' deployment of a new weapon. According to guerrilla and diplomatic sources, Frog–7 rockets were fired during the fighting. These weapons were designed as battlefield nuclear rockets, with four issued per division. But in Maidan they were fired with new sub-munition warheads, achieving the result of a cluster bomb. Smaller calibre multiple batteries of BM-27 rockets were also seen on the battlefield.

The other point of note about this Maidan operation was that it took Soviet forces some way into the Hazara Jat. Later in the year (in June) there was an operation in the Helmand valley which also leads into the remote central mountains. Hitherto they had not ventured into these areas on search-and-destroy operations.

Synchronised with the Maidan operation were smaller sweeps in the Paghman area and Koh-e-Safi. During the latter the noted guerrilla commander Shafiullah was killed.[16] As in Balkh the previous December, the death of a key commander did lasting damage to the resistance in this area. The series of operations around the capital during spring 1985 accelerated rural depopulation in areas where the peasants had resisted the temptation to move to safer 'government' villages on the outskirts of Kabul.

Guerrilla retaliation came in its predictable form of rocket and mortar attacks. On 27 April, there was a mortar raid on Charikar, between Kabul and Bagram. Thirty-five rounds were fired and casualties were estimated at 39 killed and 100 injured.[17]

KABUL'S INITIATIVE

It is apparent that Babrak Karmal and his PDPA colleagues were well aware of the need to broaden support. In his speeches he told of his disappointment with the poor progress of the revolution and the failure to extend its control. It was also apparent from his New Year's address that Karmal considered the broadening of support for the revolution as the key to military victory. This view was shared by his Soviet advisers. It is worth noting, though, that such views were expressed publicly by Karmal some months before they were seen in the pages of *Pravda*.

The quest for wider appeal took different forms. As mortar rounds fell on Charikar, Karmal hosted a *Loyah Jerga* (Grand Assembly) of rural leaders from around the country. According to the government 1796 delegates attended this meeting. Karmal told them that there would be new local elections that would be open to non-party members. It was hoped that the establishment of this new tier of local government would lead to national reconciliation.

Ideologically the campaign for locally elected councils was a significant concession by Kabul. In theory, popular contact with Kabul was through 200 local PDPA committees, as well as local branches of the non-party National Fatherland Front. In fact the 200 committees covered only about half of the districts in the country, and many existed more on paper than in reality. As for the National Fatherland Front, this organisation had never lived up to the hopes expressed for it. Its large central apparatus meant that it was regarded as an instrument for disseminating Kabul's views rather than acting as a conduit for grass-roots feelings.

The *mujahadeen* threatened to kill delegates to the *Loyah Jerga*. Their powers of intimidation remained considerable. Early in April, there was news that Jom'a Khan from the Andarab, one of the most important defectors to the government cause, had been assassinated.[18]

Plans were also announced for a major *jerga* of tribal leaders later in the year. Kabul had always been aware of the possible role of Pushtun tribes in sealing the border with Pakistan, but cash and persuasion had brought the cooperation of only a few groups. Central Committee Secretary Dr Mohammed Najeebollah was put in charge of a new campaign to win over the chieftains. The difference between Najeebollah's new efforts and previous ones was that now he started trying to influence tribes on the Pakistani side of the border.

Najeebollah was a natural choice for this task. As well as commanding the intelligence service, KHAD, which had built up a network of contacts across the border, he also had over-all responsibility for security. Najeebollah's origins as the son of a high-caste Pushtun family boosted his credibility in the eyes of tribal leaders. The potential benefits of a tribal strategy were enormous. The Pushtun tribal areas lay across most of the *mujahadeen* supply routes. Various military operations of late 1984 and early 1985 had already shown a determination to disrupt this system.

Another element of the interdiction strategy was the bolstering of border forces under Major-General Muhammed Faruq. He stated in May 1985 that 'the numbers of border troops have increased considerably and their combat capability and technical level have improved. They are armed with tanks, artillery and mortars.'[19] In fact it appears that the number of border brigades doubled during the period 1983–85. New brigades were identified in Kunar, Paktika and Kandahar provinces. A number of independent battalions were also deployed. With each new offensive near the frontier, posts were being constructed for these troops; numbers were climbing slowly but surely. Of course these isolated garrisons remained vulnerable and were constantly under siege. The situation of the border garrison near Barikot was about to change.

THE RELIEF OF BARIKOT

In mid-May, Soviet/Afghan forces launched another campaign in the Kunar valley. The Soviet element was larger: two air assault regiments rather than one. There was a sizeable Afghan force drawn largely from the 9th and 11th Divisions. The combined strength may have been as high as 10 000 men. The aim of the operation was to reach Barikot, and disrupt guerrilla infra-structure in the Kunar and its western tributary valleys. In particular the Kantiwar valley (which had been attacked during the Panjsher 7 offensive) was a key stretch of the '*jihad* trail', the *mujahadeen* supply route to the Panjsher and further north.

On 19 May, Soviet transporters started airlifting troops into Jallalabad airport.[20] By so doing they avoided the possibility of ambush on the 'black road' from Kabul. The offensive was launched on 21 May. By all accounts the operation was conducted efficiently. The Soviet air assault troops took part in a series of heliborne landings, securing various key points along the route of advance.

Afghan troops formed the bulk of the ground column. Towards the end of May there were attacks up the Wama and Kantiwar side valleys (see Map XII). There was heavy fighting for about ten days and then resistance sources in Pakistan announced that they had 'abandoned' the valley.[21] The task-force reached Barikot, bringing supplies and fresh troops. They only stayed for a day before beginning their journey down the valley.

RESISTANCE POLITICS

That June there were attempts to improve the cooperation

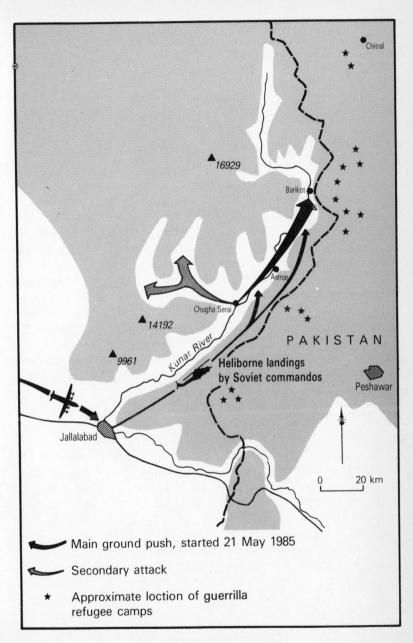

Chitral

16929

Barikot

Asmar

Chugha Serai

14192

9961

Kunar River

PAKISTAN

Heliborne landings
by Soviet commandos

Peshawar

Jallalabad

0   20 km

Main ground push, started 21 May 1985

Secondary attack

★ Approximate loction of guerrilla
    refugee camps

XII Relief of Barikot, May 1985.

amongst both Pakistan- and Iran-based groups. News of the Kunar operation reached resistance party HQ in Peshawar. Resistance leaders had gathered there for another attempt to unify their forces. There was general concern among the resistance parties at the new strength of Soviet/Afghan operations, particularly in the borderlands. The *mujahadeen* could no longer expect the relatively free access enjoyed until 1984–85.

The new Islamic Unity of Afghan Mujahadeen included all of the main Peshawar-based parties: Hekmatyar's IJP, Khalis' IP, Rabbani's ISA, Gailani's NIFA, Mujadidi's NLF, Mohammedi's IRM and Sayaf's IAAM.[22] The usual obstruction to these alliances, Gulbuddin Hekmatyar's prickly independence, was overcome by making the Islamic Party head their spokesman.

The front signalled a new determination on the part of the Pashawar-based leaders. There was also improved *ad hoc* cooperation in the field. Joint operations by 'Ettehad' (Unity) forces became more common. But the new alliance in Peshawar failed to reconcile the fundamental ideological differences between the groups.

The lack of consensus on basic objectives became apparent at a press conference to launch the new front. The remaining differences between the parties had not only prevented any agreement on the shape of post-war Afghanistan but also blocked any decision on who should be the new alliance's leader. (Later they agreed that it should alternate between them). Questioned about the differences, Hekmatyar replied in typical style, 'It will be on the battlefield that the Afghan nation and the *mujahadeen* will choose their destiny and leader.'[23]

In Iran there was an attempt by the ayatollahs to make peace between warring Hazara factions. While 1985 saw a genuine increase in cooperation between the Pakistan-based Sunni groups, the Shia bands were involved in destructive in-fighting. The succession of the Revolutionary Guards (Pasdarans) over the Victory (Nasr) front had been a bitter affair. In the chaos a number of groups had been able to establish themselves with a large degree of independence. The resistance in the Hazara Jat was actually less united than it had been under the Shura front in 1979–80.

The new groups, by and large, espoused even more extreme forms of Khomeinism than their predecessors. Among them was the Party of God (Hazbollah), the Guards of the Islamic Jihad and the Islamic Unity (Vahdat-e-Islami). Throughout early 1985 there had been fighting between these groups and the less radical Nasr and Islamic Movement bands. The extent of the conflict and the number of casualties is unknown; the impression given to the author at the time by some Hazara students in Europe was that many were killed. The situation was serious enough to provoke an initiative by Ayatollah Montazeri.

Unlike the new Peshawar-based 'alliance', the agreement which Montazeri drew up was described as a 'complete cease-fire'. the document stated 'in order to safeguard the interests of Islam and the oppressed Afghan Muslims,...any armed conflict between the Muslim *mujahadeen* should cease and...unity and understanding should be established among Islamic forces'. It went on to warn, 'needless to say, anyone violating the cease-fire will be tried and punished in accordance with Islamic injunctions'.[24] It was signed by most of the groups in the Hazara Jat.

Official Iranian involvement with the Hazara guerrillas seems to have deepened in 1985. One possible reason for this may have been the Soviet offensives in Maidan and Helmand. Most of the aid probably went to the Revolutionary Guards and the Party of God. The stepping up of supplies and increase in training of Shia refugees led to official complaints by Kabul early in 1986.[25]

One area where the pro-Khomeini Shia groups hoped to make inroads was in the northern provinces of Balkh, Samangan, Jowzjan and Fariab. Until the end of 1984 there had been considerable unity under the umbrella of Commander Zabiullah's Marmoul Front. After his death there was noticeable decline in large-scale *mujahadeen* operations in the north – particularly in Balkh. Perhaps seeing this opportunity, Soviet/Afgan forces in Mazar-e-Shariff were increased and a new belt of defences constructed around the city. Diplomatic telexes during 1985 consistently refer to Mazar-e-Shariff as being 'quiet'.

In Mazar, as in Kabul, the improvement in defences resulted in the guerrillas' adoption of terror weapons: bombs, rockets and mortars. On 6 June, a large bomb demolished an apartment block in central Mazar-e-Shariff. The official toll was 17 dead and 39 injured.[26] According to resistance sources the building was home to various party functionaries; when the bomb exploded it was mainly wives and children who were there.

A CASE OF SABOTAGE

During the night of 12 June, there was a series of major explosions at Shindand air base in western Afghanistan. Although men of Ismael Khan's Herat ISA front had staged 107mm rocket attacks on the base before, it soon became apparent that the damage done was more than the *mujahadeen* were normally capable of. According to different reports either 12 or 20 aircraft were destroyed by the blasts.[27]

The conclusion of diplomats in Kabul, and analysts elsewhere, was that the destruction was the work of people inside the base. This demonsration of discontent within the ranks of the air force provoked a major KHAD investigation. According to unconfirmed reports several air force officers were executed following the incident.[28]

PECHGUR AND PANJSHER 9

Since the massive Panjsher 7 offensive of March 1984, government activities in the valley had been restricted to 'aggressive patrols', mainly by helicopter-landed forces. The finger-shaped area of Kabul control extended as far as the village of Pechgur. The area from Pechgur to the mouth of the valley had been garrisoned by the Afghan army. The forces tied down in this role probably amounted to three brigades: the 10th Brigade (of the 20th Division), an unidentified brigade of the 8th Division and the 38th Commando Brigade. These units may have been transferred from their original commands to a new divisional HQ – possibly designated 2nd Division. Although ambushes were common as trucks and helicopters made their way up the narrow corridor to Pechgur, the network of forts had not come under any real threat.

At the beginning of June, Ahmad Shah Massud launched a campaign against government positions in the Panjsher. The base at Rokka was attacked and an ammunition dump set on fire.[29] This activity further down the valley may well have been a part of a deception plan for the assault on Pechgur.

The fort at Pechgur was held by a full strength army battalion of around 500 men. Their fire support weapons included ten mortars, four 76mm guns, two T-55 tanks and five BTR-60 personnel carriers. They were protected by sandbagged emplacements, minefields and barbed wire. The chances of Massud's guerrillas against such a fortress could not have seemed very high. There were fewer than half a dozen occasions in seven years of war when *mujahadeen* had taken a base of more than company size (90–120 men) purely by their own skill and without relying on a revolt inside.

Massud's men were well organised for the attack. One party of 60 were detailed to lift mines and cut through wire entanglements. Another 100 men operated artillery and rocket fire support. The total number of *mujahadeen* involved was probably about the same as the strength of the garrison. At 18.30 on 15 June the attack began. Moving under cover of darkness the 'sappers' began picking their way through the defences. other men put suppressive fire on to army positions.

Undoubtedly the Afghan commanders under-estimated the seriousness of the situation, perhaps expecting that they could use airpower to beat off the attack the following day. But the garrison did not survive that long. At dawn Massud's men moved through clear lanes in the minefield and stormed Pechgur. Such was the measure of surprise that they found a senior Afghan army delegation inside the base. The group, under Central Corps Chief of Staff Brigadier Ahmaddodin, included six colonels and several other officers. Ahmaddodin and one of the colonels were killed during the attack. His death was confirmed by official Kabul sources.[30] Massud's haul of booty was supplemented by 110 officers/NCOs and 350 enlisted prisoners. It appears that Massud's men seperated the POWs, taking a group of 130 (almost all officers) to a prison higher up the valley. Guerrilla accounts do not mention any Soviet advisers among those captured.

Pechgur was a notable victory, not just of Panjsheri courage, but also of organisation and tactics. Government forces, on the other hand, had failed to provide adequate artillery or air support for the base. In the process they had lost senior officers, nearly 500 prisoners and a big haul of arms.

The fall of Pechgur triggered Panjsher 9. This offensive was not comparable to the large-scale 6th or 7th operations, but to the 8th; it was a punitive raid involving mainly heliborne landings. A Soviet motor rifle regiment was sent to the Panjsher, along with two battalions from the 8th Division.[31] There were two main objectives: to retake Pechgur and to recover the prisoners.

The first was achieved without any difficulty. Massud did not contest Pechgur; he had already made his point. The second was not to be achieved. A Soviet heliborne force was landed high in the valley near Dasht-e-Rawat to intercept the prisoners who were being force-marched towards a pass out of the valley. According to the guerrillas, the 130 captives were killed by Soviet bombing. Other reports indicate that they were murdered by their guards as the Soviet rescue force approached. The fact that every one of the prisoners was found dead supports the latter theory.

At the same time as the Pechgur fighting, the Central Corps launched a brigade-level operation into the Paghman hills west of Kabul. Diplomats watched repeated airstrikes by Mil–24s and armed Mil–8s. Despite these efforts the capital suffered a rash of rocket attacks during July. On 17 July, 16 rockets fell including near misses on the Pakistani embassy and a large hospital.[32]

THE SIEGE OF KHOST

Following their new alliance the *mujahadeen* in eastern Afghanistan set out to demonstrate their power. Their target was the provincial capital Khost. Despite the government's offensive in January, the *mujahadeen* still enjoyed wide freedom of action on the Khost plain. In the mountains that surround it they had built major bases at Jaji Maidan and Zhawar.

The bid to take Khost involved men from different parties. Generally the largest contingents were drawn from Jallaladin Haqqani's IO Paktia front and from the NIFA. As the forces concentrated around the city, a NIFA spokesman claimed that 10 000 guerrillas would attack the city.[33] In fact it is unlikely that the forces ever exceeded half this number. Their arms included a number of heavy weapons. News film showed a battery of Chinese-made Type-63 multiple rocket launchers being fired against government defences.

This guerrilla power on the Khost plain was making the city increasingly difficult to supply by air (convoys by road had been virtually impossible for years). Only a few months previously the Soviet journal, *Literaturnaya Gazeta*, had printed a telling account of the dangers of flying into Khost. It noted that the airfield was littered with burnt out aircraft.[34]

Attacks continued throughout July, but the city's defences did not appear to be in immediate danger of crumbling. The force defending Khost consisted of the 25th Division and the 2nd Border Brigade. As in past battles for the city, the garrison was quickly reinforced by the 37th Commando Brigade which was flown in from Kabul.[35]

Just how the *mujahadeen* hoped to take the city with a force no larger than the defending one is unclear. Especially when all previous attempts to capture it had proven fruitless. Their initiative triggered an unexpectedly large response.

SOVIET OFFICERS PROFIT FROM WAR EXPERIENCE

On 25 July, the Soviet Southern Theatre of Military Operations (TVD) gained a new commander: Army General Mikhail Zaytsev. A series of promotions and transfers during 1985 showed the value of Afghan experience for Soviet officers. General Yuri Maksimov left after five years' service in the region, first as Turkestan District commander and then in over-all control. Before the Afghan intervention the Turkestan District was an unimportant posting, and Maksimov's own progress unimpressive. He left to command the Strategic Rocket Forces, the USSR's senior service. In doing so he leapt from around 25th to 6th in the military hierarchy. His rise provided evidence of the Communist Party's continued faith in the military conduct of the war.

His replacement, Mikhail Zaytsev had been Commander-in-Chief of the Soviet garrison in East Germany, and thus of the Central European theatre. Zaytsev's move was not a demotion and this showed that a move to the Southern TVD was considered on a par with, or better than , control of the USSR's biggest field force (19 full strength divisions) in the front line against NATO. Zaytsev tackled his new job with vigour, taking a fact-finding trip to Afghanistan two months after his appointment. He appeared at a government reception in Kabul on 6 November.

As other officers were relocated there was further proof of the importance of experience on the 'Afghan front'. Zaytsev's replacement in Germany, Pyotr Lushev had commanded the Central Asian Military District in December 1979. His successor in Central Asia, Dmitri Yazov had in turn gone on to command the Far Eastern Military District (the second biggest field command). Yazov's former deputy, Vladimir Vostrov, was appointed in command of the Siberian district.

Within a year of his appointment as Defence Minister all of Marshal Sergei Sokolov's key colleagues in the Southern TVD had been elevated to more senior positions. His Chief of Staff during the events of 1979, Valentin Varennikov, was Chief of Operations (a post that customarily leads to the top job of Chief of Staff for the armed forces as a whole). Sokolov's two subordinate district commanders at the time (Lushev and Maksimov) were running the Strategic Rocket Forces and the Central European TVD. Three of the officers who had subsequently served under Sokolov in the Southern TVD had been appointed military district commanders. A year later Lushev got another promotion – to First Deputy Defence Minister.

Thus in the summer of 1985 it became apparent that a new group – an 'Afghan Brotherhood' – had come of age in the Soviet officer corps. Their cohesiveness was explained by Russian novelist Alexander Prokhanov, writing that summer in the *Literaturnaya Gazeta*: 'All of those who have served in Afghanistan, soldiers and civilians alike, are united in spirit and character in a special "Afghan Brotherhood". Their service or their work in Afghanistan completed, they return to their homeland...and yet they remain a "limited contingent", as it were. They recognise one another at once, through some specially indentifiable "Afghan" habit, look, gesture, expression. That experience is already part of us.'[36]

In the pages of other Soviet journals there was confirmation that a tour in the DRA gave a significant boost to an officer's career. Lieutenant Colonel Yu Kuznetsov ran an air assault unit in Afghanistan. He returned with promotion to colonel and command of the prestigious 8th Guards 'Panfilov' Motor Rifle Division in Central Asia.[37] Other officers return from field service to attend high-flying academies. Captain Alexander Solyanov (Air Assault Forces) and Captain Alexander Filyasov (a helicopter gunship pilot) both returned with promotion to major and places at the M.V.Frunze Military Academy.[38] Training at this institution is a passport to further promotion and senior commands. Many similar stories have appeared, confirming a significant trend in the officer corps.

The record of Sokolov's colleagues and the feelings expressed by Prokhanov show that this 'Afghan Brotherhood' is an identifiable and increasingly important element in the Soviet elite. Whereas the armed forces have been led since the war by people who fought in 'the West', key positions were now being taken by those whose experience was in 'the South'.

THE SECOND EASTERN OFFENSIVE OF 1985

On August 20, Soviet/Afghan forces launched their second eastern offensive of 1985. It was much larger than January's effort and involved up to 20 000 men – the biggest operation since Panjsher 7 in 1984. The forces were committed in three seperate axes (see Map XIII).

A mechanised column was dispatched from Kabul via Bagrame to the Logar valley. Another was sent from Jallalabad south-west into the mountains. These two groups were to meet on the Pakistani border near the 'parrot's beak'. This indentation is the closest guerrilla infiltration point to Kabul. The border itself is the inhospitable White Mountain (Spin Ghar) barrier, but about 15 km to the west are the populous upper Logar, Nawa and upper Hessarak valleys. This area served as an extensive support facility for thousands of guerrillas. Groups of the IP (Khalis), IAAM (Sayaf), and NIFA (Gailani) had stored large amounts of equipment and food in the area. Its inaccessibility (being far from the main roads) but closeness to the capital (only 50 km 'as the crow flies') made it an ideal base of operations. Until 1985 its distance from the metalled roads had kept the area safe from government attack.

A third task-force was to drive out of Khost to attack guerrilla bases in the mountains around the city. It would go first to Jaji and then south to Zhawar.

The Soviet forces committed to these actions included at least one motor rifle regiment of the 108th Motor Rifle Division, much of the 103rd Guards Air Assault Division, and the 66th Motor Rifle Brigade. Afghan elements came from the 25th, 12th, 11th and 8th Divisions as well as the 37th Commando Brigade, 1st, 2nd and 8th Border Brigades, and the 466th Commando Battalion (flown in from Kandahar). Afghan and Soviet numbers were approximately equal at 10 000 men each.

The offensive was launched on 21 August with attacks on resistance positions around Bagrame. This fighting continued for two days. By 23 August, the task-force had reached the Logar region. At this point Soviet commanders launched a major heliborne operation, which proved one of the most successful to date. At least a regiment of air assault troops were involved; they were deployed to nine landing zones. They formed a cordon around the large guerrilla bases and villages of the upper Logar. Having placed this noose around the neck of at least one large *mujahadeen* group, it was slowly tightened. The battle lasted five days. According to guerrilla sources at least 100 *mujahadeen* were

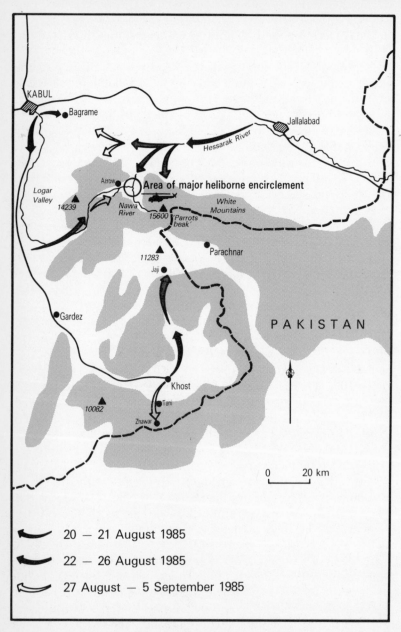

XIII Second Eastern Offensive of 1985.

killed, 40 injured and 116 weapons lost. Enemy losses were reported as 41 Soviets and 12 Afghans killed.[39]

While operations in Logar were going on, the Khost force launched an attack in the direction of Jaji. Government forces apparently pinned down a force of guerrillas loyal to Professor Sayaf. They were saved by the arrival of 400 Hekmatyar IP fighters who beat back the attack.

Approaching Hessarak, the column reached a large IP (Khalis) supply dump, which had apparently been abandoned by its defenders. Three hundred weapons were captured here.[40] This task-force then launched a large heliborne cordon operation. It did not trap any big *mujahadeen* parties, but did take another IP (Khalis) dump: 172 weapons and large quantities of grain were lost.[41]

On 28 August, the Khost force moved south to attack the major resistance concentrations around Tani. There can be little doubt that their objective was Zhawar, the huge guerrilla base close to the border. Stiff opposition slowed the advance to a crawl. It took ten days for them to fight through to Zhawar and by 11 September they were only one or two kilometres from the centre. *Mujahadeen* resolve was such that the attack did not penetrate this last distance. Guerrillas flooded across the border to save the base and, as at Jaji, men from different parties cooperated in the heat of battle.

By mid-September the offensive was complete. The pincer attack on the 'parrot's beak' was successful in that the two forces met up and flushed out large numbers of *mujahadeen* on the way. Soviet and Afghan forces had gone far from the main roads to attack the enemy where they must have considered themselves safe. The operations around Khost did not achieve their probable goals. While the guerrilla 'siege' was broken (it had from the beginning seemed something of a non-starter), large bases, notably Zhawar, did not fall. Both the Afghan army, by their participation in offensive operations close to the Pakistani border, and the *mujahadeen*, with their improved cooperation and determination in defence, could be considered to have shown an improvement.

A long-term consequence of the operations around Khost was that the guerrillas believed themselves invulnerable to government attack. If they had survived such an onslaught, they reasoned, why not proclaim Paktia as a liberated Islamic Republic? Jallaladin Haqqani taunted the Soviets: 'I want them to come and fight me on my own ground, on my own terms.'[42] The base at Zhawar became a symbol of resistance, playing host to increasing numbers of foreign journalists. Recounting the recent fighting the commander told one of them, 'the base had never been in serious danger, and the enemy could not take it as he asserted'.[43] Such confidence was proved ill-founded six months later.

THE SITUATION IN HERAT AND KANDAHAR

Although there was a detectable improvement of security in Mazar-e-Shariff, in other large cities it was still possible for groups of guerrillas to operate in daylight 'down town'. There were reports on 3 July that heavy fighting had erupted in Herat. The situation had become so bad that the governor was apparently withdrawn.[44] In Kandahar, despite the support of Esmatullah Moslem, government security was still bad enough to allow operations by contingents of fighters inside the city. A visiting American journalist, Jeff Harmon, estimated that there were 4500 *mujahadeen* there under the command of Haji Latif.[45] Their bitterest battles were fought against Esmatullah Moslem's militiamen.

Harmon discovered evidence of widespread brutality. Latif claimed to have executed thousands of government POWs. Brutal attacks on even distant relatives of men in Esmatullah Moslem's force caused the government to move it outside the city. Moslem's new responsibility was to protect a stretch of the Kandahar–Kabul road.

On 3 September guerrillas in Kandahar shot down a Bakhtar Airlines (the Afghan internal carrier) Antonov turbo prop. It crashed, killing all 52 people on board. According to Kabul, US-made Stinger surface-to-air missiles were used in the attack.

NAJEEBOLLAH'S TRIBAL STRATEGY

September also saw the arrival in Kabul of 3700 delegates for a *jerga* of tribal leaders. Having tested opinion at the *Loyah Jerga* earlier in the year, the government was ready to boost its tribal strategy. Presiding at the *jerga* was the architect of this *démarche*, Dr Mohammed Najeebollah.

This gathering of Pushtun leaders, from both sides of the border, endorsed a plan to prevent *mujahadeen* infiltration. Leaders from the Pakistani North-West Frontier Province would never have attended such a meeting in 1980–81, but they were approaching Najeebollah's plan with interest. What had changed?

Years of fighting without a guerrilla victory had convinced many that the PDPA were not going to go away and that they would have to start talking to them eventually. More important, though, was the growing antagonism between the original inhabitants of the North-West Frontier Province and the huge expatriate Afghan population. There were quarrels about land and the refugee population had taken over the traditional arms market. The *mujahadeen* and their dependants were also providing serious competition in the heroin business. Feuds between resistance parties and between 'newcomers' and original inhabitants resulted in assassinations and bombings.

General Zia's government in Islamabad provided no comfort for those who objected to the *mujahadeen* presence. His martial law regime had become progressively less popular; to some people the closeness of the Islamic Party factions and Islamic Society of Afghanistan to his regime now counted against them. All of this led a number of Pushtun chieftains to realise that the only people who would listen to their complaints about the refugees were the government in Kabul.

Even during his early years at KHAD, Najeebollah had started a network of agents in the Pushtun area of Pakistan. Through his informers he became aware of the discontent with the resistance parties. It is also likely that he had a role in exacerbating matters through his KHAD agents. Najeebollah asked the Pushtun leaders from Pakistan to stop the *mujahadeen* using their land. He offered them guns and cash so that they could form militias to enforce this ban. Some agreed to do so. How many is unclear – but at this stage they probably represented no more than a small proportion of Pushtun leaders. But Najeebollah's attempt to woo them was about to receive an enormous boost from the unlikeliest of quarters.

THE SARANDOY UNDER FIRE

Although the intelligence service, KHAD, found itself enjoying increasing influence across the border, and the army was taking part in larger-scale operations, the position of the third element of

Kabul's security triad – the Minstry of the Interior *gendarmerie* (Sarandoy) – was deteriorating. Najeebollah's growing power over all elements of security allowed him to undermine the Sarandoy. His main motive for doing so lay in the long-term institutional rivalry bewteen his own KHAD and the Ministry of the Interior.

The sub-text to this organisational conflict (common enough between security agencies in most countries) was the fact that the Sarandoy was still a haven for Khalqis. KHAD on the other hand was solidly Parchami and was putting its full weight behind the campaign to broaden the government's base of support. There were Khalqi elements who believed that this Soviet-sponsored initiative to bring non-party leaders into government was a betrayal of the revolution.[46]

Najeebollah's longer-term objective was that the Ministry of the Interior should be absorbed by the KHAD, and a new super-ministry of security created. This plan had been reported with remarkable foresight by the British Chargé d'Affairs a year previously.[47]

Najeebollah started investigations of high-ranking Sarandoy officials. An early victim of his campaign was Deputy Interior Minister Mur Mohammed Zurmati who was reportedly removed in July 1985 on evidence of helping the resistance.[48] Zurmati's demise was a secret, but KHAD investigators were preparing a spectacular public humiliation for the Sarandoy.

On 3 October, Kabul Radio announced the arrest of several important Sarandoy officers from Logar Province. They were accused of running a secret 'anti-party group' which also included leaders from the provincial Democratic Youth Organisation of Afghanistan hierarchy. Their litany of crime indicates that they were guilty of anti-Soviet Khalqi nationalist sentiments; 'This group has stood against party unity, internationalist unity and against friendship with the people of friendly countries; and has spread seditious rumours; has broken legality and has undermined the people's beliefs and traditions'.[49]

Among the casualties of this investigation were Abdorrashid Azizi, Logar Sarandoy commander, two of his department chiefs, Logar DYOA chief Abdol Mohammed, provincial governor Abdol Gafur Basim, and the local PDPA secretary Mohammed Aslam who received a severe reprimand.

The publicity given to these misdemeanours was a mark of the PDPA Politburo's determination that dissident Khalqis who objected to the new strategy of broadening the revolution's base could expect severe punishment. In the process it would weaken public faith in the Sarandoy and prepare the ground for the forthcoming security reorganisation.

In January, the formation of the Ministry of State Security was announced. Its chief, Ghulam Faruq Yaqubi, was formerly Najeebollah's deputy at KHAD. The new ministry absorbed the Sarandoy provincial commands but a national Ministry of the Interior, with Mohammed Golabzoy at its head, survived. The Interior Ministry remains responsible for some units, training and personnel matters. Operational power was, by and large, placed in the hands of the Ministry of State Security provincial commands. These HQs united Operational Battalion/Brigades (which remained 'cap-badged' to the Sarandoy) with the intelligence service's networks of agents.

EXTERNAL CATALYSTS

In the last weeks of 1985, a number of external developments altered the Afghan political environment. There were developments in the two foreign capitals which have the greatest influence over Afghan affairs: Islamabad and Moscow.

That December General Zia ul-Haq decided to act against the so-called Free Tribes: the Pushtuns of the North-West Frontier Province (NWFP). The official reason for sending the army into these tribal areas was to crack down on the heroin business. The suspicion of many observers was that the army was going in to teach the wayward tribal leaders, some of whom had been to the *jerga* in Kabul, a lesson.

Several heroin 'laboratories', little more than shacks with presses and simple distilling equipment, were shut down in the Khyber Agency. But the army's visit to the NWFP could not have any major effect on the heroin trade. One Pakistani drug-enforcement official pointed out that there were plenty of laboratories out of reach, in resistance-held areas of Afghanistan across the border.

But the high cost of General Zia's raid soon became apparent. In the process a number of armed Pushtuns who tried to oppose the army had been killed. More importantly their honour had been affronted. It was very rare for the regular Pakistan army to be sent into the NWFP, even rarer for them to enter this semi-autonomous area in order to punish the population. Zia had offended against custom; the result was fury with Islamabad.

Mohammed Najeebollah lost no time in taking advantage of the situation. He was able to consolidate and expand his bridgehead in Pushtun Pakistan. Among the outraged Afridi, Shinwari and Mohmand tribes of the Khyber Agency there were new takers for Najeebollah's offers of weapons. Kabul's media launched a campaign to win over the tribesmen. There was no shortage of people to provide Kabul Radio with suitable propaganda: 'Hayat Khan stated that the Pakistani regime, which is surviving by force of bayonet, brutally attacked our brothers in Khyber region, destroying their homes and killing women, children and old men. This situation will never be tolerated by any free tribal persons...he added that the Afridi and Shinwar brothers are in need of emergency aid.'[50]

Within weeks the Afghans had stolen a march in the war of words. Tribal 'leaders' (whose real status was difficult to confirm or deny) appeared in Kabul denouncing the Pakistani government. Soviet television was able to show pictures of refugees fleeing from fighting on the Pakistani side of the border, something of a scoop in the reporting of the long war.[51] Undoubtedly Kabul exaggerated the scale of the disturbances, but news of the trouble spread by word of mouth among Pushtuns on both sides of the border: the damage had been done.

In Moscow, *Pravda* published outraged accounts of the events in the Khyber Agency, but also a critical look at the PDPA's achievements.[52] The authoritative paper urged a further broadening of the base of government support. The appearance of this article started speculation among foreign correspondents in Moscow that the Politburo was losing patience with Babrak Karmal and the Afghan party. There were rumours that Mikhail Gorbachev wanted to pull Soviet troops out, or replace the Afghan leader. Though the tone of the *Pravda* piece was mild compared with the criticisms that Karmal himself made in his speeches, the fact that it was being aired in Moscow was evidence that changes were ahead.

Notes

1.   *The Guardian*, 14 January 1985.
2.   *Daily Telegraph*, 3 January 1985.
3.   *The Guardian*, 14 January 1985.
4.   *Daily Telegraph*, 14 January 1985.
5.   *Pravda*, 14 February 1985.
6.   *Afghan Information Centre (AIC) Bulletin*, February 1985.

7. *Afghan Realities*, 28 Febaruary 1985.
8. *Afghan Realities*, 31 January 1985.
9. *AIC Bulletin*, January 1985.
10. *Afghan Realities*, 31 December 1985.
11. Kabul Radio, List of Officer Promotions, 27 April 1985.
12. British Chargé d'Affairs, Kabul Situation Report, 19–25 February 1985.
13. Kabul Radio, 20 March 1985.
14. *The Guardian*, 29 March 1985.
15. *The Guardian*, 17 April 1985.
16. *The Guardian*, 22 April 1985.
17. British Chargé d'Affairs, Kabul Sitrep, 7–13 May 1985.
18. *Daily Telegraph*, 2 April 1985.
19. Major A. Oliynik, 'By the Spurs of the Spin Ghar: Afghan Border Guards' Uneasy Days', *Krasnaya Zvezda*, 21 May 1985.
20. British Chargé d'Affairs, Kabul Sitrep, 4–11 March 1985.
21. *International Herald Tribune*, 4 June 1985.
22. *Afghan Realities*, 1 June 1985.
23. Gulbuddin Hekmatyar's press conference, *Afghan Realities*, 1 June 1985.
24. Tehran Home Service, 17 June 1985.
25. Kabul Radio, 10 February 1985.
26. Kabul Radio, 7 October 1985.
27. *Jane's Defence Weekly*, 29 June 1985.
28. *The Guardian*, 26 June 1985.
29. *Afghan News* (ISA Newletter), no. 10, 2 July 1985.
30. Kabul Radio, 28 June 1985.
31. *The Times*, 10 July 1985.
32. British Chargé d'Affairs, Kabul Sitrep, 16–22 July 1985.
33. Rahim Wardak's press conference, *AIC Bulletin*, 16 July 1985.
34. *The Guradian*, 7 June 1985.
35. *AIC Bulletin*, 16 July 1985.
36. Alexander Prokhanov, translated and reproduced in *The Guardian*, 28 September 1985.
37. *Kraznaya Zvezda*, 7 May 1985.
38. Solyanov's story: B. Borisov, 'The Blue Beret', *Ogonyok*, 9 February 1985. Filyasov's story: Lt-Col Yu. Kryukov, 'Test of Maturity', *Aviatsaya i Kosmonavtika*, 6/1986.
39. *AIC Bulletin*, no. 54, September 1985, gives a very full guerrilla account of the offensive.
40. Ibid.
41. Ibid.
42. *Sunday Times*, 8 September 1985.
43. *International Herald Tribune*, 13 December 1985.
44. British Chargé d'Affairs, Kabul Sitrep, 9–15 July 1985.
45. *Sunday Times*, 11 August 1985.
46. Anonymous Afghan-regime diplomat to author, April 1986.
47. British Chargé d'Affairs, Kabul Sitrep, 11–17 December 1984.
48. British Chargé d'Affairs, Kabul Sitrep, 2–8 July 1985.
49. Kabul Radio, 3 October 1985.
50. Kabul Radio, 12 January 1986.
51. 'Vremya', transmitted 15 January 1986.
52. *Pravda*, 22 December 1985.

Nine: 1986

SOVIET SAPPERS AT WAR

In Afghanistan, as in many other conflicts, the protagonists spent much of their time trying to inflict casualties with mines. The Soviets made extensive use of them. Huge numbers – some estimates say one million – of PFM–1 butterfly mines had been dropped on guerrilla infiltration routes by the seventh year of the Soviet presence. Buried mines were also used in large numbers along strategic highways, in an attempt to make ambushes more difficult.

But the Limited Contingent of Soviet Forces in Afghanistan also fell victim to enemy mines on may occasions. Early in 1986 several articles appeared in the Soviet military press which highlighted the problems faced by the combat engineers.

One article described the activities of the sapper battalion commanded by Lieutenant Colonel Nikolai Antonenko.[1] His battalion (almost certainly the organic engineer force of the 201st Motor Rifle Division) operated in a large area of north-eastern Afghanistan – in the provinces of Konduz, Takhar and Badakhshan. In five years his men had disarmed 30 000 mines and explosive devices in this area. The battalion had cleared 1000 km of roads of mines, and repaired a further 9000 km of tracks. In the course of these operations the battalion chief of staff had been killed.

Another engineer, Lieutenant-Colonel Gennady Loshkaryov, was featured in the Soviet press. He described the changing nature of the engineers' war: 'How many kinds of mines the sappers have to deal with in Afghanistan!...previously the sappers' mine detectors had often spotted 'home-spun' gadgets – sometimes even a PVC bag fitted with a primitive fuse. In these days the sappers have been dealing more and more often with mines of overseas manufacture.'[2]

Loshkaryov was injured by an Italian-made anti-personnel mine. These devices, made by the firm Technovar, are nicknamed 'easter cakes' by the Soviet troops. According to the Soviet account, Loshkaryov's men disarmed nearly 70 of the distinctively shaped Italian mines on the day that he was injured. Loshkaryov was the first army officer to be decorated with the Order For the Service of the Motherland in all three classes.

The supply of other types of mine made by the Italian firm Technovar was confirmed in another Soviet journal. A photograph clearly shows Soviet sappers in flack-jackets stacking captured Italian anti-tank mines.[3] Technovar is known to have sold large numbers of mines to Arab countries. It is believed that these countries then passed them on to guerrilla parties.

Blowpipe missiles were supplied by the Americans and British through the Middle East. By mid-1986 scores of missiles had arrived, many gong to the Islamic Party of Yunis Khalis.

THE STRUGGLE FOR THE BORDERLANDS

PDPA Central Committee Secretary Mohammed Najeebollah's campaign to close the Pakistani border continued into the New Year. Kabul kept up its propaganda in support of the Pushtun groups of the Free Tribal area. On 24 January, the Afghans claimed that an Afridi group militia on the Pakistani side of the border had siezed 100 *mujahadeen*.[5]

There can be little doubt that truth was one of the first casualties in Kabul's accounts of the turmoil in the tribal areas. Despite their exaggeration there were certain irreducible facts. There was widespread discontent with President Zia among the tribes and there were some tribal leaders who switched to Kabul.

It was, for example, quite certin that an influential chieftain of the Afridi group, named Wali Khan, sided with the DRA. The defection of Khan, who led the Kulikhel clan, was even acknowledged in guerrilla sources.[6] It is more difficult to discover the real depth of support for Kabul and the degree to which the chieftains were prepared to fight their brother Pushtuns in the guerrilla parties.

Late in January, Afghan security forces launched an operation against guerrilla bases in eastern Nangrahar Province. On 28 January, a force of 1600 border troops and militiamen attacked the *mujahadeen* near the villages of Nazian and Sarobi (not to be confused with the Sarobi in Kabul Province) close to the Pakistani border, in the foothills of the White Mountains.[7] On 2 February a task group from the 11th and 9th Divisions, numbering 4000 men, joined the fray.[8]

It appears that the Afghan forces were able to overcome guerrilla positions for a short period. The *mujahadeen* counter-attacked and the army returned to its bases sometime after 23 February.

THE WAR IN HERAT

Late in January, Colonel Joma Asak's 17th Division launched an attack on *mujahadeen* positions near the Zendejan pass in Herat Province. They destroyed an Islamic Society of Afghanistan (ISA) base there, killing an estimated 120 enemy.[9]

Colonel Asak stressed that his headquarters unified elements of the army, Sarandoy, Border Troops and Revolution Defence Groups. He said that all forces had 'been mobilised around one command of the Herat garrison, and have been directed and led by one command'.[10] Asak was evidently so pleased with the performance of his troops that he added, 'the enemy's command and operational capability has been completely disrupted and, as combat commander, I assure you that the enemy's combat capability in the country's north-west zone has been eliminated forever'.

In view of the resilience of Commander Ismael Khan's ISA Front, Asak's claim was a rash one. His headquarters was rocketed within a few hours of his radio broadcast. According to some accounts, the rocket was a Soviet one aimed at *mujahadeen* who were attacking the post. The resistance rumour-machine soon inflated the story, claiming that Asak was killed in the barrage.[11] In fact not only did the colonel survive, but he was promoted to brigadier and transferred to Major-General Shahnwaz Tani's increasingly powerful General Staff.

In view of his promotion it appears that Kabul's verdict on Joma Asak's campaign of January and February was favourable. But the basic security situation in Herat, Badghis, Farah and Ghowr Provinces (the ones under 17th Division jurisdiction) had improved little.

Years of heavy fighting had depopulated the area, giving the guerrillas some problems, but they had evolved into a comparatively efficient organisation. In the dangerous open ground near Herat the guerrillas used tunnels – many of which had been dug for drainage and irrigation – to move between villages.[12]

Just as the Americans in Vietnam found themselves trying to flush an unseen enemy from an underground haven, so the Soviets tried to hunt them. Sergeant Sergei Kuznetzov recounts an engagement: 'They were shooting at us from the house. We were shooting at that house, nobody came out, we went in and found this tunnel. Somebody had to go in. I was deputy commander of the platoon and crawled inside. I tripped over a rocket launcher, passed it back and crawled further...Andrei Trofimovich was lucky. He was going down the passage and a bandit's buttet missed him.'[13]

KARMAL IN DECLINE

By February there were signs that Babrak Karmal's position was faltering. A government news agency press release of 17 February noted that the leader 'did not appear in the best of health'.[14] At the end of the month he went to Moscow, where he was dealt a more ominous humiliation at the hands of Mikhail Gorbachev.

Unlike Fidel Castro, Le Duan and the leaders of other socialist countries, Karmal was not invited to address the 27th Congress of the Communist Party of the Soviet Union. To add to his discomfort, Karmal had to listen to Mikhail Gorbachev call Afghanistan a 'bloody stump' from the platform.

Karmal's health was suffering and after the congress he went for medical treatment. He had suffered for some years from respiratory disorders, spending up to six weeks each year in Soviet clinics. But his treatment at the 27th Congress left no doubt that there was a more serious problem in the relationship.

The Afghan leader was regarded as weak by Moscow – not just in health, but in his ability to impose tighter discipline on the party and state machine. Articles in *Pravda* hinted at Soviet frustration with the slow growth of support for the government. It was also quite possible, given his congress speech, that Gorbachev wanted to frighten the Afghan party by raising the prospect of a withdrawal and installing a stronger leader.

With Afghan power structure so closely modelled on the Soviet one, it is also worth mentioning the changes that Gorbachev made to his own machinery of power. Under Brezhnev, one man headed the three arms of Soviet power: the Party, the Supreme Soviet (legislature) and the Council of Ministers (the executive or government). But Gorbachev took only the title of Party General Secretary. Initially there were signs that he believed that Afghanistan could benefit from a similar division of labour.

As Karmal's position became uncertain, the Soviets seemed to give greater prominence to Soltan Ali Keshtmand, the Chairman of the Council of Ministers. Keshtmand published a major article in *Izvestia*[15] and received a high-level reception at Moscow airport a high-level reception at Moscow airport during a visit in April. All of this led many Western analysts to conclude, wrongly, that Keshtmand was Karmal's chosen successor.

In fact the Soviets were probably aware that as a member of the Hazara minority it might make good sense, within Afghanistan, to give Keshtmand prominence, but it would have made little sense to make him leader. The grip of the Pushtuns on national political life – even under the PDPA – remained too strong for a Hazara to be acceptable as leader. Nevertheless the more prominent treatment accorded to Keshtmand was a sign of changes to come in the division of power in the DRA.

On 27 March, Karmal appeared at the 17th Plenum of the PDPA Central Committee in Kabul. He presented his report on the 27th Congress. On 2 April, he addressed the expanded Revolutionary Council. It was his last appearance in Kabul for several weeks, for he returned to the USSR – officially for medical treatment.

THE ZHAWAR CAMPAIGN

In September 1985, a task-force narrowly failed to take the guerrilla base at Zhawar, close to the Pakistani border. By their failure they increased the standing of Jallaladin Haqqani, the local IP (Khalis) commander. Haqqani added to the fortifications, in the belief that the base was impregnable.

Visiting journalists saw several tanks, underground workshops and an impressive system of trenches around Zhawar. Inside the tunnels there were generators and a field telephone system linking different areas. Air defence consisted of three 40mm anti-aircraft guns, dozens of heavy machine guns and several SA-7s.[16] Haqqani's investment boosted his status, giving him a degree of authority over men in other groups in Paktia. He declared Zhawar and its surrounding area to be liberated.

All of this doubtless infuriated the Soviets and their Afghan allies, who were waiting for another opportunity to attack the fortress. The new offensive involved a degree of organisation superior to anything the Afghan army had managed before.

The plan involved the pooling of units from throughout the east of the country. Although this pattern was sometimes used by Soviet units (for example in Panjsher 7), the idea was to involve as little of the 40th Army as possible. Control was exercised by the General Staff of Major-General Shahnawaz Tani. He gave his first deputy, a talented officer from the Baluchi minority, command of the operation. This man, Brigadier Abdol Gafur, set about preparing the army for its toughest challenge to date.

Throughout March, units were concentrated in Paktia for the operation. Elements of the 8th, 14th, 12th, 7th and 25th Divisions were pooled. According to one rumour a unit was even brought from the 18th Division, hundreds of kilometres to the north.

The 37th Commando Brigade, Shahnawaz Tani's old unit, was built-up to full strength of around 1500 men in three battalions. The brigade, along with the 466th Commando Battalion from Kandahar and a Soviet air assault regiment were flown into Khost. The Soviet unit (probably designated 40th Guards Air Assault Regiment) belonged to the 103rd Guards Air Assault Division in Darulaman.[17] The 2200 man unit was the only Soviet regiment involved in the ground fighting.

The Afghan and Soviet commandos flown into Khost - about 4200 men - amounted to one third of the 12 000 men or so committed for the operation. They would spearhead the drive into the mountains.

The new offensive was timed to coincide both with a new round in the Geneva talks and with another *jerga* of tribal leaders in Kabul. In the first week of April, forces set out from Khost on their way to Tani. They engaged various pockets of resistance on the Khost plain. The government claimed 120 guerrillas were killed during this phase of the operation.[18] They reached Tani, which was held by the 907th Battalion of the 2nd Border Brigade.

As the force progressed beyond Tani, towards Zhawar, resistance became very heavy. Groups which were still on the plain started to rocket Khost airfield in an attempt to disrupt heliborne operations. During the three weeks of fighting they fired nearly

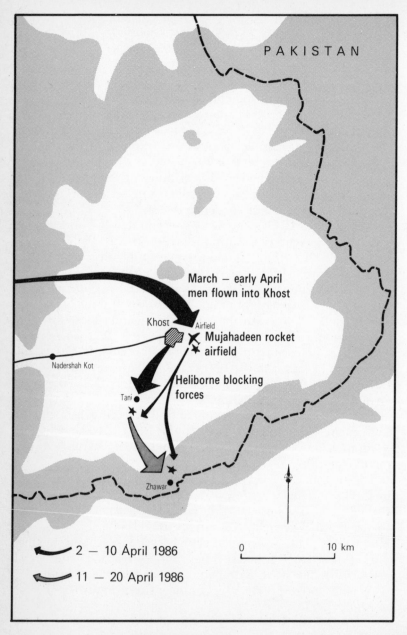

XIV Zhawar Campaign, 1986.

2500 107mm rockets at the town.[19] *Mujahadeen* from the NIFA, ISA and Sayaf groups combined with Haqqani's Khalis forces to resist the onslaught.

They succeeded in stalling the advance just south of Tani for several days. Brigadier Gafur then used what he described as 'hammer and anvil' tactics – driving the *mujahadeen* against the mountains to prevent their retreat, and then smashing them.[20] His usual device for doing this was the battalion heliborne landing. Afghan and Soviet commandos launched several of these during the second week of April.

It took ten days to fight from Tani to the outer defences at Zhawar. The rate of advance averaged only two or three kilometres a day. Haqqani appealed for help and fighters came across the border. Resistance forces were heavily armed and skilful, imposing one notable humiliation. A battalion of the 37th Commando Brigade landed in a guerrilla killing zone and was almost completely destroyed. About 80 men of the 400-strong landing force surrendered, the rest died.

As the 'hammer' approached Zhawar, the fortress was subjected to increasingly heavy air attack. Su-25s dropped laser-guided bombs into cave mouths, killing many.[21] Pakistan reported dozens of violations of its airspace as fighters wheeled over the fortress, only three kilometres from the border. Zhawar's anti-aircraft defences claimed at least three helicopters and a fighter.[22] After several days of pounding, the anti-aircraft fire became increasingly inaccurate – the defenders had fired so many rounds that they had worn out their gun barrels. In one air attack Haqqani himself was injured. He was taken across the border.

Informed of the imminent fall of the fortress, Major-General Nazar Mohammed, the Defence Minister, flew into Khost on 19 April.[23] By the next day Afghan and Soviet commandos were in the caves of Zhawar. The *mujahadeen* used their tanks in the battle – apparently two were destroyed and two captured. After four days of hand-to-hand fighting, the base was cleared. Gafur's men then flushed out several other bases in the area. During the first week of May, Afghan/Soviet forces launched attacks round Jaji (Alikhel), further north in Paktia province.

According to Kabul Radio, "252 independent enemy fortifications were destroyed. 6000 anti-tank mines and 12 000 anti-personnel mines were neutralised; and hundreds of rockets and rocket launchers, thousands of 107mm rockets and millions of rounds of tank and machine gun ammunition were siezed.'[24] They also claimed 2000 enemy dead and 4000 injured for the whole operation. While these figures are exaggerated, it is quite probable that the *mujahadeen* lost around 1000 killed during the entire operation. A guerrilla source admits that 250 were killed in the caves of Zhawar alone.[25]

Abdol Gafur's plan to force the *mujahadeen* to stand and face an unequal fight succeeded – due as much to the guerrillas belief that their fortress was impregnable as to the brigadier's skill. The most important aspect of the battle was that it proved that the Afghan army, when well organised and well supported, could win against heavily armed *mujahadeen* close to their source of spply.

The performance of the Afghan army in the battle for Zhawar is remarkable when compared to its dismal efforts in 1980-81. Only 200-300 men deserted Gafur's force, even though they were within sight of the Pakistani border. They overcame a strong and well-coordinated resistance. Cooperation in the field by men of different *mujahadeen* parties was very good. The cost to the Afghan army was high – perhaps 600 dead.

At first resistance sources tried to deny that the fortress had fallen.[26] When it became obvious that it had, they tried to belittle the army's achievement. But the smouldering shambles at Zhawar was testimony enough. A force composed mainly of Kabul troops had brought death to the *mujahadeen* where they believed they were safe. On the night of 23 April, men of the 37th Commando Brigade held positions in Jallaladin Haqqani's bunkers – a place where they had not set foot in eight years of war. The architect of victory, Brigadier Abdol Gafur, boarded a plane to Kabul and celebration.

A GATHERING OF THE TRIBES

While the Sukhois were pounding Paktia, tribal leaders from Pakistan arrived for a *jerga* in Kabul. According to the official communiqué, 1540 Pushtun and Baluch tribal leaders from Pakistan and 200 from Afghanistan attended the gathering.[27] A message from Babrak Karmal was read *in absentia*.

The leading light at the *jerga* was Mohammed Najeebollah. He urged them to return to Pakistan with the mission of helping Afghan refugees: 'Save them from the pressure of rebel hands and discharge your fraternal duty for their return to this country so that they can continue their peaceful life in their country.'[28]

With no apparent sense of irony, Najeebollah also stressed that the DRA would never interfere in Pakistan's internal affairs. The *jerga*, like the one in 1985, was a victory for Kabul and for Najeebollah.

OPERATIONS IN FARIAB

The province of Fariab, near the Soviet border, in northern Afghanistan had never offered ideal territory for the guerrillas. Much of the area was too flat – particularly near the frontier. Government posts had already made rebel attacks difficult in the provincial capital, Maimana. The men still fighting were mostly loyal to the ISA's local commander, Ujjur Pahlevan, and the Islamic Movement.

In March, matters deteriorated for the resistance when several rivers flooded. Soviet and Afghan commanders planned an opertion to clear guerrillas from around the town of Andkhoy. An estimated 3000 Afghan troops were assigned – the bulk of the 18th Division, Sarandoy and Border Troops. A Soviet force numbering around 1000 was also committed.

What caught the *mujahadeen* off-guard was that the Soviet ground column launched its attack from Aqina, inside the USSR. The combined forces surrounded Andkhoy and the cluster of villages around it. They tightened the encirclement, clearing villages one by one. This continued for over a week until guerrillas started running out of ammunition. At this point a number of commanders defected.

Several hundred fighters were probably able to escape the encirclement, but others were trapped, In a letter to party leader Rabbani, Ujjer Pahlevan estimated losses in the disastrous battle. The enemy lost 400–600, the *mujahadeen* 1000. He added '17 of the best local commanders drank the cup of martyrdom.'[29] The remnants of Pahlevan's force fled south to the Astana Baba mountains, on the edge of the Hazara Jat. The offensive succeeded in neutralising the resistance around Andkhoy – with defections perhaps as many as 1400 men were lost to them. It also created a large flow of refugees internally and some even as far as Pakistan – a month-long walk.

NAJEEBOLLAH TAKES OVER

On 25 April, Brigadier Abdol Gafur, hero of Zhawar, appeared in
Kabul. Like other senior military and party men who came to the
city for the annual April Revolution day celebrations he did not
want to miss the big day. But Babrak Karmal was conspicuous by
his absence. Rumours of his imminent demise were rife, but many
diplomats and PDPA men still believed that he would appear on
the reviewing stand for the 27 April parade.

When Karmal did not show up, most Kabulis realised that there
was something seriously wrong. Karmal was not disgraced –
people in the parade carried his picture and he was still referred to
as Party General Secretary.

On 4 May, the PDPA Central Committee met for its 19th
Plenum. According to the official account 'after talks and
discussions in a completely free and democratic atmosphere, votes
were taken and the resignation of comrade Babrak Karmal on
health grounds was approved unanimously. Najeebollah was
appointed his successor as General Secretary in a climate of
complete unity of views.'[30]

Diplomatic reports say that tanks took up key positions in Kabul
for the announcement of Karmal's resignation. There were also
reports of demonstrations in favour of Karmal at several schools in
the capital.[31] Karmal stayed on as President of the Revolutionary
Council. Initially he was cast in the role of elder statesman and it
was believed he would stay in Kabul. But in time, following
interference by Karmal's supporters, he was removed to a safer
distance.

For a few months the division of power between Karmal,
Najeebollah and Keshtmand mirrored that between Gromyko,
Gorbachev and Ryzhkov. In these early days, the idea that there
was too much work for one man and that a broadening at the top of
the power structure paralleled the broadening of the revolutionary
base were added to Karmal's poor health as reasons for the change.

Undoubtedly Najeebollah's physical strength counted in his
favour – his nickname was 'the bull'. He took over as General
Secretary when only 38 years old, but his appeal to the Soviets was
as a strong man in the political sense. His control of KHAD gave
him power over politburo colleagues. Charm and family
background boosted his credibilty in the eyes of Pushtun leaders.

But Najeebollah was also perceived as one of the few men in the

PDPA who was more pro-Soviet than Karmal; as such his choice could have been controversial. Not only would he annoy nationalist Khalqis (some of whom still held senior army posts) with his mandate to broaden the base of the revolution still further, but he also had many rivals from his past battles with the Sarandoy.

In short there were factions in the security forces who might have plotted against Najeebollah. But although there were some unconfirmed reports of shooting in Kabul, it is quite clear that there was no *coup* attempt, and that Najeebollah's accession to power was the smoothest of any Afghan leader for 20 years.

In many ways this near flawless transition was the greatest tribute to Babrak Karmal. There were murmurings among old party adversaries, but the PDPA behaved itself. Perhaps Najeebollah's enemies understood that the ex-chief of intelligence knew too well who they were, or perhaps Gorbachev's implied threats of Soviet withdrawal prevailed. Whatever their reasons, party rivals kept quiet and the organisation was seen to behave maturely. Karmal's long campaign against factionalism paid off – to that extent anyway.

The President himself returned to Kabul a few days later. He attended public meetings, shared the platform with Najeebollah and took up his temporary mantle as party figurehead. There was no overt sign of any rift or hard feelings on his part. Perhaps Karmal was happy to enjoy the fruits of his own labour, as the first Afghan leader in 13 years to leave office alive.

NAJEEBOLLAH ON THE ROAD

Within days of his promotion Najeebollah (now referred to by the Kabul media as Dr Najeeb) began a hectic programme of visits and speeches. He talked to tribal leaders, army officers, Sarandoy units, members of the clergy, farmers and party workers. He travelled around the country. The contrast with Karmal was obvious: the 'bull' had energy and he would use it to galvanize the party.

At the same time the Foreign Minister, Shah Mohammed Dost, led a delegation to Geneva for another round of talks. After Mikhail Gorbachev's remarks many observers thought the Soviets might accept any deal for a withdrawal. In fact the talks produced no progress, remaining deadlocked on the timetable issue.

Najeebollah did not offer any new political programme, just a more energetic application of the existing one. Soviet television said he would 'be steadily implementing the resolutions adopted by previous plenums of the Central Committee concerning the expansion and strengthening of the social base of the revolutionary order.'[31]

Speaking on 14 May, Najeebollah criticised the party for weakness in the practical sphere.[32] His first real political initiative was launched during a visit to Mazar-e-Shariff in June. He announced the setting up of a second house for the legislature – a Council of Nationalities. This chamber, like its Soviet counterpart, would include representatives from all national minorities.[33]

Najeebollah also used his visit to Mazar to reassure local clergymen that his government was pro-Islamic. His speech included Koranic sayings and claimed that 127 mosques had been built since the April Revolution. State radio told listeners that Najeebollah's first stop when he returned to Kabul was to attend Friday prayers at the mosque.

Najeebollah's likely opponents in the further broadening of government support were certain Khalqi nationalists who felt the PDPA was 'diluting' the revolution under Soviet pressure. There were some rumours that Major-General Nazar Mohammed, Defence Minister and veteran Khalqi, would lose his job immediately. In fact the new leader waited several months before replacing him with former minister Brigadier Mohammed Rafi.

At the 19th Plenum of the Central Committee there was an expansion of this important body. Some 49 full and 40 candidate (non-voting) members were appointed. Many of them were undoubtedly Najeebollah supporters. One full and two candidate members were appointed to the Politburo. These included two of Najeebollah's old allies: Tribal Affairs Minister Suleiman La'eq and Minister of State Security Ghulam Faruq Yaqubi.

On the whole, the 19th Plenum was generous: Najeebollah had involved more people in high-level party work and promoted a few allies in the process. There was only one notable casualty – army political chief Major-General Yasin Sadeqi. He lost his position as a Central Committee secretary, and his job.

General Sadeqi had achieved a great deal as political chief. Whereas just over a third of units had political organisations in 1981, this figure had risen to a claimed 85 per cent in 1986. Writing earlier in the year Sadeqi summed up the achievement: 'A harmonious structure of the party political apparatus has now been established in our army. Its basis is the nearly 7000-strong detachment of political-worker officers, many of whom have been trained at higher military political schools in the Soviet Union.'[34]

That structure of political control had been every bit as important in Najeebollah's smooth assumption of power as the coercive apparatus of the Ministry of State Security, which also penetrated most units. Unlike the presence of State Security agents in units, which prevented wayward officers from plotting, the political workers also had a role in motivating troops on the battlefield.

The likely reason for Sadeqi's removal is that he had become too powerful. He may well have opposed the further expansion at senior levels of the party. The unfortunate General was the only obvious victim in Najeebollah's early months in power. In many ways he did not deserve it, having played a bigger part in improving army effectiveness than most officers.

MASSUD GOES NORTH

The leader of the Panjsher resistance, Ahmad Shah Massud, chose to spend much of the summer of 1986 fighting outside his home valley. There were several reasons for this. Soviet/Kabul forces garrisoned on the lower floor of the valley were operating more effectively. The loss of Pechgur the previous summer had alerted them to the vulnerability of some of their fixed positions.

Faced with the strength of this garrison Massud did what ISA spokesmen said he might do following the 1984 Panjsher 7 offensive: he looked for targets outside the valley. Another reason for the expedition was the weakness of the ISA Marmoul Front since the death of Zabiullah. Previously Zabiullah had working agreements with many other groups in the northern provinces. But in the eighteen months after his death rebel effectiveness in this area declined noticeably. Massud's well organised expedition that summer was to prove once again that the Lion of the Panjsher was in a class of his own.

Massud took several *motoraks* out of the Panjsher, as well as other ISA men from Salang and Baghlan, and went north to Badakhshan and Takhar.

In June he operated in Badakshan and a Soviet operation was launched to trap him and his ISA forces in the Khejob valley. An air assault regiment was committed to operations here, a battalion of which operated from a forward base in Konduz. As the Soviets went up the valley they were supported by 60–70 helicopters.[35] Parties of men were landed by helicopter on high ground and worked their way down the valley, clearing it of enemy.

ISA fighters staged at least one costly ambush on an air assault forces reconnaissance party. The group was being landed by two Mil-17 helicopters when it was ambushed – 20 Soviet commandos were killed in the action. Maps taken from an officer showed that the commandos had a very good intelligence picture of guerrilla forces in the area.[36]

Massud then went to Eshkamish, base of the army 75th Brigade. He launched a number of attacks there, but did not succeed in taking the town.[37]

Following their operations in Khejhob and Eshkamish, Massud's group moved south to attack a government fort at Ferkhar. Coordinated by radio, Massud's men eliminated outlying posts one by one until the central fort was isolated. This outpost, which included a contingent of State Security men, resisted for some time before being overcome.[38] Up to 300 government troops were killed or captured in the fighting.

A LIMITED WITHDRAWAL

On 28 July, during a speech in Vladivostock, Soviet leader Mikhail Gorbachev surprised the world by announcing a limited withdrawal of Soviet forces from Afghanistan. The initiative was part of a package aimed at improving relations with China.

The General Secretary announced that two motor rifle, one tank and three anti-aircraft regiments were to be withdrawn. While Western commentators stated that a pull-out of 7000 would hardly effect the capabilities of a force of 118 000 (a US State Department figure; see Appendix II for a discussion of LCSFA strength), the move did have military significance. Two motor rifle regiments out of 11 (nine divisional and two independent) was important. No military commander would happily give such forces up.

By pulling men out, Gorbachev was also signalling his willingness in principle to withdraw all Soviet troops. The initiative was welcomed by a Pakistani foreign ministry spokesman.[39] While the move had obvious significance for the peace talks in Geneva, some Soviet commentators were anxious to reject the idea of linkage. One pointed out angrily that the issue of Soviet withdrawal was still a bilateral one between Moscow and Kabul.[40] The six regiments eventually departed in October, amid Pentagon claims that other Soviet troops had been brought into the DRA to make up for them.

In November, it was announced that Babrak Karmal had relinquished the title of president and other party titles. Kabul media gave details of his pension and the retirement that awaited him. However poor Karmal's health, it would have been easy for Najeebollah to have kept him on in a figurehead role. The move must therefore be seen as a consolidation of Najeebollah's personal power. Karmal's move into the wings and Najeebollah's strengthening of his own position mark a watershed in Afghan politics. The new leader came from a younger, harder generation. He had served for six years near the top of an embattled regime before coming to power. In time the differences in his approach will be felt by all Afghanistan.

Notes

1.   Col V. Filatov, on Radio Moscow, 17 January 1986.
2.   G. Miranovich, 'Doing His Bit', *Soviet Military Review*, no. 12, 1985.
3.   See *Ogonyok*, 13 March 1986.
4.   See author's article, *The Independent*, 17 June 1987.
5.   Kabul Radio, 24 January 1986.
6.   *AIC Bulletin*, no. 60, March 1986.
7.   *AIC Bulletin*, no. 59, February 1986.
8.   Ibid.
9.   British Chargé d'Affaires, Kabul Sitrep, 21–27 January 1986.
10. Kabul Radio, 23 February 1986.
11. Tehran Radio (home service), 26 February 1986.
12. Commander Allaladin, of Herat ISA Front, interviewed by author, 7 April 1986.
13. Moscow Radio (home service), 23 March 1986.
14. Bakhtar News Agency, report of 18 February 1986.
15. Soltan Ali Keshtmand, *Izvestia*, 13 March 1986.
16. David Isby, who visited Zhawar, interviewed by author, March 1986.
17. *AIC Bulletin*, no. 62, May 1986.
18. Kabul Radio, 8 April 1986.
19. Rahmatullah Safi, NIFA commander who took part in Zhawar battle, interviewed by David Isby, information given to author, September 1986.

20. Abdol Gafur, interviewed in Tass release, 22 April 1986.
21. Rahmatullah Safi, see note 19.
22. *Voice of Afghanistan*, 19 April 1986.
23. Kabul Radio, 15 April 1986.
24. Kabul Radio, 3 May 1986.
25. Rahmatulah Safi, see note 19.
26. Karachi Radio (home service), 25 April 1986.
27. Kabul Radio, 9 April 1986.
28. Najeebollah's speech to *jerga*, Kabul Radio, 10 April 1986.
29. Copy of letter from Pahlevan to Rabbani obtained through Afghan Support Committee, London.
30. Kabul Radio, 4 May 1986.
31. Soviet TV broadcast, 5 May 1986.
32. Bakhtar News Agency, 14 May 1986.
33. Kabul Radio, 28 May 1986.
34. Gen. Yasin Sadeqi, *Kraznaya Zvezda*, 20 February 1986.
35. Arthur Kent, a journalist, was eyewitness at the Khejob fighting, interviewed by author, 15 October 1986.
36. *Jane's Defence Weekly*, 18 October 1986.
37. *AIC Bulletin*, no. 65, August 1986.
38. Report by Sandy Gall, transmitted on ITV News at Ten, 22 September 1986.
39. Karachi Radio (home service), 28 July 1986.
40. Yuri Kornilov, Moscow Radio, 25 July 1986.

Analysis

A COUP OR A REVOLUTION?

When officers loyal to the PDPA seized power in Kabul in April 1978, their act was described by many foreign observers (for example Louis Dupree, an American academic expert on the country) as a *coup*. For the tiny Afghan party, on the other hand, the events of that month were elevated to the 'Great April Revolution'.

The PDPA found themselves in power with a membership of only 18 000 (by their own estimate, others say 8000–10 000). With this tiny constituency they hoped to change an independent, obstinate, conservative people. Their aims – redistribution of land, equality for women and equal ethnic opportunity – were revolutionary. They declared these aims very quickly; some Soviet theorists were to say too quickly.

If tumultuous events are the index of revolution, then the bombing of President Daoud's residence ranks ahead of the storming of the Winter Palace in Petrograd in 1917. The violence that has followed has, to paraphrase Mao, been no dinner party. The smallness of the PDPA and their reliance on a small segment of the armed forces was not in itself the main reason for the failure of the Khalqi regime. Castro's revolution in Cuba began with half a dozen followers. Lenin himself led a tiny party when the tsar was overthrown.

In the case of the Russian Revolution there was a centralised structure of authority to be seized. In Afghanistan there was none. If Taraki and his followers did not face trouble sooner in 1978, it was because it took months for peasants to feel the change in Kabul. As the idealists in Kabul unveiled their programme they succeeded in alienating the key social force in the country: leadership at the village level. These leaders, whether spiritual, tribal or landowners, could all agree on the threat to their interests posed by the 'communists' in the big city.

Had the Khalqis managed to keep the army together they might have imposed their will more successfully. Instead Taraki and Amin neglected party control of the forces and alienated growing numbers of even their own small band.

In a very narrow sense, the PDPA succeeded in creating a

revolution in Afghanistan: they unleashed the colossal latent tension in Afghan society. Their revolution, and the bloodshed that has followed, is about the transformation of a backward society, a 'nation' only in its xenophobic perception of outsiders. The record of Afghanistan's leaders until 1978 was a pitiful one: they had failed to give the country any of the attributes of the modern centralised state.

Since the Soviet intervention the issues have, of course, altered. There are Kremlin ideologists who see the napalming of villages as a justifiable action against CIA-sponsored 'counter-revolution'. There are Americans who believe that giving Stinger rockets to 'freedom fighters' so that they may shoot down airliners is justifiable, because it imposes a cost on 'Soviet exapansionism'. Such beliefs are trading in Afghan lives. But when the fighting is over Afghanistan must still struggle with its backwardness. Whether it is communism or Islamic fundamentalism that eventually triumphs, the April Revolution will probably be seen as the starting point of that struggle.

WHY DID THE SOVIETS INVADE?

The committal of the Soviet army to the war in Afghanistan in December 1979 marked a turning-point not just in the conflict, but in superpower relations. This event is seen by many as the death of detente, the birth of a new Cold War.

There is no way of knowing the relative weight given to various factors when the Poltiburo discussed the issue throughout the summer and autumn of 1979. Our experience of Western cabinet memoirs tells us that, even had the protagonists published accounts of these deliberations, they would probably have differed. Hindsight presents us with a list of possibilities; one day they may be repeated by schoolchildren in the way that history presents convenient classification of the 'causes of the English (or American) Civil War':

(a)   the preservation of a friendly government in Kabul;
(b)   the removal of Hafizullah Amin and his narrow-based group
       of Khalqi supporters;
(c)   the desire to secure strategic real estate (bases, etc.);
(d)   the wish to alter the regional balance of power;

(e) spreading Soviet ideology;
(f) absence of cost. Soviet belief in Western and Third World indifference.

All of these factors probably weighed on the minds of Brezhnev and his colleagues. Analysis of events gives us clues as to their relative significance.

Above all, the Kremlin needed to maintain a friendly government in Kabul. That government can be defined as one drawn from the People's Democratic Party, with a socialist programme and a pro-Soviet stance in international affairs.

Quite clearly though, Hafizullah Amin's leadership was unacceptable to the Kremlin. His policies were accelerating the collapse of the army and alienating the mass of the population. The vilification to which Amin was subjected posthumously, by both the Soviets and the Karmal faction, leave no doubt that they hold him responsible for many of their subsequent difficulties. There is evidence that the KGB really believed that Amin was acting on behalf on the CIA and would eventually have turned on them.

The difficult task of removing Amin, while preserving the party that had sponsored his excesses, was the key Soviet objective. In a way, everything flows from it. Certainly possessing Afghan airbases would marginally improve Soviet chances of interdicting the Gulf oil flow, but the Treaty of Friendship with Taraki's government would have given them access to those in times of crisis anyway.

Strategic bases could have been readily secured perfectly (as the intervention showed) before the outbreak of hostilities. Most Soviet aircraft lack the range to reach the oilfields from Shindand or Bagram. The types that do (such as the Tu–22M Backfire and Su–24 Fencer) have not been based in the DRA. To suggest that a lust for facilities prompted the intervention is to ignore the complex events that preceded the operation and that have motivated Soviet policy since.

The maintenance of a 'friendly' regime in Kabul does not neccessarily mean exporting Soviet-style revolution. Undoubtedly the PDPA had been strongly influenced by Marxist–Leninist thought, but until they took power the Soviet party virtually ignored them. There were no delegations to congresses, very little training of cadres and scant material support. On the contrary the Soviets gave considerable aid (including military and internal security equipment) to the very regimes which Karmal, Taraki and Amin were plotting to overthrow. What was important to the Kremlin was having good relations with its southern neighbour.

Since the arrival of the Limited Contingent of Soviet Forces, it has become obvious that Soviet theorists do not believe the country is ready for a complete Marxist transformation. They rank Afghanistan, along with many other developing nations, as a revolutionary country in its 'national democratic phase'. Soviet treatment of other regimes in this category shows that they are prepared to tolerate military dictatorships without party infrastructure or orthodox Marxist aims.

The ideological aim in Afghanistan has been expressed recently, not in terms of an East European satellite closely modelled on Soviet socialism, but (in Mikhail Gorbachev's words) of 'expanding the social base of the April national democratic revolution right up to the point of creating a government with the participation of political forces which have been outside the country but are ready to participate sincerely in the nationwide process of constructing a new Afghanistan'. Far from advocating a hard-line ideological programme it is apparent, even from open sources, that the Soviets regarded Taraki and Amin's espousal of a Marxist programme as an embarrassment. Their ideological objective in invading was to ensure the survival of a leftist (as opposed to Marxist) pro-Soviet PDPA regime. Although the armed forces and certain other agencies are clearly patterned on the Soviet model, other aspects of policy (the inclusion of non-party people in government, gifts of land to supporters) clearly run counter to it.

In the context of the times (the Iranian revolution, and the wave of fundamentalism that followed it), the prospect of allowing the PDPA to fall was distinctly alarming to Moscow. Some observers believe that this in turn would have affected the stability of the Soviet Central Asian republics. It must be said, though, that those areas of the USSR bordering on revolutionary Iran do not seem to have experienced any particular upsurge in Islamic discontent.

Others on the right of Western politics saw the intervention as part of a grand geo-political strategy to alter the Near Eastern balance of power. Images of the imperialist 'Great Game' were conjured up: Afghanistan as a victim of Russia's long-held expansionist designs. All that lay between the Soviets and the warm waters of the Indian Ocean was the relatively unstable Baluchi area of Pakistan.

In fact the Indian Ocean Squadron is not short of ports. Since the introduction of Soviet forces into the DRA there has been remarkably little exploitation of the Baluchi problem. Indeed the Soviets and the PDPA have been far less active in stirring up this minority than previous Afghan governments. While there have been many minor infringements of Pakistani airspace, as well as some shelling, it must be said that the Soviets have been careful not to escalate the conflict.

It is not hard to imagine how frustrated Soviet military commanders must be that they cannot attack the huge guerrilla infrastructure in Pakistan. Compared with almost every Western nation faced with externally supported insurgency their behaviour has been the model of restraint. In South-East Asia the war expanded to Laos and Cambodia precisely because those countries were being used as a base by the Viet Cong. In southern Africa neither Rhodesia nor South Africa hesitated to launch major military 'hot pursuit' raids into neighbouring countries. And in the Middle East Israel has used massive military force against insurgents based in Lebanon. In short, the Soviets have been able to limit the escalation of the conflict and have actually destabilised the region less than the forces of 'democratic' countries operating in South-East Asia, southern Africa, or the Middle East.

Finally, it is evident that the Soviets did not believe that the operation would cost them a great deal. Here they seriously under-estimated the consequences of their actions. In the DRA itself the arrival of the Soviet army fanned the rural rebellion and accelerated the collapse of the army. The backing of Karmal's Parcham group also intensified factionalism in the party itself.

Internationally there was also a huge cost. Russian misperception of the Carter administration may have led to the belief that there would be only token objections to action in an area of traditional Soviet influence. In fact it provided the gathering American Right, many of whom did not even believe in dialogue or arms control, with a tailor-made excuse to torpedo these processes. The presence of Soviet troops continues to prevent normalisation of relations with China. Increases in defence spending might well have happened under President Reagan without Afghanistan; but there must be some, at least, in the Kremlin who wonder whether the ruinous intensification of the arms race is the price that they are paying for those barren Afghan mountains.

WHAT HAS THE PEOPLE'S DEMOCRATIC PARTY OF AFGHANISTAN ACHIEVED?

If the Soviets want a dignified withdrawal from the Afghan imbroglio, then the progress and stability of the PDPA regime is the most important factor in the conflict. The process of broadening the base of the revolution – gaining more supporters – is critical to the Afghan regime.

The core of regime support is the People's Democratic Party itself. Membership may have been as low as 5000 (with several thousand Parchamis executed or in prison) by the time Amin was ousted. By 1985, the regime was claiming a figure of 120 000. While most Western analysts believe that these numbers are an exaggeration, there is no doubt that the ranks of the party have expanded several-fold. Although membership is concentrated in the big cities, guerrilla accounts of executing party functionaries by the dozen shows that there are members even in small provincial centres.

To carry a party card is to risk summary execution by the *mujahadeen*. Whatever motivates people to do so, the PDPA and their Soviet backers must take comfort from the expansion of membership. A critical element of this cadre is in the armed forces. Some estimates put the number of members in the security forces at 60 per cent of the total.

When Taraki and Amin ordered the army into battle they had not taken the trouble to build any kind of party machine in the forces. Even in 1980–81, most units were without party organisation. By 1984–85 it was evident that the majority now had them. The importance of this in improving discipline and reducing factionalism should not be under-estimated. In Kunar in January 1985, and Paktia in April 1986, predominently Afghan forces carried out major offensives. The Afghan army is still a poor and unreliable one, but its recent performance is in a completely different class to that of the dark years (1979–81). Numbers have grown; there have been no mass desertions, nor major revolts; and fewer violent episodes of factionalism.

A network of Soviet 'advisers' remains in the Afghan forces command. The degree to which they control or merely support Afghan operations is hard to divine with certainty. But in 1985 and 1986 there have been a number offensives which have involved mainly Afghan troops. They still depend for much of their air and logistic support on the Soviet contingent, but clearly in recent years the Afghan sodiers and commanders have borne the brunt in most of the country.

Factionalism still exists – and it is more complex than simple Khalqi/Parchami rivalry. There is deep institutional antagonism between the various security agencies. The establishment of joint security HQs, and then of the Ministry of State Security, were measures aimed at lessening this. Compared to what Babrak Karmal called the 'horrific scenes' where Sarandoy fought paratroops at Balar Hissar, or Khalqi officers of the 14th Division revolted in 1980, the problem undoubtedly has lessened. Rivalries remain and they may still result in the occasional killing; but compared to the ideologically atomised resistance there is a clear community of interest among the PDPA's factions.

Attempts to broaden support have also involved the introduction of mass organisations: the National Fatherland Front, the Democratic Youth Organisation of Afghanistan and the Democratic Womens' Organisation of Aghanistan. Claimed membership for these bodies runs into hundreds of thousands. However much the resistance may pour scorn on them, there is evidence that these organisations have enlarged the regime's constituency.

One genuine achievement of the revolution has been the emancipation of (mainly urban) women. There is no doubt that thousands of women are committed to the regime, as their prominent participation in Revolution Defence Group militias shows. Eyewitnesses stated that militant militiawomen played a key role in defending the beseiged town of Urgun in 1983. Four of the seven militia commanders appointed to the Revolutionary Council in January 1986 were women.

The youth organisation is also widening government support. It will be an important source of new members for the party too. Many thousands have been sent for education and training in the USSR. While some may not have been enthusiastic about this, the author spoke to a young Parchami militant who was committed and keen about this instruction.

The PDPA have improved national literacy. They have also gone to great lengths to cultivate sections of the Islamic clergy. There are more mullahs, now, who endorse the government line. Time has allowed the government to prove that Islam is not under threat in areas they control. In the process both schools and mosques (those with a pro-Kabul clergy) have become targets for guerrilla attacks. In this way the government is able to point to the *mujahadeen* as wreckers of schools and mosques, thus polarising local communities.

Since mid-1985 there has also been a concerted effort to bring non-party people into government. They have been widely elected in local councils, appointed to the Revolutionary Council, and to the cabinet. In many ways this marks weakness rather than strength on the part of the part of the regime. Strict party direction of national affairs is being compromised in a partial return to traditional Afghan consensus politics.

In many other ways, too, the party has compromised its initial idealism. Land reform has been moderated. Some big landowners have secured their estates by promising to support the government. Other gifts of land have been made to officers and party members. The emancipation and education of women has been abandoned in conservative rural areas. In tribal lands the government has failed to break traditional practices. Now they safeguard tribal privileges and offer large cash incentives to those who will fight on their behalf.

In much of rural Afghanistan, in Babrak Karmal's own words, 'no fundamental transformation has taken place'. Guerrilla power remains unchallengeable in the Hazara Jat, parts of the north-east and north-west. Critics jibe that the PDPA has succeeded in creating 'socialism in one city', i.e. Kabul. They remain a highly urbanised group, but there has been some expansion. Government power is now more secure in towns like Mazar-e-Shariff, Jallalabad and Khost. In others, notably Herat and Kandahar, their power is not yet consolidated even within the city.

The PDPA has made headway in expanding its base of support. In 1979 they relied on a few thousand. Today if party cadres, armed forces officers, members of mass organisations, those involved with local councils, and their dependants are added up, the total is nearly one million. The cost has been enormously high: huge loss of life; depopulation of large tracts of countryside; and the presence of a foreign army. There is evidence that the Soviets want a faster expansion of support – certainly the pace so far has frustrated them. In future the PDPA will be under even more pressure to compromise and broaden their support. The trend has been in their favour, but the pace has been disappointing.

WHAT ARE THE MILITARY LESSONS OF THE CONFLICT?

The Soviet army entered Afghanistan completely unprepared for this kind of war. As an institution it is a good learner; it is possible to trace the development of operations during the years of the war.

During 1980–81, the Soviets conducted conventional operations in pursuit of limited military objectives (the defence of certain key points – particular towns, bases and the roads which connect them). They re-organised their forces from highly centralised armour-heavy elements into integrated combined-arms battalions, brigades and division task-forces. The need for large numbers of helicopters was realised. Afghan army strength dwindled to its lowest point and they remained incapable of actions above battalion level. In the second half of 1981, the Soviets launched several 'experimental' operations with newly formed combined arms regiments/brigades.

In 1982, the LCSFA launched two divisional offensives in the Panjsher and one in Herat. These large-scale actions did not succeed in destroying guerrilla forces in those areas, but did force Massud to negotiate a cease-fire. Soviet forces were used to create a breathing space for rebuilding the Afghan army.

In 1983, there was increased reliance on airpower, and no Soviet divisional operations. There were attempts to improve the security of the capital. In general there were few offensives, probably because the Soviets were re-evaluating their strategy.

In 1984, a new interdiction strategy involving greater use of helicopter-landed troops was practised. There were major offensives in the Panjsher and the east of the country. Afghan forces were demonstrating greater reliability.

During 1985–86 there was an expansion of the area of operations, indicating that Soviet key points were by then considered reasonably secure. Air mobility was used to attack previously safe guerrilla havens near the Pakistani border. The Soviet army also challenged guerrilla power in parts of Hazara Jat for the first time.

For Western counter-insurgency experts, the Soviet learning process in the DRA does not contain any earthshaking new experience. The principal lessons: vital importance of small actions, need for decentralised and flexible control of support assets, increased responsibility for junior officers/NCOs, and expanded use of helicopters, had all been noted in Vietnam. For the Soviets there was a difference in that they learnt these lessons at first hand. Undoubtedly the war will have a lasting effect on the officer corps.

In prosecuting their war against the '*dushmans*', the Soviets have deployed new military technology. In particular infantry fire-power has been massively increased in Afghanistan. The AGS–17 automatic grenade launcher gives infantry companies accurate suppressive fire. Similarly the RPO rocket flame-thrower provides the foot soldier with a portable napalm strike. At closer range, the new AK–74 rifle with its attached BG–15 grenade launcher and RPG–16 rocket both allow the infanteer to neutralise hard targets.

The growth in Soviet infantry firepower, in particular of these suppressive fire systems, has important implications for NATO. Western defence in the central front ascribes a vital role to anti-tank missiles. Weapons such as the AGS–17 and RPO allow Soviet commanders at the platoon level to neutralise such defences hundreds of metres away, quickly and without resort to artillery or air support.

Other weapons have also been fielded which provide long-range suppressive firepower. The Vasilek 82mm and Air Assault Forces BMD–mounted 120mm automatic mortars both provide flexible quick firing support. BM–27 and Frog–7 artillery rockets have been used with sub-munition warheads – a development with important implications for anti-tank as well as anti-personnel missions.

In the air, the Mil–24 has been used extensively as close air support, supplanting lightweight fighter bombers in the role. Gunship pilots have accumlated a huge fund of combat experience, including evasion of heat-seeking missiles. The Su–25 (Frogfoot) was used for the first time in Afghan skies. The air force has used airborne forward controllers to direct fire; introduced new cluster and retard bombs.

While the Soviets have taken the opportunity to test their latest defence technologies in the Hindu Kush, the most important lesson of the war for them is in the need for flexibility in command. They arrived in the country with huge standard divisions. Very soon they found these organisations, and the way that they used resources, of limited use. They began to use combined-arms battalions and regiments with much more flexible organisation and command procedures.

Units like the 70th Motor Rifle Brigade and 191st Independent Motor Rifle Regiment were established with combat resources (such as multiple rocket launchers) normally found at division or army level. Units have also had helicopters attached under their direct command for long periods. This decentralisation, particularly of helicopters was soon being copied in Soviet first-echelon forces based in Eastern Europe. Divisions in East Germany began receiving organic helicopter squadrons. More responsive artillery and air support procedures were also introduced widely. General Maksimov highlighted the need for forward observers with combat units to ensure efficient coordination.

Attitudes have also been changed. Around 60 000 Soviet officers have now served in Afghanistan. This 'Afghan Brotherhood', as they have been described, form a pool of combat-experienced leaders. They have emerged from the fog of war with an understanding of the difference between textbook solutions and the real battlefield. There is evidence that these men are being given preferential treatment: courses at the M. V. Frunze and other prestigious academies, promotion, decorations and key command appointments. By 1987, veterans of this conflict not only commanded the largest field forces of the Soviet army, but, at the lower level, controlled gunship helicopter regiments, motor rifle divisions, and air assault brigades that might be sent to fight in other theatres.

The war has spawned a new breed of heroes. An estimated 75 (by late 1986) servicemen had recieved the Hero of the Soviet Union gold star for service there. Of these, nearly 70 are still alive and most are officers. They give a new, contemporary example for Soviet cadets traditionally weaned on tales of the Second World War.

The conflict has also presented evidence of the weakness of junior command and of poor morale in the ranks of the Soviet army. It is hard to imagine a war to which Russia's conscript army would be less well suited than a counter-insurgency in mountainous Afghanistan. Under the stress of operations soldiers have resorted to indiscriminate killing, looting, alcohol and drug abuse. Brutality among the soldiers – principally bullying by the 'old soldiers' of more recently arrived draftees – has produced a high desertion rate. It is impossible to know just how many men have deserted, but the number may be 200–300.

As well as boosting desertion, the brutality of 'old soldiers' also undermines NCOs' authority. Nowhere has the Soviets' lack of a sizeable professional NCO corps been more painfully felt than in Afghanistan. As a result the burden is placed on junior officers, who find themselves attempting to deal with the soldiers emotional problems as well as the tactical situation. There is evidence that many officers have risen to the challenge and are respected, but that others have failed. The Soviet army normally relies on mass and firepower to compensate for this and in the DRA this allowed it to achieve a respectable operational record.

In its first six years in the country the Limited Contingent of Soviet Forces (and the Afghan services) have improved the security situation. Their progress in Kabul, Parwan, Balkh, Samanagan, Jowzjan, Fariab, Logar, Laghman, Nangrahar, Kunar, Paktia and Paktika Provinces means that, whereas government control only extended to around 10 per cent of the country when they arrived, it can be estimated (early in 1987) to amount to about 35 per cent with a further 20 per cent dominated by neither side. Areas under government 'control' are, of course, still operated in by guerrillas. In Kabul for example the improvement of the security situation has resulted in the adoption of terror weapons: unguided rockets, bombs and assassination. Although the UK security forces can be said to 'control' nearly all of Northern Ireland it does not mean that the IRA cannot mount terror attacks. Total security in areas with a large civilian population remains virtually impossible.

Further evidence of the Soviet/Afghan forces' success is in the expansion of the area of operations. In 1985–86, they destroyed guerrilla bases (such as Zhawar in Paktia Province) which had never been threatened before in five years of war.

The Soviet/Afghan forces have achieved this operational success under the tightest possible political control. Some comparisons with Vietnam are worth making. In six years (according to US State Department figures) Soviet forces in the DRA grew from 85 000 to 118 000 men. By comparison, US strength in Vietnam grew from 16 000 in 1964 to 539 000 in 1969. While the USA unleashed B-52 raids, heliborne landings and covert operations against communist bases in Laos and Cambodia, there has never been a major Soviet incursion into Pakistan.

Although the Soviet and Afghan forces combined are less than half the size of US forces at their peak in Vietnam, their area of operations is three and a half times as big.

The Soviets' achievement indicates that they have conducted their campaign efficiently. Where comparisons with Vietnam do not stand up is in the quality of insurgent forces that they have faced.

HOW HAS THE RESISTANCE DEVELOPED?

The word 'resistance' best sums up the nature of the opposition. The Afghan guerrillas come from many different ethnic groups and belong to parties with totally different (and conflicting) objectives; what unites them is the will to resist the godless Soviets and their servants in Kabul. The strength of this patriotic fervour is such that the resistance has shown remarkable resilience in confronting a highly organised enemy army.

That the resistance is still fighting after civilian casualties estimated in the hundreds of thousands, and that millions of Afghans chose to be refugees rather than return, is a dramatic testimony to the strength of the Islamic nationalism that, first, the April Revolution and, then, the Soviet invasion generated. If you take away this anti-Soviet feeling the resistance is exposed as leaderless, disorganised and lacking coherent ideology.

Some of the guerrilla parties (notably the ISA and Hekmatyar IP) were fighting well before the April Revolution for an Islamic fundamentalist republic. Others (such as NIFA) favour the restoration of the monarchy. Among the Shia Hazaras there are groups whose passionate devotion to Khomeinite ideas involves union with Iran. As the struggle has gone on, one might have expected to see some dominant ideology and leadership emerge. But the Afghan resistance has produced no Ho Chi-Minh, no Colonel Grivas, no Ahmed Ben Bella. While the Sunni Pakistan-based parties have moved just perceptibly closer together, the Shia resistance is actually less united than in 1979.

Looking back at the years of warfare since April 1978, it is apparent that the period from March 1979 to December 1980 marks the peak of resistance achievement. In March 1979, the Herat garrison joined the rebels and the entire city was under their control for several days. This is the only time in all the years of war that the *mujahadeen* managed this. Following those events the army disintegrated and the rebels filled the vacuum. Their success prompted the Soviet intervention and in the aftermath of that there was a huge increase in support for the *mujahadeen*.

As garrisons defected there were huge hauls of booty. During 1980, the resistance was unchallenged in up to 90 per cent of the country. They were backed by a national moral consensus: outrage at the invasion provided far more recruits than they could arm. The tide has never reached such heights since: the *mujahadeen* have not succeeded in overcoming any brigade-sized Afghan garrison, nor in holding an entire provincial capital.

What is remarkable about the resistance is that in many years of war only a handful of commanders have appreciated, and still fewer acted upon, the basic principles of guerrilla war. Most *mujahadeen* understand the value of surprise. They have relied on the ambush as their basic tactic, and they are reasonably good at it. They have destroyed thousands of trucks in their war of the roads. Other basic principles such as the need to concentrate forces to gain a decisive tactical advantage, the need to organise mobile forces for such operations, the requirement for a highly organised support apparatus among local people, and the value of specialisation among troops, have been grasped only by Ahmad Shah Massud and a handful of others.

The *mujahadeen* remain locally based. They rarely communicate with other groups, do not operate outside their own valley or province, and resist any kind of discipline or strategy – even from their own party leaders. Repeated failed attempts by large groups of *mujahadeen* to take towns such as Asadabad, Barikot, Urgun, Khost and Ali Khel are evidence of the guerrillas' inability to take any kind of tactical, let alone strategic, initiative.

Among the groups only a few (notably Massud's and Ismael Khan's) have organised full-time guerrilla cadres. Above all, it is a lack of training that prevents the resistance from achieving greater cohesion. They like to blame their troubles on Soviet firepower and lack of support from the West, but the Afghans alone are responsible for the failure of basic organisation. Tito in Yugoslavia (in the early days at least) took on a mechanised enemy army with almost no help. Tito formed a competent partisan army from a nation which, like Afghanistan, contained several feuding ethnic groups. In the modern era, tiny cadres of Polisario fighters in the Western Sahara and Kurds have imposed a cost completely disproportionate to their numbers, and they have done so with little outside support. Some analysts have said that this disorganisation is a strength, because it means that the resistance cannot be decapitated. It is nothing of the sort: without unity and organisation they cannot take the initiative. If they cannot take the initiative, victory is impossible.

There is one case study that shows what the *mujahadeen* can achieve if they are organised: the Panjsher Front of Ahmad Shah Massud. This group has taken a heavy toll on enemy convoys and resisted nine major Soviet army offensives – three of them at the divisional task-force level. Yet the number of fighters is well below that in the ISA Herat or Marmoul Fronts, perhaps as few as 3000. These men have been organised into mobile and local groups. Massud has used the mobile groups to take the initiative: attacking the Salang road, Bagram airbase, and providing the *mujahadeen* with their major victory of recent years – the capture of Pechgur fortress.

Some fronts have sent men to Massud for training, others have copied certain features of his organisation. The Ismael Khan Herat Front is also well organised, being run by ex-army officers. The continued impotence of government forces in large parts of western Afghanistan is due to their efforts. They are one of the very few guerrilla fronts to use radio communications. The disproportionate influence of these two fronts is evidence of what can be achieved with even a small amount of organisation. Why have they not been copied more widely? Fierce local independence, party rivalry and ethnic prejudice (Massud and Kahn are from the minority Tajik group) probably all play a part.

It is wrong to suggest that the *mujahadeen* have been isolated. Military aid from the USA and conservative Arab states amounts to hundreds of millions of dollars. Chinese arms supplies began earlier and have increased. For many years the guerrillas saw the shoulder-launched surface-to-air missile as a high-tech panacea. By 1986 large-scale supplies of Stinger and Blowpipe anti-aircraft missiles were having an effect. Some time will be needed to assess their significance in the over-all struggle. On the other hand, the Vietnamese communists shot down nearly 4000 helicopters during their long war – almost all of them with low-calibre anti-aircraft guns and small arms. The Chinese have supplied the very same 12.7mm, 14.5mm and 23mm anti-aircraft guns to the *majahadeen*, but even when they have been concentrated in large numbers (such as at the siege of Urgun) they have not been used to any great effect.

For all its inadequacies, the resistance has imposed a cost on the Soviet army. In the first five years of the war the Americans estimate that they lost 12 000 men. Averaged over the whole period this amounts to 46 men a week. Estimates of *mujahadeen* strength range from 90 000 to 250 000 men. Can 100 000 or 200 000 Afghan fighters with their boundless devotion to the cause only account for 46 Soviets a week?

One cannot escape the conclusion that despite the moral righteousness of their war against the invader, many *mujahadeen* spend little time fighting him. Thousands, perhaps tens of thousands, have perished in inter-group feuding. Some groups, such as Nasr in the Hazara Jat during 1984–85, seem to have devoted all their energies to fighting other parties. The competition for fighters' allegiances between Peshawar-based parties means that the war is still run on a cash basis in much of the country. Some clearly fight for the money, others have to spend their time accumulating booty to provide their parties with that cash. The mercenary attitude of many fighters is exemplified by the number who have been bought out by the government. Fazel Ahmad (in Herat Province), Jom'a Khan (in the Andarab) and Esmatullah Moslem (in Kandahar) all deserted the *jihad*, with large numbers of followers, for cash. Many more have been hired for the tribal militias. No serving government generals have gone over to the *mujahadeen* for ideological reasons during the last few years.

It remains to be seen whether this chaotic resistance could impose a defeat by exhaustion on the Soviets. They talk about the Sovietisation of their own Central Asian provinces, against 'bandit' opposition in the 1920s. 'Give us twenty years and we'll finish them', a serving Soviet sergeant told the author. At their current rate of progress they may need more time. Thirty years? Forty? How many Soviet lives will the *mujahadeen* claim in the meantime?

WHAT SHOULD THE WEST DO?

In Western countries there has been a pro-*mujahadeen* consensus since the early days of the war. Their moral case against an invading army cannot be faulted. Ultimately, the end of the Afghan war will be judged when that army leaves. Their struggle is just; surely they deserve whatever help we can give?

But also operating in the minds of many Westerners, particularly Americans, is a certain *schadenfreude*. They are delighted at the Soviets' difficulties and they want to exacerbate them. The popular vilification of the Soviets is such that the Western media often accept the guerrilla view as truth. Flimsy evidence such as gas masks and the testimony of illiterate peasants has been used to convince large sections of the public that the Soviets are guilty of using chemical weapons. In fact not a single gas shell or bomb has been recovered (it only took a few weeks for such evidence to be found in the Gulf War), and the Americans have now abandoned these claims. But the damage has been done. For the congressmen voting funds for the guerrillas, their ability to humiliate the Soviets is more important than the cause they wish to help.

Which is what? Few Westerners ever bother to ask themselves the question. It is not just a matter of evicting a foreign army (who would disagree with that?), but what follows when that army has gone? Only one or two parties are fighting for freedom in any Western sense. The programmes of the fundamentalist parties would undermine the freedom that many women have achieved under the PDPA. They are not struggling for Western democratic institutions, but for an Iranian-style theocracy. It remains for the Afghans to decide how they define freedom, not the West, but the decision they reach should affect whether supplies to them are continued.

Mujahadeen definitions of just means and legitimate targets may well differ from Western ones. At their own admission the guerrillas have planted bombs in city streets, killed mullahs, destroyed schools, hospitals and mosques. It is also evident that they have used the heroin trade as a source of finance. Does anybody in America care? The deeds of fanatical commanders on the battlefield should not affect humanitarian aid to the huge refugee population, but there should be a debate about military assistance. However just their cause, the *mujahadeen* are guilty of precisely the same 'crimes' as the PLO or the IRA. Democracies, we are told, do not talk to 'terrorists' – let alone supply them with the means of terror.

If one forgets the moral questions and concentrates on the superpower contest, then the aim of causing the Soviets as much trouble as possible is logical and necessary. In following such an aim the West expends Afghan lives and prolongs their suffering with the same cynicism and self-interest as the Soviets.

IS A COMPLETE SOVIET WITHDRAWAL LIKELY?.

The Soviets have paid a high cost in Afghanistan. It is measured not just in casualties, but in continued poor relations with the USA and China, and the intensification of the arms race. It is the greatest paradox of the war that the Soviet army both supports the PDPA regime and yet by its very presence prevents it from gaining wider popular support.

Victory or defeat will be measured in terms of the opposition that remains after the Soviet army goes home. If the PDPA survives, then the whole enterprise will have been worth it for the Soviets. Throughout 1986 there were signals that Mikhail Gorbachev and the Politburo were anxious to do a deal that would allow them to begin withdrawing their army. Whilst there is certainly a new urgency in Gorbachev's initiatives, the fundamental Soviet condition for withdrawal, i.e. an end to external aggression (principally from Pakistani territory), has not changed. In backing the Afghan/Pakistani withdrawal talks, the Soviets have forced General Zia's regime into *de facto* recognition not just of the PDPA regime, but also of the fact that it has been interfering in Afghanistan. Their readiness to withdraw may also be a sign of the strength of their position in Afghanistan, rather than its weakness. It should be remembered that under Gorbachev, the Soviet army has expanded its area of operations and pursued a more aggressive interdiction strategy. Perhaps the Afghan army is now strong enough to fight the war with progressively less Soviet help; they have been holding the line in large parts of the country anyway.

One factor which inhibits the withdrawal is the unpredictable effect of any deal with Pakistan. Firstly, it is far from certain that General Zia could enforce a pledge to halt guerrilla operations: *mujahadeen* leaders have already said that they would fight on. Zia might face civil war if he sent the army into the border provinces to stop them. Secondly, it is uncertain what effect the withdrawal would have on support for the Kabul regime. On the one hand, people might regard the Soviets as being on the run and go all out to defeat the PDPA. On the other, support for the *mujhadeen* might decline to pre-1980 levels if the people saw that the main aim of the *jihad*, i.e. the expulsion of the invader, had been achieved.

The scale of the Kremlin's commitment to Afghanistan (which includes massive economic as well as military aid) means that a quick, immediate withdrawal is highly unlikely. It could only happen if either the West has under-estimated Mikhail Gorbachev's desire to get out at any cost or, conversely, if the West has under-estimated the strength of the Kabul regime.

WHO WILL WIN?

Victory of the war in Afghanistan will be defined as the circumstances under which the Soviet army (or the bulk of it at least) leaves. If the PDPA regime survives and continues a slow expansion of support, then the Soviets will have won. If the regime collapses, even within a year or two of the withdrawal, the USSR will be judged to have experienced a humiliation on the scale of Vietnam.

In purely military terms the Soviets and their Afghan allies are winning. They control considerably more territory now than they did in 1980. their confidence in this base allowed them to expand the area of operations in 1985–86. By then they were destroying guerrilla strongholds in the upper Logar, White mountains, fringes of the Hazara Jat, and close to the Pakistani border that had not previously been under threat since 1978.

The *mujahadeen*, on the other hand, have failed (with the exception of one or two areas) to create a coherent unified military force. They are incapable of taking even small provincial centres. In flatter areas such as the Koh-e-Safi plain and lower Maidan valley near Kabul, the Oxus valley in the north, and the Khost plain, their power has been rolled back. In 1979 government mobile forces chased from one end of the country to the other trying to stamp out rebellion: the *mujahadeen* held the initiative. Today they hold the initiative only in the upper Panjsher, parts of Herat province, and the central Hazara Jat. Even in those areas their disunity and poor organisation prevents them either from extinguishing the few remaining government positions, or from expanding their operations.

Undoubtedly the re-vitalization of the Afghan armed forces has been a critical factor in the gains of 1985–86. Under Najeebollah their operations have been fused with a cunning strategy to enlist the support of Pathan dissidents in Pakistan. It is unlikely that this army could survive without Soviet support at the moment, but it is progressing.

But the growth in popular backing for Najeebollah's regime is still very slow. There have been signs of Soviet frustration that after years of fighting their success has not been greater. If current trends do continue they will win; but it will take a very long time – perhaps another 15 years. Militarily they can cope for that period, but will the Soviets accept the international costs?

In the Soviet army there is a large vested interest in Afghanistan. Their advice to the party must be that an ignominious withdrawal would be more costly than a continuing war. While there has been some evidence of isolated discontent, there is no anti-war movement in the USSR to undermine their position. Mikhail Gorbachev has shown a willingness to withdraw forces, but his regime has also stepped up the pace of operations. There has been no Tet offensive to convince the Politburo of the ultimate futility of their struggle. Their forces hold the military initiative and for that reason a defeat on the battlefield is highly unlikely.

Appendix I: Kabul Forces Order of Battle

(As at 1 January 1985)

1st (Central) Corps: HQ Kabul

2nd Corps: HQ Kandahar

3rd Corps: HQ Gardez

7th Division: Moqor[1]
  65th Brigade

8th Division: Kargha garrison, Kabul
  4th Regiment: Kabul
  5th Regiment: Kabul
  72nd Brigade: Kabul[2]
  32nd Brigade: Kabul

9th Division: Chugha Serai (also called Asadabad), Kunar Province[3]
  31st Mountain Brigade: Asmar
  51st Brigade: Barikot
  69th Brigade: Chugha Serai
  46th Artillery Regiment: Chugha Serai

11th Division: Jallalabad, Nangrahar Province
  66th (?) Brigade: Jallalabad[4]
  81st Brigade: Hadda
  71st Brigade: Ganikhel
  91st Artillery Regiment: Jallalabad

12th Division: Gardez, Paktia Province
  67th Brigade: Gardez
  36th (?) Regiment: Ali Khel (Jaji)
  24th (?) Brigade: Chamkani

14th Division: Ghazni, Ghazni Province
  3rd Brigade: Ghazni
  u/i regiment: Bamiyan, Bamiyan Province

223

15th Division: Kandahar, Kandahar Province
  36th Brigade: Kandahar
  43rd Mountain Regiment: Kalat, Zabol Province
  u/i Brigade: Girishk, Helmand Province

17th Division: Herat, Herat Province[5]
  28th Brigade: Herat
  33rd Brigade: Qala Yi-Naw, Badghis Province
  2nd Regiment: Chakhcharan, Ghowr Province

18th Division: Mazar-e-Shariff, Balkh Province
  62nd Mechanised Regiment: Mazar-e-Shariff
  35th Regiment: Shebarghan, Fariab Province
  u/i Mountain Battalion: Mazar-e-Shariff

20th Division: Nahrin, Baghlan Province
  10th Brigade: Panjsher valley[6]
  23rd Brigade: Nahrin
  75th Brigade: Eshkamish, Takhar Province

25th Division: Khost (also called Matun), Paktia Province
  19th Brigade: Khost
  59th Brigade: Nadershah Kot
  u/i Brigade: Khost
  6th Artillery Regiment: Khost

Non-Divisional Units

4th Armoured Brigade[7]: Pol-e-Charkhi garrison, Kabul
7th Armoured Brigade[7]: Kandahar
15th Armoured Brigade[8]: Pol-e-Charkhi garrison, Kabul
21st Mechanised Brigade[9]: Farah, Farah Province
21st Guards Regiment[10]: Kabul
22nd Guards Regiment[10]: Paktia Province
15th Brigade: Urgun, Paktia Province
37th Commando Brigade[7]: Rishkoor garrison, Kabul
38th Commando Brigade[11]: Kabul
u/i Paratroop Regiment[11]: Kabul
466th Commando Battalion[12]: Kandahar
88th (?) Artillery Brigade[13]: Rishkoor camp, Kabul
10th Engineer Regiment: Hussein Kut, Parwan Province
5th Transport Regiment: Siah Sang garrison, Kabul
119th Transport Regiment[14]: Sherpur barracks, Kabul
52nd Signals Regiment: Kabul
235th Independent Signals Battalion: Kabul
203rd Reconnaissance Battalion[7]: Kabul
212nd Reconnaissance Battalion[15]: Gardez
u/i Reconnaissance Battalion[8]: Kandahar

AIR FORCE

322nd Air Regiment: Bagram Airbase
  3 Fighter squadrons (with 40 MiG-21s)

321st Air Regiment: Bagram Airbase[16]
  3 Fighter-Bomber squadrons (with Su-7, Su-22)

393rd Air Regiment: Dehdadi Airbase, Balkh Province
  3 Fighter-bomber squadrons (with MiG-17s)

355th Air Regiment: Shindand Airbase, Farah Province
  3 Bomber squadrons (with IL-28)
  1 Fighter-bomber squadron (with MiG-17s)

232nd Air Regiment: Kabul Airport[17]
  3 Helicopter squadrons (with 12 Mil-4, Mil-8, Mil-6)
  (1 squadron of 8 Mil-8 detached to Shindand)

377th Air Regiment: Kabul Airport[18]
  4 Helicopter squadrons (with 6 Mil-25, 25 Mil-17)

u/i Air Regiment: Kabul Airport
  2 Transport Squadrons (with 10 An-2, 15 An-26/30)
  1 VIP Transport Squadron (with 1 IL-18, 12 An-14)

u/i Attack Helicopter Squadron (with c.15 Mil-24): Jallalabad
u/i Attack Helicopter Squadron (with c.15 Mil-24): Kabul

Air Force Academy (with Yak-18s and L-39s)[19]: Kabul

Air Defence Forces[20]
  99th SAM Regiment: Kabul
  92nd (?) SAM Regiment: Kabul
  66th AAA Battalion: Kandahar
  u/i Radar Regiment: Kabul

Border Command[21]
  1st Border Brigade: Jallalabad, Nagrahar Province
  2nd Border Brigade: Khost, Paktia Province
  3rd Border Brigade: Konduz (?) Badakshan Province
  4th Border Brigade: Nimroz Province
  5th Border Brigade: Herat, Herat Province
  u/i Border (Training) Brigade: Kabul
  u/i Border Brigade: Kandahar Province
  8th Border Brigade: Paktika Province
  10th Border Brigade: Asadabad, Kunar Province

UNIT STRENGTHS

The terms 'brigade' or 'division' need to be used with caution with the Afghan forces. During the nadir of 1979–81, average divisional strength may have been as low as 1500, with some below 1000. Since then the army has had more success in keeping men in the ranks. Some divisions remain small, probably around 1500 men – the 7th and 14th Divisions, for example. Others such as the 25th, 8th and 11th Divisions may number around 4500 men each.

MINISTRY OF INTERIOR

These forces are divided into *gendarmerie* (Sarandoy) made up of conscripts and organised along conventional lines, and Revolution Defence Group militias. By 1985 there were 20 identified Sarandoy Operational Battalions and Mountain Battalions. They were attached to provincial Sarandoy commands and include armoured vehicles and light artillery. The Kabul Security Command deployed two mobile regiments (the 1st and 2nd) and controlled a system of 12 security wards with observation posts, check points, etc. A further four Sarandoy brigades/regiments have been identified in Badakhshan (24th Sarandoy Brigade), Kandahar, Baghlan and Parwan. At the beginning of 1986, operational control of certain Sarandoy mobile provincial units passed to the new unified Ministry of State Security headquarters.

MILITIAS

Much of the militia force (those called Revolution Defence Groups) fell under Ministry of Interior control. In Kabul their activities were closely integrated with the Security Command. Other militias have been hired by different agencies. There are at least six tribal regiments (in Kandahar, Zabol, Paktia, Kunar, Herat and the Andarab valley). They are made up of locals who are basically tribal mercenaries. These elements are normally paid by the Ministry of Frontier and Tribes and often cooperate with the border troops. Other local militias have been hired by the KHAD. Youth militia forces have been raised by the Democratic Youth Organisation of Afghanistan. Although there are reports of them fighting they are a lightly armed force designed primarily to prepare men for military service. A strongly Parchami party militia called the Revolutionary Guards operates on a similar principle (although it did send men to fight in the 1982 Panjsher campaign, with poor results). The Revolutionary Guards are very much a Kabul-based youth militia. Like many guerrillas, most militiamen are militarily effective for intermittent short periods, and their loyalties are often questionable. The militia total reached approximately 20 000 to 25 000 by 1986.

Notes
1. Based at Rishkoor garrison south of Kabul until April 1981. It was, and possibly remains, a Central Corps assigned unit.

2.   One brigade is thought to be in the Panjsher and may no longer be part of the 8th Division (see note 6). The 8th Division was considerably re-organised in 1980–81 forming new brigades (the 4th and 5th) to replace others (the 69th and 32nd) sent to the provinces.

3.   The 9th Division had to be rebuilt after the mass desertions of 1979–80. Two entire brigades (the 5th and 30th Mountain) which joined the *mujahadeen* were not reformed. The 60th Brigade was detached from the 8th Division in 1980.

4.   The 32nd Brigade was identified as fighting under the 11th Division HQ in 1982. It subsequently returned to 8th Division control.

5.   Until the April 1979 Herat Revolt, the 17th Division also included the 70th and 11th Brigades. However, no report has been found of them since and it is believed that they were not reformed.

6.   This brigade has been in the Panjsher since May 1984. According to unconfirmed reports the units garrisoning the Panjsher were formed into a new formation – 2nd Division – late in 1984. The 2nd Division reportedly consists of two brigades (one ex-20th Division and one ex-8th Division) and the 444th Commando Battalion.

7.   Central Corps assigned.

8.   2nd Corps assigned.

9.   In the 1940s, the 7th Division was based in Farah. Its designation changed to the 16th Division during reorganisation in the 1950s. This division may have existed until Daoud's time, but the author has found no evidence to support its existence since the April Revolution.

10.   The guards regiments (also sometimes referred to as mountain units or commandos) were formed in the early 1970s. They were probably dissolved during 1979–80, perhaps to provide manpower for the 8th Division's new brigades. With the growth in army strength during 1983–84 they were reformed. The 22nd Guards Regiment was identified in Paktia during the 1986 Zhawar operation. A third such regiment, the 44th existed until 1979, and may have been reformed.

11.   An unit designated the 26th Airborne Regiment (which was upgraded from the 262nd Airborne Battalion) was at Balar Hissar fort until 1980. It was subsequently moved and reformed, possibly at Bagram.

12.   Formed late 1984.

13.   The brigade includes one gun battalion (with M-1946 130mm guns), two howitzer battalions (with 152mm M-1937s), one anti-tank battalion (with Snapper guided missiles), and a multiple rocket launcher battalion (with BM-13 MRLs).

14.   Formed in late 1980 or early 1981.

15.   3rd Corps assigned.

16.   The 321st Air Regiment was formed in 1984–85 to provide improved bombing capability. Two Su-22s shot down over Pakistan in 1986 came from this regiment.

17.   This regiment may have been split up to provide detachments for units in the provinces.

18.   Formed in 1984 with the supply of 70 Mil-17s to the DRA air force. According to a captured pilot from this regiment, 26 of these Mil-17s had been lost in combat by June 1986.

19. Some of these planes are held at Dehdadi.
20. The Air Defence Forces are part of the air force. Until 1979–80 there was an anti-aircraft gun division – the 77th, based in Kabul. It had 100 85mm KS-12 guns, and 75 100mm KS-19 weapons. The division was 'mothballed' during this period of acute manpower shortages. However the SAM units have been retained, albeit below strength. Why they have bothered with them at all, given the nature of their war against the *mujahadeen*, remains something of a mystery.
21. The Border Troops are believed to have been transferred to Ministry of Frontiers and Tribes control in 1983. Since then they have been built up and given importance by the regime.

Appendix II: Soviet Forces in Afghanistan

40th Army/Turkestan Military District Forward: Tari-Tajbeg camp, Kabul

103rd Guards Air Assault Division: Darulaman camp, Kabul

5th Guards Motor Rifle Division[1]: Shindand, Farah Province

108th Motor Rifle Division: Khair Khana camp, Kabul

201st Motor Rifle Division: Konduz, Konduz Province

66th Motor Rifle Brigade: Jallalabad, Nagrahar Province
70th Motor Rifle Brigade: Kandahar, Kandahar Province
u/i (may be 56th)[2] Air Assault Brigade: Gardez, Paktia Province
345th Independent Guards Air Assault Regiment: Bagram, Parwan Province
191st Independent Motor Rifle Regiment: Ghazni, Ghazni Province
866th Indepedent Motor Rifle Regiment: Feyzabad, Badakshan Province
181st Motor Rifle Regiment[3]: Bagram, Parwan Province
187th Motor Rifle Regiment[4]: Mazar-e-Shariff, Balkh Province
u/i Special Designation (*Spetznaz*) Brigade: Kandahar[5]
u/i Special Designation (*Spetznaz*) Brigade: Kabul
u/i Special Designation (*Spetznaz*) Brigade: Shindand
u/i Artillery Brigade[6]: Kabul
40th (?) Airfield Defence Battalion, Bagram, Parwan Province
u/i Guards Independent Commandants Service (military police) Battalion:
    Pol-e-Khumri, Baghlan Province (?)
u/i Motor Transport Regiment: Khair Khana camp. Kabul (with detachment
    at Pol-e-Khumri)
u/i Construction Regiment: Bagram, Parwan Province
u/i Construction Regiment: Shindand, Farah Province
40th (?) Signal Regiment: Balar Hissar Fort, Kabul
u/i Pipelaying Battalion: Pol-e-Khumri (?), Baghlan Province
u/i Engineer Battalion: Jallalabad, Nangrahar Province

AIR FORCE

Bagram
u/i Fighter Aviation Regiment
u/i Fighter Aviation Regiment
50th Independent Composite Aviation Regiment
262nd Independent Reconnaissance Helicopter Squadron

229

Kabul
263rd Independent Tactical Reconnaissance Squadron

Shindand
u/i Fighter Aviation Regiment
200th Independent Guards Attack Squadron
u/i Independent Tactical Reconnaissance Squadron
u/i Independent Helicopter Regiment

Kandahar
u/i Fighter Aviation Regiment
280th Independent Helicopter Regiment

Jallalabad
355th Independent Helicopter Regiment

Konduz
181st Independent Helicopter Regiment (a squadron-sized detachment serves
    at Feyzabad)

Aircraft
80 MiG-21 (Bagram, Kandahar, Shindand)
40 MiG-23 (Bagram)
80 Su-17 (Shindand and Kandahar)
30 Su-25 (Bagram, Shindand)
15 MiG-21R (recce at Kabul)
12 MiG-25 (recce at Shindand)
140 Mil-24 (at Bagram, Shindand, Jallalabad, Konduz)
105 Mil-8/17 (Bagram, Shindand, Jallalabad, Konduz, Feyzabad)
40 Mil-6 (Shindand, Kandahar, Konduz)
40 Mil-2 (Bagram, Shindand, Kandahar)
7 An-26 (Bagram).

INTERNAL SECURITY FORCES

In addition to these Soviet Ministry of Defence elements there are also four
regiment-sized internal security forces in use. There are two border guard mobile
detachments (one at Torghundi in Herat Province, the other in the north-east)
which fall under KGB control. Their main task is to prevent infiltration into the
Soviet Union, but they have conducted aggressive patrolling some miles inside the
DRA. Also under KGB control is a Security Troops Brigade. This unit is stationed
in Kabul where it guards key installations, regulates traffic and maintains
discipline – a form of military police. The USSR Ministry of Internal Affairs also
has a motor rifle regiment serving in Afghanistan.

FORCES IN THE USSR

There are several divisions in the Turkestan Military District bordering the DRA. Their likely designations and locations are:

54th Motor Rifle Division: Termez
346th (or 357th) Motor Rifle Division: Kushka
66th Motor Rifle Division: Samarkand
84th Guards Motor Rifle Division: Kizyl Arvat
280th Training Division: Ashkabad

Some of these formations took part in the intervention and were subsequently reformed. None of them is at full strength, the 280th and, to a lesser degree, the Termez-based division have a role in pre-Afghanistan training for recruits. Elements from these divisions (not usually exceeding battalion strength) are sometimes used for operations inside the DRA. It is also practice to use air assault units for particular operations. Some of these have been flown in from European Russia for a few weeks at a time.

HOW MANY SOVIETS?

There has been some controversy as to how many Soviets troops are actually serving in Afghanistan. Guerrilla claims of 150 000 to 200 000 are rightly discounted. US State Department figures are generally relied upon by most analysts. They plot a slow growth in Soviet troop numbers from around 85 000 in late 1980 to 118 000 in 1986 (prior to Mr Gorbchev's withdrawals). In fact the State Department has as great an interest in exaggerating these figures as the *mujahadeen*. Almost all Western sources agree that the main combat power of the Limited Contingent is composed of one air assault and three major rifle divisions, and five to six independent regiments/brigades (see above). If one adds the strength of these units to the support elements identified in the DRA, it simply does not add up to the State Department's figure of 118 000.

1 Army HQ	500
3 motor rifle divisions (11 000 each)	33 000
1 air assault division	6 500
1 indep. air assault brigade	2 000
1 indep. air assault regiment	1 500
2 indep. motor rifle brigades (2600 each)	5 200
2 indep. motor rifle regiments (2200 each)	4 400
3 *Spetznaz* brigades (1000 each)	3 000
1 airfield defence battalion	350
1 artillery brigade (gun and rocket)	2 200
1 transport regiment	1 500
2 construction regiments (1200 each)	2 400
1 indep. engineer battalion	400
1 pipelaying battalion	280
1 signals regiment	740

Army-level support (includes medical, MPs, maintenance, bakeries, etc.)	3 000
2 border troops regiments (2000 each)	4 000
1 security troops brigade	2 000
1 MVD rifle regiment	2 000
Advisers in Afghan units (several hundred in defence ministry, academies, plus units down to company level)	3 000
Air force personnel	10 000
Total	88 370

The figure of 88 370 is so far below the State Department estimate that it suggests more than a methodological disagreement. The author understands unofficially that State Department figures include many Soviet civilian advisers, and some units based in the southern USSR. The figure is higher than the 76 000 in the author's controversial *Jane's Defence Weekly* article for two reasons. Firstly there was a small increase in forces between late 1984 (the baseline for the *Jane's* calculation) and June 1986 (the baseline for the figures above). New air assault and artillery brigades were identified. Secondly the author accepts that his air force personnel figure was too low, and that the average divisional strength (prior to the 1986 troop withdrawal) is 11 000 rather than 10 000 as previously quoted.

Notes

1. The 5th Guards was the formation most affected by the October 1986 withdrawal. It lost its tank regiment, anti-aircraft regiment and possibly one of its motor rifle regiments. Other anti-aircraft regiments were withdrawn from Kabul and Konduz.
2. Formed late 1983 or early 1984.
3. Under command of the 108th Motor Rifle Division.
4. Under command of the 201st Motor Rifle Division. Other analysts classify this as an independent regiment. The testimony of prisoner Pte G. Dzhamalbekov, from this unit, indicates that it is part of the 201st Division.
5. The Kabul *Spetznaz* unit was the first deployed. The others followed in 1983–84.
6. Although an army-level artillery brigade was withdrawn in June 1980 there was evidence of 130mm guns and BM–27 rocket launchers in use during 1984. These weapons are normally army-level assets. It is likely that a special composite unit with a battalion of each of these types of weapon was formed in 1984.

Appendix III: The Afghan Cabinet

	PDPA Gen. Sec.	President	Prime Minister
30 April 1978	Nur Mohammed Taraki (K)	Nur Mohammed Taraki (K)	
17 August 1978			Hafizullah Amin (K)
31 March 1979			
27 July 1979			Hafizullah Amin (K)
14 September 1979	Hafizullah Amin (K)	Hafizullah Amin (K)	
27 December 1979	Babrak Karmal (P)	Babrak Karmal (P)	Babrak Karmal (P)
June 1980			
August 1980			
September 1980			
February 1981			
January 1982			
October 1983			Soltan Ali Keshtmand (P)

	Deputy PM	Deputy PM	Deputy PM	Deputy PM
30 April 1978	Hafizullah Amin (K)	Aslam Watanjar (K)	Babrak Karmal (P)	
17 August 1978				
31 March 1979	Shah Wali (K)			
27 July 1979				
14 September 1979				
27 December 1979	Asadullah Sarwari (K) Mohammed Ziray (K) Abdorashid Arian (K)	Soltan Ali Keshtmand (P)		
June 1980				
August 1980				
September 1980				
February 1981		Abdol Majid Sharboland	Gol Dad	Khalil Ahmed Abawi
January 1982				
October 1983				

	Education	Finance	Commerce	Higher Educ	Inf. & Cult.
30 April 1978	Distagir Panjsheri (K)	Abdol Qader Misaq (P)		Mahmud Suma (K)	Suleiman La'eq (P)
17 August 1978	Abdorashid Jalili (K)				
31 March 1979					Malek Katawazi (K)
27 July 1979					
14 September 1979	Anahita Ratzebad (P)	Abdol Wakil (P)	Mohammed Jallalar	Gol Dad	
27 December 1979					Abdolmajid Sarboland
June 1980					
August 1980					
September 1980	Abdol Samad Qayumi				
February 1981				Sarwar Mangal	
January 1982				Burhanuddin Ghaisi	
October 1983					

	Justice	Planning	Mines & Ind.	Transport
30 April 1978	Abdolkarim Shara'i	Soltan Ali Keshtmand (P)	Mohammed Ismail Danesh (K)	
17 August 1978		Shah Wali (K)		
31 March 1979		Sadiq Alemghir (K)		Hussein Mubarak Shafi (K)
27 July 1979				
14 September 1979				
27 December 1979	Abdorashid Arian (K)	Soltani Ali Keshtmand (P)		Sherjan Mazduryar (K)
June 1980				
August 1980				
September 1980		Abdol Qarizada Soltan Ali Keshtmand (P)		
February 1981	Abdol Wahad Safi			
January 1982	Mohammed Bashir Baghlani			
October 1983				

	Pub. Works	Power & Water	Trade	Social Welfare
30 April 1978	Mohammed Rafi (P)	Mahmud Hashemi	Abdol Qudus Ghorbandi	Anahita Ratzebad (P)
17 August 1978				
31 March 1979	Distagir Panjsheri (P)			
27 July 1979				
14 September 1979				
27 December 1979	Nazar Mohammed (K)	Raz Mohammed Paktin		
June 1980				
August 1980				
September 1980				
February 1981				
January 1982				
October 1983				

NOTES

Under Babrak Karmal the cabinet was expanded. In January 1982 additional posts for Irrigation, Light Industry, Public Works and Local Government were created. A Ministry for Islamic Affairs was started two years later.

Under Karmal the use of the cabinet as central decision-making body declined. The PDPA Central Committee gained greater power. During the period 1983–87 increasing use was made of a Politburo and the Central Committee expanded. In mid-1986 Politburo membership was as follows:

    Mohammed Najeebullah (P),
    Babrak Karmal (P),
    Nur Ahmed Nur (P),
    Soltan Ali Keshtmand (P),
    Mohammed Ziray (K),
    Anahita Ratzebad (P),
    Mohammed Watanjar (K),
    Suleiman La'eq (P),
Candidate (non-voting) members were:
    Mohammed Baryalai,
    Nazar Mohammed (K),
    A. Razmjo (Kabul PDPA chief),
    Mir Sahib Karwal,
    Gulam Faruq Yaqubi (P).

Appendix IV: Resistance Parties

ISLAMIC SOCIETY OF AFGHANISTAN (Jamiat Islami Afghanistan)

Leader: Burhanuddin Rabbani
Estimated strength: 5000 (cadre) 30 000 (all supporters)
Ideology: Sunni Islamic fundamentalist. In favour of a theocratic republic.
Membership mainly Tajik with some other Dari-speakers (Turkmens, Aimaks) and a few Pushtuns.
Main fronts: Ahmad Shah Massud: Panjsher valley
                 Ismael Khan: Herat, Farah, Badghis Provinces
                 Zabiullah Khan (killed Dec. 1984): Balkh and Samangan
                 Provinces
Other areas of operation: Badakhshan, Fariab, Jowzjan, Baghlan, Kabul Provinces
Notes: Probably the most efficient party in the resistance. They have received arms from the USA, China, Pakistan and conservative Arab governments (Saudi Arabia, Kuwait). Their northern, Turkie power base is solid, but at the same time prevents a large Pushtun following.

ISLAMIC PARTY OF YUNIS KHALIS (Hezbe Islami)

Leader: Yunis Khalis
Estimated strength: 3000 (cadre), 20 000 (all supporters)
Ideology: Sunni Islamic fundamentalist. In favour of a theocratic republic.
Membership almost entirely Pushtun, mainly from tribal groups.
Main fronts: Jallaladin Haqqani: Paktia and Paktika Provinces
              Abdol Haq: Kabul area
              Unknown: Nangrahar Province
              Qari Samad (killed Jan. 1985): Logar Province
Other areas of operation: Konduz (mostly eliminated in spring 1984); Ghazni, Zabol
Notes: An effective organisation by Afghan standards, receiving help from the British, Americans, Chinese, Pakistanis and certain Arab countries. Their power limited to eastern Afghanistan and was damaged during the border offensives of August 1985 and April 1986.

ISLAMIC PARTY (Hezbe Islami)

Leader: Gulbuddin Hekmatyar
Estimated strength: 2500 (cadre), 20 000 (all supporters)
Ideology: Conservative Sunni Islam. In favour of a centralised Islamic republic.

Main fronts: Mahmood: Nangrahar Province
                        Unknown: Laghman Province
Other areas of operations: Kabul (Paghman hills), Balkh, Fariab, Paktika, Farah
Notes: The most controversial party, widely despised by other groups. Mainly
Pushtun, but with some support in northern areas. Backed by Pakistan and the
USA.

NATIONAL ISLAMIC FRONT OF AFGHANISTAN (Mahaz-i-Melli-i-Islamiye-Afghanistan)

Leader: Pir Sayed Gailani
Estimated strength: 2000 (cadre), 15 000 (all supporters)
Ideology: Sunni, monarchist and pro-pre-revolutionary Pushtun establishment.
Main fronts: Amin Wardak: Maidan valley, Wardak Province
                        Haji Latif: Kandahar Province
                        Rahmatullah Safi: Paktia Province
Other areas of operation: Nimroz, Paktika (Mohammed Nasim)
Notes: A mainly Pushtun group run in the field by ex-army officers. The recipient
of large amounts of CIA funds.

ISLAMIC REVOLUTION MOVEMENT (Harakat-i-Enqelab-i-Islami)

Leader: Mohammed Nabi Mohammedi
Estimated strength: 2000 (cadre), 20 000 (all supporters)
Ideology: Sunni, conservative, pro-pre-revolutionary establishment.
Main fronts: Sayed Murtaza: Logar Province
                        Mohammed Shah: Farah Province
                        Shafiullah (killed Apr. 1985): Koh-e-Safi
                        Qari Taj Mohammed: Ghazni
Other areas of operation: Herat, Helmand, Kandahar, Paktia
Notes: Strength mainly among Ahmadzai Pushtun tribal groups. A belt of
support across southern and western Afghanistan with very little backing in the
non-tribal, non-Pushtun areas. A 'moderate' alternative to the fundamentalist
Sunni groups.

ISLAMIC ALLIANCE OF AFGHAN MUJAHADEEN (also Islamic Unity for
Afghan Liberation)

Leader: Adbur-Rabbur Rasul Sayaf
Estimated strength: 900 (cadre), 4000 (all supporters)
Ideology: Sunni, conservative, in favour of an Islamic republic.
Main fronts: Unknown: Paktia Province
                        Chakari: Kabul
Other areas of operation: Paktika
Notes: This force grew out of various attempts to unify the Pakistan-based
resistance, and its name has changed with these different alliances. It is US-
backed and relies on Pushtun fighters.

NATIONAL LIBERATION FRONT (Jabha-i-Nejat-i-Melli)

Leader: Sibghatullah Mujaddidi
Estimated strength: 1500 (cadre), 3500 (all supporters)
Ideology: Sunni, monarchist, pro-pre-revolutionary Pushtun establishment.
Areas of operation: Kunar, Kandahar
Notes: A small group of Pushtuns.

SHURA

Leader: Sayed Ali Beheshti
Estimated strength: 4000 (cadre), 8000 (all supporters)
Ideology: Shia, in favour of autonomous Hazara region.
Area of operations: Bamiyan, Baghlan, Balkh, Ghazni Provinces
Notes: The independent Shia front reached the peak of its strength in 1979–80. It remains a well organised group, but has lost supporters to radical parties.

ISLAMIC MOVEMENT (Harakat Islami)

Leader: Sheikh Muhsini
Estimated strength: 2000 (cadre), 15 000 (all supporters)
Ideology: Shia, in favour of Islamic republic.
Area of operations: Fariab, Jowzjan, Balkh, Badakhshan
Notes: Combines some Shia Hazara support with backing from Shia Dari–speakers in northern Afghanistan.

NASR

Estimated strength: 1500 (cadre), 4000 (all supporters)
Ideology: Shia Hazara separatists
Area of operations: Helmand, Ghowr, Bamiyan
Notes: Received Iranian backing during the early 1980s. Nasr was used to undermine Shura, but subsequently became too independent-minded.

REVOLUTIONARY GUARDS (Sepha-e-Pasdara)

Leader: Mohsen Reza'i
Estimated strength: 3000 (cadre), 8000 (all supporters)
Ideology: Shia Hazara Khomeinite, in favour of union with Iran.
Area of operations: Ghowr, Helmand, Bamiyan, Jowzjan, Herat
Notes: A strong Iranian-backed group. They have received the bulk of Tehran assistance since 1984.

HEZBOLLAH (Party of God)

Estimated strength: 1500 (cadre), 3000 (all supporters)
Ideology: Shia Hazara Khomeinite, in favour of union with Iran.
Area of operations: Herat, Ghowr, Helmand
Notes: An Iranian-backed group linked to Hezbollah in other countries.

Note on numbers of mujahadeen

The figures listed above represent, in places, educated guesswork. The cadre figure represents the residual minimum number of men under arms, in-country. In well-organised parties like the ISA most of these men are actual cadre fighters, i.e. the 5000 will, for the most part, be made up of the same men throughout the year. In other organisations (e.g. IAAM) there is constant movement across the border, and the cadre figure is the minimum number that can be counted on to be in-country at any given time.

The 'all supporters' figure represents the total who would take up arms for the party if, hypothetically, all its force and villages came under attack at the same time. It does not include villagers who may provide food, who may even carry a party card, but who would not be prepared to take up arms if the Soviet army appeared in their valley. It is the maximum number the party could call to arms.

The total figures for the parties listed above add up to 28 900 cadre and 150 500 all-comers. To them should be added several thousand men who are part of unaffiliated local organisations, or fight merely for reward or pleasure. The total of guerrillas that would be operating on any given day would therefore not be below 35 000 and not above 175 000. This represents a reduction on the period 1980–82 when the total number fighting for the resistance may have reached 250 000.

Index

245